WHALES
DOLPHINS AND PORPOISES

WHALES
DOLPHINS AND PORPOISES

CONSULTING EDITORS
Sir Richard Harrison MD FRS
Dr M. M. Bryden DSc FAIBiol

ILLUSTRATIONS BY
Tony Pyrzakowski

Ken Lucas/Seaphot Limited/Planet Earth Pictures

MEREHURST PRESS
LONDON

Published in Great Britain by
Merehurst Press
Ferry House, 51-57 Lacy Road, Putney, London SW15 1PR

Produced by
Weldon Owen Pty Limited
43 Victoria Street, McMahons Point NSW 2060, Australia
Telex 23038; Fax (02) 929 8352
A Member of the Weldon International Group of Companies
Sydney • Hong Kong • London • Chicago • San Francisco.

First published in 1988
Reprinted 1989 (twice)
ISBN 1-85391-034-1

Managing Editor: Kim Anderson
Project Coordinator: Lesley Dow
Picture Editor: Kathy Gerrard
Editors: Tony Bishop, Claire Craig, Carson Creagh
Captions: Carson Creagh
Index: Diane Regtop
Maps: Greg Campbell
Design: Sue Burk
Layout: Greg Campbell, Moyna Smeaton, Lisa Kryger
Production Manager: Mick Bagnato

© 1988 Intercontinental Publishing Corporation Limited
© 1989 Weldon Owen Pty Limited

Typeset by Keyset, Sydney, Australia
Printed by Kyodo-Shing Loong Printing Industries Pte Ltd
Printed in Singapore

A Weldon Owen Production

Colin Monteath/Hedgehog House, New Zealand

Cover:
A humpback breaches in the icy waters of the Northern Hemisphere.
Photo by Al Giddings/Ocean Images Inc/Planet Earth Pictures.

Endpapers:
An orca surfaces for air, exhalating just before breaking the water.
Photo by Ken Balcomb/Earthviews

Page 1:
A characteristic of right whales is the prescence on the head of whitish excrescences known as
callosities. Several are seen on this view of the top of a right whale's head, including one at the tip of
the upper jaw, often called the bonnet, and one on either side of the chin.

Page 2:
Spinner dolphins are fast and agile swimmers and congregate in pods of up to several
hundred individuals.

Page 3:
Killer whales (orcas) were so called because they herded and often attacked other whales and not as
is often believed, because they killed humans.

Page 4-5:
Whale watchers gaze on as a humpback prepares to dive in the icy waters
of the Lemaire Channel.

Page 6-7:
Bottlenose dolphins are often seen in oceanaria, which have been improved markedly since the first
enclosure was opened in the early 1940s.

Page 8-9:
A female humpback swims in close proximity to her calf off the coast of Hawaii.

Page 10-11:
A spotted dolphin plays with the photographer's bandanna.

CONSULTING EDITORS

Professor Sir Richard Harrison MD FRS
Emeritus Professor of Anatomy, University of Cambridge, UK, Honorary Fellow,
Downing College, Cambridge

Dr M. M. Bryden DSc FAIBiol
Professor of Veterinary Anatomy, University of Sydney, Australia

CONTRIBUTORS

Dr Lawrence G. Barnes
Curator and Head, Vertebrate Paleontology Section, Natural History Museum of Los Angeles
County, Los Angeles, California, USA

Dr M. M. Bryden
Professor of Veterinary Anatomy, University of Sydney, Australia

Peter Corkeron
Tutorial Fellow, Department of Zoology, University of Queensland, Australia

Carson Creagh
Editor and natural history writer, Sydney, Australia

Dr W. H. Dawbin
Honorary Research Associate, Australian Museum, Sydney, Australia

Hugh Edwards
Marine photographer and author, Perth, Western Australia

Dr R. Ewan Fordyce
Senior Lecturer, Department of Geology, University of Otago, New Zealand

Sir Richard Harrison
Emeritus Professor of Anatomy, University of Cambridge, UK, Honorary Fellow,
Downing College, Cambridge

Dr Kaiya Zhou
Dean, Department of Biology, Nanjing Normal University, Nanjing, People's Republic of China

Dr Victor Manton
Curator, Whipsnade Park, Dunstable, Bedfordshire, England

Dr Margaret Klinowska
Scientific consultant and Member, Research Group in Mammalian Ecology and Reproduction,
Physiological Laboratory, University of Cambridge, United Kingdom

Dr Robert J. Morris
Principal Scientific Officer, Institute of Oceanographic Sciences, United Kingdom

Marty Snyderman
Marine Photographer, cinematographer and author, San Diego, California, USA

Dr Ruth Thompson
Author and historian, Sydney, Australia

P. Morris/Ardea London Ltd

6

INTRODUCTION

'Greatest of all is the Whale, of the Beasts which live in the waters,
Monster indeed he appears, swimming on top of the waves,
Looking at him one thinks, that there in the sea is a mountain,
Or that an island has formed, here in the midst of the sea.'

Abbot Theobaldus c1022

Since earliest times whales have been hunted by man for their oil, whalebone, meat and other products. As man's seamanship advanced so did the bloody slaughter of these large, defenceless creatures. When man called on scientific knowledge to increase the efficiency of his management of Death at Sea, he all but exterminated the Great Leviathans. The smaller dolphins and porpoises at first escaped exploitation but recently have been trapped in fishing operations, taken for culinary delicacies or as fertiliser, and captured to do tricks in dolphinaria.

Some explorers and observant whaling captains, seafaring naturalists and snuff-taking scientists in museums began to suspect that whales and dolphins were very remarkable animals, and produced more and more reasons for arriving at their opinion. In some ways cetaceans seemed, with their distinctive attributes and surpassing skills, perfect examples of evolutionary adaptation, yet they could also be considered aberrant mammals that had lost external ears, hair, fingers and legs but which had acquired flippers, a dorsal fin and strange tail flukes. They posed biological puzzles as to what bit of their anatomy did what — and we are still not exactly sure.

In this book, some fourteen experts with unique qualifications tell you what they have discovered, seen and experienced, and what they think about fascinating aspects of the evolution, history, structure, physiology and senses, sex life and behaviour of a superb Order of the Mammalia. It is not easy to study cetaceans, they swim and dive too well, so it is with pleasure and not a little pride that I present to you the contributions of my very able colleagues.

Richard Harrison

Professor Sir Richard Harrison MD FRS

Male orcas lack the small hooked dorsal fin and can grow up to twice the length of a female.

WHALES OF

THE WORLD

EVOLUTION

R. EWAN FORDYCE

The origins of cetaceans are still uncertain. Many aspects of cetacean anatomy are obvious adaptations for a marine existence and indicate little about ancestry, but biochemical and genetic studies suggest cetaceans are related to hoofed mammals (ungulates). This relationship is also supported by the fossil record, which extends back 50 million years. Thus it is among land mammals of this age or older that we must seek the ancestors of cetaceans. The most likely ancestral group is the Mesonychidae, a family of primitive terrestrial hoofed mammals that lived in North America, Europe and Asia. Mesonychids ranged in size from small dog-sized to large bear-sized animals. Cetacea probably arose from a small form — most evolutionary radiations start off from small rather than large ancestors. Mesonychids included animals with rather simple teeth, possible adaptations to fish eating, as well as large carnivores. We can speculate that one of these (possibly) fish-eating animals became adapted to feed on abundant food in shallow waters around the edge of the Tethys — the large sea that once stretched eastwards from the present Mediterranean to beyond India — and quickly took to an amphibious life. (The early stages of any evolutionary radiation seem to be fast as animals move into previously unoccupied niches.) Initially the animal would have been rather like an otter or fur-seal in habit, using all four limbs to move around in the sea. The tail probably became adapted for vertical beating very quickly, but we do not know how this affected the use of the hind limbs, or how the end of a mesonychid tail might become flattened. While the early whales probably bred on land for many millions of years, there were probably rapid physiological changes to life in water, for example, eyes and kidneys becoming used to different salt balance, loss of hair, development of insulating blubber, ability to hear underwater (even the most primitive whale, *Pakicetus,* had a tympanic bulla that seems to have functioned in underwater hearing) and development of nasal plugs to close the nostrils on diving.

► The grey whale's ungainly appearance may suggest a 'primitive' cetacean but, in fact, the only grey whale fossils known are little more than 100 000 years old.

▼ Despite its wolf-like appearance, the *Mesonyx* of 50 million years ago had five small hoofs rather than claws. Relatives of these paradoxical mammals appear to be the most likely ancestors of archaeocetes and toothed and baleen whales.

14

THE EARLIEST WHALES

The earliest whales are the protocetids, a family of archaic whales or archaeocetes. The most primitive is the recently discovered *Pakicetus*, a fossil 50–53 million years old from Pakistan. Its small incomplete skull indicates that it is little removed from land mammals, yet it has a distinct earbone (bulla) probably adapted for underwater hearing. *Protocetus*, 50 million years old, comes from Egypt and is known positively only from a small skull. Like modern cetaceans, it has a long slender upper jaw with a blowhole behind the tip, simple cheek-teeth, widely separated eyes, and a long brain-case. The bulla is inflated like those of living whales, and probably functioned in underwater hearing. The body form of *Protocetus* is uncertain, but it may have had external hind limbs.

Other protocetids are known mostly from less complete material from Asia, Africa and North America. None is younger than 50 million years, and all are from northern localities. It seems likely, therefore, that the earliest phases of cetacean evolution were restricted to the Tethys.

Rocks from the same period in India have recently yielded a few unusual primitive archaeocetes with a long narrow skull and a long junction between the lower jaws. They are markedly more advanced in their feeding apparatus than the protocetids, indicating an unsuspected ecological diversity among early cetaceans. They are superficially similar to odontocetes and the first specimens discovered were in fact identified as odontocetes. However, the similarities are now thought to be an example of evolutionary convergence.

THE ADVANCED ARCHAEOCETES

Basilosaurus (Zeuglodons), or yoke-toothed archaeocetes, are perhaps best known through a fossil 38–45 million years old that belongs to the advanced archaeocete family Basilosauridae. Basilosaurids are more advanced than protocetids in that their cheek-teeth have multiple cusps, and the sinuses in the skull base are enlarged. These features are also seen in early toothed whales (odontocetes) and baleen whales (mysticetes) and suggest that living whales evolved from basilosaurids. *Basilosaurus*-like bones from rocks in New Zealand and Seymour Island, Antarctica, suggest that advanced archaeocetes had reached far southern waters by about 40 million years ago.

▼ A speculative reconstruction of *Protocetus*, a 2.5 metre archaeocete from the Mediterranean of 50 million years ago. *Protocetus* may have had external hindlimbs, but they were probably non-functional vestigial projections.

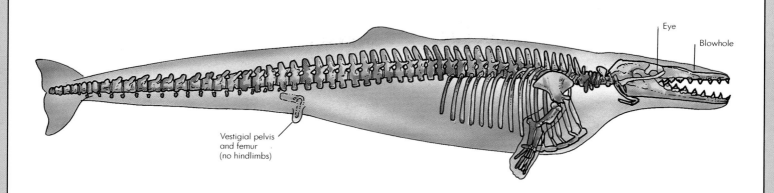

Eye

Blowhole

Vestigial pelvis
and femur
(no hindlimbs)

BASILOSAURUS (ZEUGLODON)
AN ANCESTRAL WHALE

IN 1832, 28 giant vertebrae were unearthed in Louisiana, in the southern United States, and identified as the remains of a reptile by the American geologist James Harlan. He named the animal *Basilosaurus,* from the Greek *basileus,* a king, and *sauros,* a lizard.

By 1839 a fragment of skull and some incomplete teeth had been discovered, and Sir Richard Owen, Hunterian professor of the Royal College of Surgeons in London, recognised that it belonged not to a reptile but to an ancient marine mammal. He described its complex, many-cusped teeth in detail and suggested the common name Zeuglodon, from the Greek *zugotos,* yoked or joined, and *odous,* a tooth.

During the next few years many similar fossils were discovered in the Eocene beds of Alabama; an American fossil-hunter named Albert Koch collected a number of specimens and strung the vertebrae from several individuals together to produce a monster 35 metres long, which he exhibited as a 'sea serpent' in New York in 1845.

Zeuglodon was, in fact, a fairly large cetacean, averaging 15 metres in length, with a maximum recorded length of 21 metres and a weight of at least 5000 kilograms. The proportion of head to body was lower than in any living whale; the skull represented only 7 per cent of the animal's total length, giving it a truly serpentine shape. The neck was short and compact, relatively mobile in comparison with most modern cetaceans, with seven completely independent cervical, or neck, vertebrae. The rest of the spinal column was extraordinary long because each of the vertebrae was elongated.

Of course, it is impossible to do more than guess at the external appearance of this impressive basilosaurid, but we know from its skeleton that its forelimbs were modified as short broad paddles that, unlike those of living whales, were still hinged at the elbow. The pelvis was pronounced, with a distinct

and possibly functional ball-and-socket joint holding a well-developed femur. In some cases these hind limbs could be large enough to appear as humps beneath the skin or even, perhaps, as stumpy hind paddles, but they were too small to be of much use.

The vertebrae lack the massive processes that in modern whales make the spine rigid and provide support for the powerful movements of the tail flukes; these ancient whales may have been sufficiently flexible enough to allow rapid bending and they may have 'wriggled' through shallow waters — but it is equally likely that they had already adopted the horizontal tail flukes and up-and-down body movements that characterise living cetaceans. It seems likely that these animals had a dorsal fin; they were also streamlined and had almost certainly lost most or all of their body hair.

As Sir Richard Owen discovered, the teeth of this ancient whale were differentiated into sharp incisors and canines for grasping struggling prey, such as fish, and robust cheek teeth with rather delicate cusps, adapted for dealing with small bones but not hard-bodied crustaceans or thick molluscs.

This mixture of tooth shapes suggests a similarly mixed diet, and probably indicates that most of their time was spent foraging in warm, shallow coastal waters. They were buoyant but might have been more at home in the shallows along the 5-metre line, from where, seal-like, they could haul themselves on to beaches to breed. The nostrils lay at the top of the snout a short distance from the tip, making it possible for them to breathe without surfacing completely.

It has been speculated that the centre of gravity in *Basilosaurus* was so far forward that it could raise its head and shoulders above the surface of the water to look around, as many modern whales do.

▲ Based on measurements from dozens of specimens, this reconstruction of a 15 metre Zeuglodon is as accurate a 'portrait' as possible of an early ancestor of today's whales.

▲ The 5 metre dorudontines of 40 million years ago were already taking on the streamlined appearance of modern dolphins. By this stage of cetacean evolution, the nostrils had migrated back a little towards the top of the skull.

Advanced archaeocetes also include the more generalised dolphin-like dorudontines. At least six species are known from the USA, Europe, Africa and probably New Zealand. Dorudontines were about 5 metres long and had vertebrae of more normal proportions than *Basilosaurus*. Dorudontines lack the broad upper jaw, which might allow filter-feeding, or the long narrow upper jaw, which might allow very rapid forceps-like prey-catching. Like many living toothed whales, dorudontines probably fed indiscriminately on fish, squid and birds.

EXTINCTION AND THE LAST ARCHAEOCETES

About 38 million years ago, dorudontines and basilosaurines largely disappeared from rocks where they might otherwise be expected in the Northern Hemisphere. It has been suggested that at this time the archaeocetes became extinct as the result of a global mass extinction that is thought to have affected many other groups of organisms, but this is uncertain. Does the lack of specimens in younger rocks really indicate extinction, or have palaeontologists just not looked in the right place to find fossils? Cetaceans are marine mammals, and have evolved mostly in the open ocean from which we have few fossils. Most fossils come from ancient shallow-water marine sediments originally deposited around continental margins and now exposed on land. Although these occurrences probably give a biased view of cetacean history, they are all that we have.

What, then, of the last archaeocetes? *Kekenodon,* a fossil about 30 million years old found in New Zealand, may be the youngest identified archaeocete. Archaeocetes probably declined as the odontocetes and mysticetes evolved rapidly during this period. Odontocetes, which probably ate similar food, may have been more efficient feeders than archaeocetes. They could hunt and navigate using echolocation, and are likely to have been wholly aquatic even in the birth of young; archaeocetes, like seals, may have returned to land for birth. Whether odontocetes caused the demise of the archaeocetes through active ecological displacement or whether they merely replaced a group already in decline is still uncertain.

THE RISE OF ODONTOCETES AND MYSTICETES

Odontocetes use echolocation to hunt their single prey, while mysticetes filter-feed on large shoals of prey. These feeding strategies apparently arose when the two suborders evolved from the archaeocetes, which neither echolocated nor filter-fed.

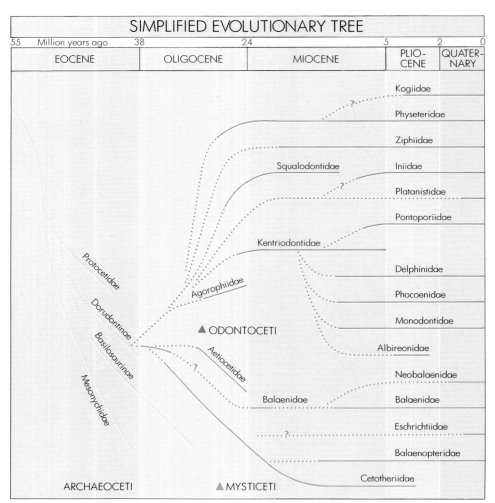

SIMPLIFIED EVOLUTIONARY TREE

55 Million years ago	38	24	5	2	0
EOCENE	OLIGOCENE	MIOCENE	PLIO-CENE	QUATER-NARY	

Kogiidae
Physeteridae
Ziphiidae
Squalodontidae
Iniidae
Platanistidae
Pontoporiidae
Kentriodontidae
Delphinidae
Phocoenidae
Monodontidae
Albireonidae
Neobalaenidae
Balaenidae
Eschrichtiidae
Balaenopteridae
Cetotheriidae

Protocetidae
Dorudontinae
Basilosaurinae
Mesonychidae
Agorophiidae
▲ ODONTOCETI
Aetiocetidae
Balaenidae
ARCHAEOCETI
▲ MYSTICETI

Odontocetes and mysticetes probably evolved from basilosaurids 30–40 million years ago, but unfortunately this period has a poor fossil record. Perhaps changing sea levels and currents resulted in less favourable conditions for the preservation of cetacean fossils. It is even possible that such changes in the world's oceans provided the new environment that favoured the rise of odontocetes and mysticetes.

The evolution of cetaceans may reflect major geological changes in the Southern Hemisphere. The former huge southern supercontinent of Gondwana finally fragmented at about this time, when Australia and South America moved northwards away from Antarctica. Until then the climate of Antarctica was rather moderate, despite the polar position of the continent. The moderate climate was probably caused by coastlines continuous to the north with the more temperate landmasses of Australia and South America, and by the lack of a circumpolar ocean. The polar climate deteriorated as Australia and South America drifted away to leave Antarctica insulated by the extensive circumpolar Southern Ocean. Certain oceanic features — temperature gradients and currents — today govern overall availability of food resources in the Southern Ocean, and probably did so in the past. Perhaps the development of the new oceanic and climatic patterns triggered the evolution of the two groups of cetaceans, with their new feeding strategies of filter-feeding and echolocation-assisted predation.

PRIMITIVE MYSTICETES

Modern mysticetes are huge toothless animals with baleen, very different from their early ancestors. At least one of the earliest mysticetes is thought to have had baleen, but several primitive specimens are toothed.

Mammalodon, a fossil from Victoria in Australia, typifies a stage through which the earliest mysticetes might have passed. This small animal is only 24 million years old and a late survivor. It has a skull equipped with a short, broad, flat, toothed upper jaw. This joins loosely with the long brain-case, and the bones on either side of the upper jaw could flex against each other — adaptations associated with filter-feeding in living mysticetes. The lower jaws in *Mammalodon* look rather like those of archaeocetes and have conspicuous teeth but, as in living mysticetes, the jaws lack a bony junction — again probably an adaptation for filter-feeding. The high-crowned teeth with small projecting cusps probably intermeshed when the mouth was closed, and formed a sieving mechanism.

Cetotheres (family Cetotheriidae) were small to medium-sized primitive baleen whales that

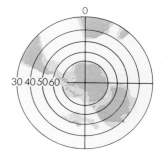

▲ About fifty million years ago, Australia and South America were linked to each other across Antarctica in the huge southern land mass of Gondwana.

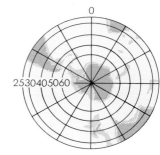

▲ The breakup of the last remnants of Gondwana, which led to the present position of the continents, has created opportunities for cetaceans to radiate into new habitats and to develop new feeding strategies.

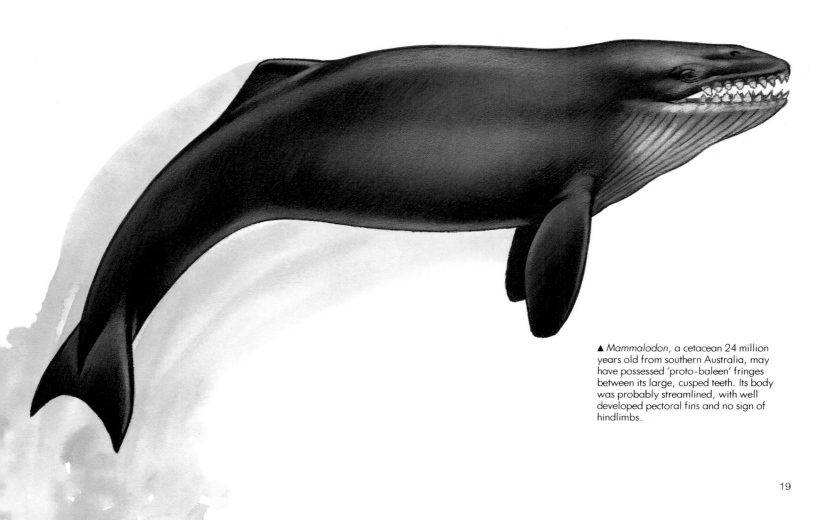

▲ *Mammalodon*, a cetacean 24 million years old from southern Australia, may have possessed 'proto-baleen' fringes between its large, cusped teeth. Its body was probably streamlined, with well developed pectoral fins and no sign of hindlimbs.

lived from 30 million years ago to as recently as 3 million years ago. They were structurally diverse, and included many genera. The earliest ones were little more advanced than *Mammalodon,* while the most recent were very similar to living rorquals (family Balaenopteridae).

The cetotheres may, like the rorquals, have been gulp-feeders, but they seem not to have reached the size of living rorquals. Perhaps their more primitive feeding apparatus (indicated by the shape of the skull) was just not as efficient as that of the rorquals.

▶ Whales had diverged into toothed hunters and toothless filter-feeders by 30 million years ago, and the many adaptations that characterise rorquals such as this minke whale were in evidence 15 million years ago.

▼ A filter-feeding strategy makes best use of large numbers of very small organisms. One of the filter feeders (centre) is the blue whale, the largest organism on the planet.

Robert Pitman/Earthviews

LIVING MYSTICETES

Living rorquals (family Balaenopteridae) range in size from the diminutive minke whale (*Balaenoptera acutorostrata*) to the large fin whale (*B. physalus*) and blue whale (*B. musculus*). The ancestors of these species probably evolved from cetotheres by about 15 million years ago. Living rorquals all have pronounced external throat grooves, to allow the mouth to expand during gulp-feeding, and have a distinctively depressed frontal bone above the eyes. The depressed frontal is seen in fossil balaenopterids, which suggests that they, too, were gulp-feeders. By 5 million years ago, balaenopterids had reached large sizes, comparable with living species. And by this stage humpback whales (*Megaptera novaeangliae*) had evolved, although it is not clear why these diverged from the other rorquals.

The living grey whale (*Eschrichtius robustus*) has sometimes been allied with cetotheres, but it is better placed alone in the family Eschrichtiidae. The short fossil record includes only a few specimens from the margins of the North Pacific and North Atlantic. They are probably the same as the living grey whale, and are little older than 100 000 years. Grey whales do not seem closely related to other living mysticetes. Fossils may

Francois Gohier/Ardea London Ltd

ultimately unravel details of their origins.

Right whale (family Balaenidae) origins are uncertain. The small *Morenocetus*, the earliest right whale, indicates that they evolved about 22 million years ago but there is no likely ancestor known among earlier mysticete fossils. Fossils of right whales, like those of rorquals, are relatively common in rocks up to 10 million years old. (Isolated ear bones, which are erosion-resistant, are sometimes abundant.) The 10–12 million year gap between *Morenocetus* and later right whales is also puzzling.

The poorly known southern pygmy right whale (*Caperea marginata*) has no fossil record, but probably evolved from ancestors linked with right whales. Nonetheless, it is distinct enough to be placed in its own family, Neobalaenidae.

PRIMITIVE ODONTOCETES

Odontocetes or toothed whales, both fossil and living, are more diverse than mysticetes. The wide range of skull forms suggests different methods of feeding and probably different uses of high-frequency echolocation. In fossil skulls, teeth may be serrated, smooth, delicate, robust, reduced in size or missing, and the upper jaw may be long and blunt, short and wide or downturned. These structures indicate a significant diversity of species by 25 million years ago, and foretell the appearance of diverse younger and better known odontocetes. Some groups that had appeared by 25 million years ago were later to become important elements in the global fauna (squalodonts and kentriodontids).

Sharp triangular teeth with serrated edges and a wrinkled surface characterised the shark-toothed dolphins (family Squalodontidae). Squalodonts were small to medium-sized dolphins and are known from many parts of the world in rocks 6–25 million years old. The robust multiple teeth suggest an active carnivorous lifestyle; indeed, some may have been similar in habit to orcas (*Orcinus orca*). Squalodonts disappeared about 6 million years ago, but we do not know why.

Kentriodontids had appeared by 25 million years ago and were abundant in some localities until about 5 million years ago. They were probably similar to small living dolphins, although their skulls are more primitive.

LIVING ODONTOCETES

Beaked whales (family Ziphiidae) are rather similar in aspects of skull form to squalodonts. However, beaked whales have far fewer teeth and their relationships with squalodonts are not clear. There are possible ziphiids dating back 22 million years and ziphiids are common fossils worldwide in marine sediments 5–10 million years old. These later beaked whale fossils include specimens belonging to the genus *Mesoplodon* which, like their living relatives, are nearly toothless. Ancestral ziphiids had many functional teeth in the upper and lower jaws and evolutionary tooth loss may be associated with the squid-eating diet probably adopted by beaked whales early in their history.

Like beaked whales, sperm whales (family Physeteridae) first appeared about 22 million years ago. Even then they had the basined, high-backed, asymmetrical skull typical of the living sperm whale (*Physeter catodon*). However, the early forms were rather small and had a tapered upper jaw with well-developed teeth. In sperm whales, as in beaked whales, the gradual evolutionary loss of teeth may be associated with a squid-eating diet.

▲ *Mesonyx*, from 50 million years ago, had the robust and relatively unspecialised skull of a carnivorous terrestrial mammal.

▲ Within 5 million years, the protocetids were displaying numerous adaptations to marine life, especially in the lengthening of the 'beak' or rostrum.

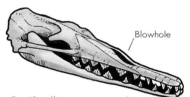

▲ By 40 million years ago, the dorudontines were well adapted to life in the sea — a definite 'beak' had appeared and the nostrils were moving backwards.

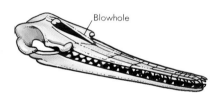

▲ The shark-toothed squalodont dolphins of 25 million years ago had many features of 'modern', toothed whales, including a blowhole close to the top of the skull.

▲ By the time modern dolphins had appeared, about 15 million years ago, the shape of the skull was well established and the teeth had become both more numerous and less complex in shape.

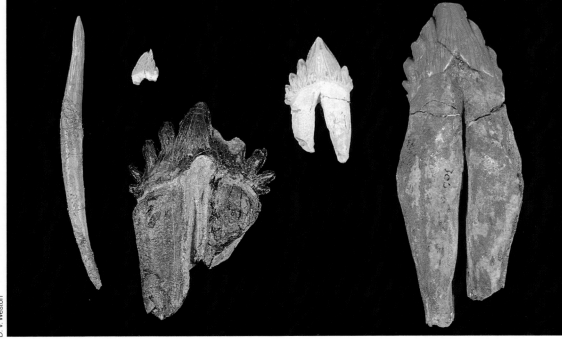

◄ Fossil teeth from New Zealand and Antarctica indicate the range of size, shape and complexity of primitive cetacean dentition. From left, an anterior tooth and a cheek tooth (top) of a primitive odontocete, a cheek tooth of an archaeocete, the tooth of a primitive mysticete and the tooth of a large archaeocete.

D. V. Weston

R. E. Fordyce

▶ The skulls of primitive dolphins were strikingly similar in appearance to those of living species, though their skulls lacked the unusual asymmetry, or 'left-handedness', that is characteristic of the skulls of most modern toothed whales.

▼ In the same way that sperm whales have 'lost' functional teeth in the upper jaw, beaked whales have adapted to a diet composed mainly of squid with a reduction in the number of teeth — most have only two teeth, both in the lower jaw.

extinct groups that include the ancestral dolphins, kentriodontids. Dolphins arose from the kentriodontids by 12 million years ago and have radiated to become the most diverse and successful group of odontocetes. They differ from kentriodontids in that the skull is asymmetrical and the air sinuses in the skull base are more complex. The fossil record still gives only moderate insight into the origins of living dolphins, with their greatly varying habits, sizes and structure.

Porpoises are small odontocetes that have been distinct from their dolphin relatives since about 10 or 11 million years ago. Early fossils from the Pacific coast of the Americas illustrate typical skull features of modern porpoises. The geographic distribution of fossils suggests porpoises originated in the North Pacific. If so, they must have spread later to the Atlantic and southern waters.

Living belukhas (*Delphinapterus leucas*) and narwhals (*Monodon monoceros*) occupy north polar waters, but early white whales (family

Pygmy sperm whales have a poor fossil record. They are probably related most closely to physeterids, from which they differ in their small size and, more particularly, in the construction of the skull basin and earbone.

Both dolphins (family Delphinidae) and porpoises (family Phocoenidae) seem to be related to the white whales (family Monodontidae) and

James D. Watt/Earthviews

Fred Bruemmer

Monodontidae) lived in warmer climates around California 10–12 million years ago and may have evolved from kentriodontids.

Living river dolphins are often treated as a single unified group, yet they may represent two or even four families. Some may be allied with squalodonts, others with true dolphins. Their similarities may merely be a case of convergent evolution — adaptations to the same environment among animals of separate origins. Fossil river dolphins were probably similar to living species, with a long upper jaw, many small conical teeth, and a small body. It is the details of the skulls and earbones that reveal their separate origins. Thus the living Indian Ganges River dolphin (*Platanista gangetica*) has possible relatives 13–15 million years old in Maryland and Virginia. The South American franciscana (*Pontoporia blainvillei*) has fossil relatives in both South and North America, and may be related to the living Chinese river dolphin (*Lipotes vexillifer*), which may in turn be descended from *Prolipotes,* a fossil from China. Finally, the living South American Amazon dolphin (*Inia geoffrensis*) has been allied, sometimes doubtfully, with a variety of small fossil odontocetes about 5–12 million years old in the family Iniidae.

In conclusion, the picture of cetacean evolution gained from the study of fossils and living animals over the past decade is much more complex than formerly suspected. Advances of similar magnitude should be expected in future.

The broad picture of evolution that we now have seems unlikely to change, but many details must be filled in. More information about fossils may ultimately tell us about rates and patterns of evolution, changing geographic patterns and changing ecological strategies. Even now, the cetacean fossil record suggests that evolution has been inextricably linked with natural extinction. The human species, however, should be careful not to interfere with and accelerate these natural processes.

▲ 'Anomalous' toothed whales such as the narwhal and the belukha may have evolved from kentriodontid dolphins. They have many features that are far removed from those of superficially similar small cetaceans.

▼ A recently discovered fossil dolphin (centre) from Antarctica has a skull that resembles a beaked whale's (left), but it is more closely related to modern dolphins (right) — an example of convergent evolution.

D. V. Weston

23

KINDS OF WHALES

LAWRENCE G. BARNES and CARSON CREAGH

Living cetaceans are divided into two major groups or *suborders,* each containing one or more smaller groups, or *families.* In all there are 13 families of cetaceans and they contain the 76 or more different species of whales. The living whales are reviewed below by suborder and family in roughly phylogenetic (evolutionary) order.

SUBORDER　　　　　　　　　　　　　　　　　**FAMILY**

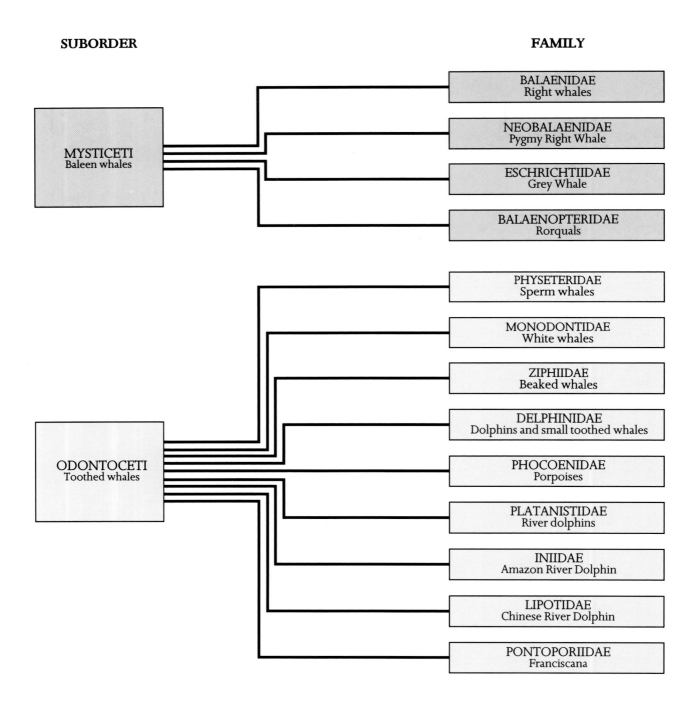

SUBORDER	FAMILY
MYSTICETI — Baleen whales	BALAENIDAE — Right whales
	NEOBALAENIDAE — Pygmy Right Whale
	ESCHRICHTIIDAE — Grey Whale
	BALAENOPTERIDAE — Rorquals
ODONTOCETI — Toothed whales	PHYSETERIDAE — Sperm whales
	MONODONTIDAE — White whales
	ZIPHIIDAE — Beaked whales
	DELPHINIDAE — Dolphins and small toothed whales
	PHOCOENIDAE — Porpoises
	PLATANISTIDAE — River dolphins
	INIIDAE — Amazon River Dolphin
	LIPOTIDAE — Chinese River Dolphin
	PONTOPORIIDAE — Franciscana

FAMILY BALAENIDAE
RIGHT WHALES

Three Species

Bowhead
Balaena mysticetus

APPEARANCE The bowhead (also known as the Greenland right whale) is the stockiest of the baleen whales, with a barrel-shaped body and a very large head (about a third of the total body size). The mouth is bowed sharply upward, the pectoral fins are small and paddle-shaped. There is no dorsal fin and the flukes are pointed. Colour is generally blue-black (young) to blue-grey (older animals) overall, with a whitish chin patch lighter underside, and mottling caused by sloughing skin. There are 325 to 360 baleen plates up to 4.6 metres long in each side of the upper jaw. The white chin patch unique to this species can sometimes be seen when bowheads swim upside down.
SIZE Between 3.5 and 5.5 metres at birth, reaching an average of 18 metres at maturity.
HABITAT AND DISTRIBUTION Confined to arctic waters, where they follow the seasonal advance and retreat of the ice. Populations are found from Spitzbergen to eastern Greenland, from Davis Strait to Hudson Bay to the Sea of Okhotsk and the Bering, Chukchi, Beaufort and Siberian Seas.
REPRODUCTION Mating takes place in late summer, and calves are born in the spring, after ten months' gestation. They are weaned after six months and calving takes place at two-year intervals.
DIET Various small crustaceans.

Southern Right Whale
Eubalaena australis

APPEARANCE Originally considered a subspecies of the northern right whale, the slow-swimming southern or black right whale looks identical to its northern congener. The body is stocky and fat, and is marked with skin thickenings or callosities (home to specialised whale lice and barnacles) on the upper and lower jaws and above the eye. The callosity on the upper jaw is often called the bonnet. The pectoral fins are paddle-shaped, there is no dorsal fin and the flukes are extremely long, narrow and pointed. The body is pale in the young, darkening in adults to black with white patches where skin has sloughed off. There are 225 to 250 baleen plates up to 2.2 metres long in each side of the upper jaw.
SIZE Calves are 5 to 6 metres long at birth and reach an average of 15 metres at maturity. Individuals up to 17.7 metres have been recorded.
HABITAT AND DISTRIBUTION Widely distributed (though rare) throughout the Antarctic, southern South America, Australia, New Zealand, South Africa and high latitudes of the Indian Ocean. The right whale was so named because of its high oil yield and its very fine silky baleen that made it the 'right' whale to hunt. It was heavily fished for at least 300 years and is rare today.
REPRODUCTION Calves are born in winter after a twelve-month gestation period and are suckled until they reach about 8.5 metres in length. Sexual maturity is reached at 15 metres in males and 16 metres in females. There seems to be a three-year calving interval.
DIET A selective feeder on copepods and krill.

FAMILY NEOBALAENIDAE
PYGMY RIGHT WHALE

One Species

Pygmy Right Whale
Caperea marginata

APPEARANCE The pygmy right whale is so called for its bowed mouth: it is only very distantly related to the right whales and the shape of the pygmy right whale's mouth appears to be an example of convergent evolution. The body is like that of the minke whale or Bryde's whale, and this species has a prominent, sickle-shaped dorsal fin. The pectoral fins are small and rounded and the flukes are broad. There is no ridge on the rostrum or the back and there are only two deep, well-marked throat grooves. Colour is dark grey above, becoming darker with age, fading to light grey below. There are 230 yellowish-white baleen plates up to 70 centimetres long in each side of the upper jaw.

SIZE From about 1.5 metres at birth to 6.1 metres and 4.5 tonnes at maturity. Females are slightly larger than males.
HABITAT AND DISTRIBUTION Known only in the Southern Hemisphere, from Australia and New Zealand to South Africa, Argentina, the Falkland Islands and the Crozet Islands north of Antarctica.
REPRODUCTION Nothing known. This is apparently a solitary species, though groups of up to eight animals have been observed.
DIET Stomach samples of two stranded pygmy right whales contained small crustaceans (copepods) but nothing further is known.

FAMILY ESCHRICHTIIDAE
GREY WHALE

One Species

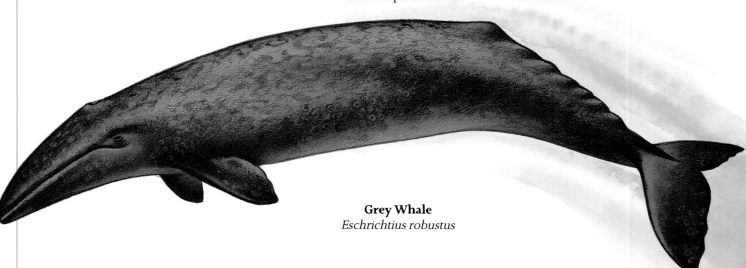

Grey Whale
Eschrichtius robustus

APPEARANCE A primitive-looking species, with a rough, clumsily shaped head, a slightly bowed mouth and small visible hairs in pits and on the rostrum. The body is moderately slender with well-developed, paddle-shaped pectoral fins, almost triangular flukes and, instead of a dorsal fin, nine to thirteen small bumps along the dorsal ridge. Colouration is mottled grey overall, but marked on the head and back by white and yellowish patches of whale lice and barnacles. There are no throat grooves. In each side of the upper jaw are 140 to 180 thick, yellowish white baleen plates up to 40 centimetres long.
SIZE Calves are 5 metres and 500 kilograms at birth, reaching 13.7 to 15.2 metres and 33 tonnes at maturity. Females are believed to be slightly larger than males, with larger heads.
HABITAT AND DISTRIBUTION At one time found also in the North

Atlantic, the grey whale survives today only in the North Pacific, where it is seen in coastal waters from Alaska to Baja California depending on the time of year. The grey whale has been recognised as influencing the topography of the seabed in the Arctic, from its 'ploughing' of bottom mud in search of food.
REPRODUCTION Mating occurs in winter during the grey whale's southward migration. Calves are born in lagoons and calm coastal areas after a thirteen-month gestation period and weaned at nine months. Calving occurs every two years and sexual maturity is reached at between five and eleven years, when males are 11 metres and females 11.5 metres in length.
DIET Bottom-dwelling amphipods.

FAMILY BALAENOPTERIDAE
RORQUALS
Six Species

Fin Whale
Balaenoptera physalus

APPEARANCE Second largest of the whales, the fin whale or finback has a long, slender and relatively narrow body with an unusual asymmetrical colouration. It is generally dark grey to brown on the back and white below. The right side of the jaw and the right baleen plates are white, while those on the left are dark. Most animals have a grey-white chevron just behind the head. The sickle-shaped dorsal fin is far back on the dorsal ridge. The relatively small pectoral fins are narrow and pointed, and the flukes are large, thin and pointed. There are 262 to 473 baleen plates, 70 centimetres long, in each side of the upper jaw and fifty-six to one hundred throat grooves.
SIZE From 6.5 metres at birth to an average of 20 metres. Females are slightly larger than males, and the largest recorded fin whale was 27 metres.
HABITAT AND DISTRIBUTION These shy animals are found solitary or in groups of up to ten in all oceans, though they avoid shallow and coastal waters.
REPRODUCTION Calves are born at two to three year intervals after an eleven-month gestation period and are suckled for six to seven months. Sexual maturity is at ten to thirteen years, when males are 18.5 metres and females 19.8 metres.
DIET Small crustaceans and pelagic schooling fishes such as mackerel and herring, and squid.

APPEARANCE The tropical and relatively infertile habitat of Bryde's whale may be a major factor in its small size and population. It is a slender, medium-sized rorqual, dark grey on the back with occasional circular scars from attacks by cookiecutter sharks, and lighter on the belly. There is a secondary ridge on either side of the central ridge of the head. The prominent, strongly sickle-shaped dorsal fin is close to the tail stock. The pectoral fins are slender and the flukes are large and pointed. There are about forty to fifty throat grooves and 255 to 365 slate-grey baleen plates up to 46 centimetres long in each side of the upper jaw.
SIZE Calves are 4.3 metres long and weigh 900 kilograms. Adults reach 14.6 metres and 20 tonnes.
HABITAT AND DISTRIBUTION Tropical and subtropical waters of the Pacific, Atlantic and Indian Oceans. Found individually or in groups of up to ten animals.
REPRODUCTION Calves are born after eleven to twelve months gestation. Males reach sexual maturity at eight to thirteen years (12 metres) and females at seven to ten years (13 metres).
DIET Schooling fishes such as herring, pilchards and sardines, krill and squid.

Bryde's Whale
Balaenoptera edeni

27

FAMILY BALAENOPTERIDAE (continued)

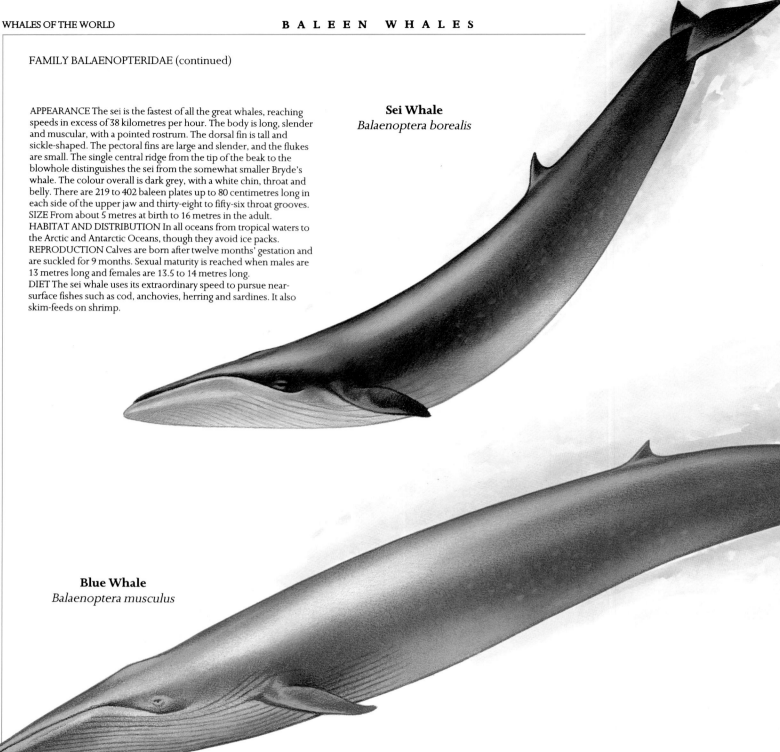

Sei Whale
Balaenoptera borealis

APPEARANCE The sei is the fastest of all the great whales, reaching speeds in excess of 38 kilometres per hour. The body is long, slender and muscular, with a pointed rostrum. The dorsal fin is tall and sickle-shaped. The pectoral fins are large and slender, and the flukes are small. The single central ridge from the tip of the beak to the blowhole distinguishes the sei from the somewhat smaller Bryde's whale. The colour overall is dark grey, with a white chin, throat and belly. There are 219 to 402 baleen plates up to 80 centimetres long in each side of the upper jaw and thirty-eight to fifty-six throat grooves.
SIZE From about 5 metres at birth to 16 metres in the adult.
HABITAT AND DISTRIBUTION In all oceans from tropical waters to the Arctic and Antarctic Oceans, though they avoid ice packs.
REPRODUCTION Calves are born after twelve months' gestation and are suckled for 9 months. Sexual maturity is reached when males are 13 metres long and females are 13.5 to 14 metres long.
DIET The sei whale uses its extraordinary speed to pursue near-surface fishes such as cod, anchovies, herring and sardines. It also skim-feeds on shrimp.

Blue Whale
Balaenoptera musculus

APPEARANCE The blue whale is the largest organism on this planet — its heart alone is the size of a small car and pumps 9.7 tonnes of blood through the huge body. Its mouth can be 6 metres long, and the flukes 4.5 metres from tip to tip. The body is slender, especially in the head and chest area. The head (like a broad, pointed arch when viewed from above) has a single central ridge from the tip to the blowhole. The extremely small, sickle-shaped dorsal fin is located well down the back and marks the end of a ridge. The pectoral fins are long, slender and curved on the leading edge, and the flukes are relatively small. There are more than 300 baleen plates in each side of the upper jaw and the highly distensible throat has forty or more grooves. Overall colour is blue-grey, mottled with light grey spots, but cold-water algae living on the belly may give this a yellowish tinge.
SIZE Calves are 7.5 metres long and weigh 2-3 tonnes at birth. Average adult size is 23 metres (males) to 24.5 metres (females), though blue whales were larger before intensive mechanised whaling brought the species to the brink of extinction. The largest blue whale ever captured was 29.4 metres. Average adult weight is 100 tonnes or more.
HABITAT AND DISTRIBUTION Formerly widespread, though never common, blue whales are today found in small populations in all open oceans.
REPRODUCTION Calves are born after eleven months' gestation, suckle an estimated 380 litres of milk per day and gain 90 kilograms per day over a seven-month period. Sexual maturity is reached at two to twelve years, at a length of 22.5 metres in males and 24 metres in females.
DIET Small krill in the Southern Hemisphere, supplemented by small schooling fishes and crustaceans in the Northern Hemisphere.

Minke Whale
Balaenoptera acutorostrata

APPEARANCE The minke whale is the smallest of the rorquals. It is well shaped and graceful, has a pointed head (with the lower jaw protruding) and a single prominent ridge from the tip of the upper jaw to the blowholes. The back is black from the beak to just behind the long, slender, pointed pectoral fins, merging to dark grey and then to black again at the flukes. The undersurface is white. There is a sickle-shaped dorsal fin and the pectoral fins have a distinctive white band. The flukes are relatively large and thin, there are fifty to seventy throat grooves and there are 231 to 360 creamy white baleen plates up to about 20 centimetres long in each side of the upper jaw.
SIZE Calves are 3 metres long and grow to about 10 metres in length and 9 tonnes in weight.

HABITAT AND DISTRIBUTION Minkes are primarily inshore solitary whales, found in coastal temperate waters of all oceans, but they are sometimes seen at sea, where they breach spectacularly, exposing the entire body.
REPRODUCTION There is a gestation period of ten months and young are suckled for less than six months. Sexual maturity is at six years, when males are 7 metres and females 7.3 metres.
DIET Small schooling fishes such as herring and cod, squid and crustaceans.

Humpback
Megaptera novaeangliae

APPEARANCE The humpback is a stocky animal with a rounded body narrowing to a slender tail stock. The head is massive and marked with protuberances containing hair follicles and providing sites for barnacles and whale lice. The pectoral fins are huge (Megaptera means 'great wing') and may be as much as a third of the total body length. They are broadly serrated on the leading edge, in contrast with the flukes, which are — uniquely among whales — serrated on their trailing edges. The body is black except for patches on the chin, throat, belly and flukes and on one or both surfaces of the pectoral fins. Southern Hemisphere humpbacks tend to have more extensive white pigmentation than those in the Northern Hemisphere. Scars, barnacles and cookiecutter shark bites are common on the body. There are fourteen to twenty-two deep throat grooves and 270 to 400 blackish brown baleen plates up to 80 centimetres long in each side of the upper jaw.
SIZE From 4 to 5 metres at birth, reaching 19 metres and 48 tonnes at maturity.
HABITAT AND DISTRIBUTION Found in all oceans to the edge of ice packs, but highly migratory between polar waters in summer and tropical waters in winter. Groups of four to twelve animals are common.
REPRODUCTION Calves are born in winter every two or three years and sexual maturity is reached at 11–12 metres in males and 12 metres in females.
DIET Humpbacks apparently feed only in cold water, on krill, sardines, mackerel, anchovies and other small schooling fishes.

FAMILY PHYSETERIDAE
SPERM WHALES
Three Species

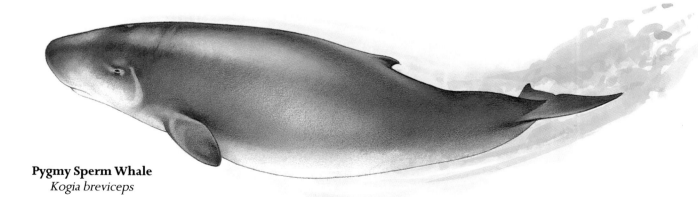

APPEARANCE Perhaps the most widely known of all cetaceans, the sperm whale is unmistakable. Its body shape is unique, with a squared, blunt head taking up almost a third of the total body length. There is a single S-shaped blowhole on the left side of the forehead and the long, narrow lower jaw fits neatly into the underside of the head. The pectoral fins are small and broad, with rounded tips. There is no distinct dorsal fin but there is a series of bumps (the first often large and triangular) along the back to the tail stock. The light brown to blue-grey skin is rippled on the back and sides. There are eighteen to twenty-five large, conical teeth in each side of the lower jaw only and these fit into sockets in the upper jaw, which has ten to sixteen vestigial teeth that virtually never erupt.

Sperm Whale
Physeter catodon

SIZE Calves are 3.7 metres to 4.3 metres at birth. Female adults grow to 13 metres in length and 16 tonnes in weight while males average 18.5 metres and weigh 32 to 45 tonnes.
HABITAT AND DISTRIBUTION All oceans except polar ice fields, although distribution is dependent upon season and sexual and social status. The sperm whale has apparently evolved to live in deep water so effectively that it is in real danger of stranding when it moves inshore.
REPRODUCTION The gestation period is 14 to 15 months and calves are suckled for up to two years. Males reach sexual maturity at about ten years, females at 8 to 11 years. Sperm whales can live for seventy years or more.
DIET Squid, especially giant squid, fish, octopus.

Pygmy Sperm Whale
Kogia breviceps

APPEARANCE Basically similar to its much larger relative, the pygmy sperm whale is stocky with a square head and the upper jaw longer than the lower jaw. The back is dark brown-black, fading gradually to a light belly. There is a dark patch, then a thin light line, behind the eye, giving the impression of a fish's gill cover. It has a small, sickle-shaped dorsal fin — large and slightly rounded pectoral fins and large, tapered flukes. There are ten to sixteen long, curved, sharp teeth in each side of the lower jaw only.
SIZE From 1.2 metres at birth to 3.7 metres and 400 kilograms.

HABITAT AND DISTRIBUTION Worldwide in tropical and temperate waters, but very little is known about the numbers or biology of this shy animal.
REPRODUCTION Calves are born in late spring after eleven months' gestation. Males are sexually mature at 2.7 to 3 metres and females at 2.7 to 2.8 metres.
DIET Principally squid and octopus, but small fishes, crabs and other invertebrates are also taken.

FAMILY MONODONTIDAE
WHITE WHALES
Three Species

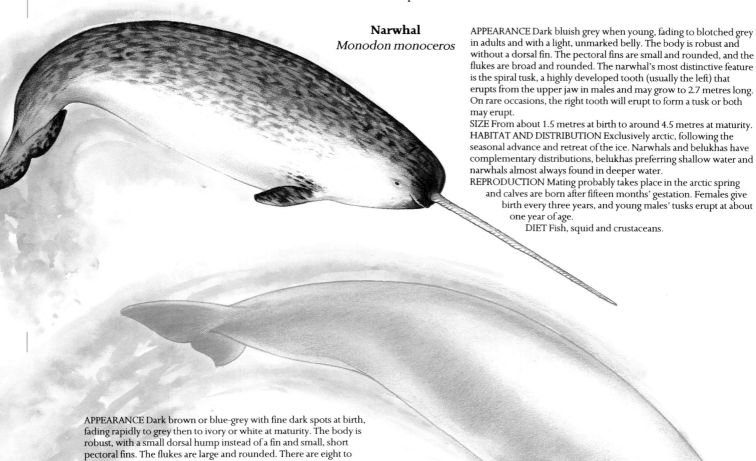

Narwhal
Monodon monoceros

APPEARANCE Dark bluish grey when young, fading to blotched grey in adults and with a light, unmarked belly. The body is robust and without a dorsal fin. The pectoral fins are small and rounded, and the flukes are broad and rounded. The narwhal's most distinctive feature is the spiral tusk, a highly developed tooth (usually the left) that erupts from the upper jaw in males and may grow to 2.7 metres long. On rare occasions, the right tooth will erupt to form a tusk or both may erupt.

SIZE From about 1.5 metres at birth to around 4.5 metres at maturity.

HABITAT AND DISTRIBUTION Exclusively arctic, following the seasonal advance and retreat of the ice. Narwhals and belukhas have complementary distributions, belukhas preferring shallow water and narwhals almost always found in deeper water.

REPRODUCTION Mating probably takes place in the arctic spring and calves are born after fifteen months' gestation. Females give birth every three years, and young males' tusks erupt at about one year of age.

DIET Fish, squid and crustaceans.

APPEARANCE Dark brown or blue-grey with fine dark spots at birth, fading rapidly to grey then to ivory or white at maturity. The body is robust, with a small dorsal hump instead of a fin and small, short pectoral fins. The flukes are large and rounded. There are eight to eleven teeth in each side of the upper and lower jaws.

SIZE About 1.5 metres at birth, growing to a maximum of 5 metres.

HABITAT AND DISTRIBUTION Mainly shallow water in arctic and subarctic waters, from bays and estuaries to hundreds of kilometres upriver during summer.

REPRODUCTION Females reach sexual maturity at about five years, males at eight or nine. Belukhas reproduce every three years or so, with a gestation period of fourteen months and a lactation period of twenty months. They live for as long as twenty-five years.

DIET A broad range of fishes (especially salmon), crustaceans and octopus.

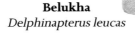

Belukha
Delphinapterus leucas

Irrawaddy Dolphin
Orcaella brevirostris

APPEARANCE The pale to dark bluish grey Irrawaddy dolphin or pesut has a robust body with a blunt, bulbous head, a distinct and functional neck, no distinct beak, a short dorsal fin that curves backwards, and long pectoral fins. The flukes are wide and distinctly notched. There are twelve to nineteen teeth in each side of the upper jaw and twelve to fifteen in each side of the lower jaw.

SIZE Smaller than the narwhal and belukha, the Irrawaddy dolphin is only around 60 centimetres long at birth and grows to a maximum of 2.2 metres.

HABITAT AND DISTRIBUTION Slow swimmers, they prefer protected environments — warm, shallow, muddy and brackish inshore waters, estuaries, mangrove swamps and tropical rivers from India to Thailand, Borneo, Papua New Guinea and northern Australia. They have been sighted more than 1400 kilometres upstream in fresh water.

REPRODUCTION Nothing known. Total population unknown, but assumed to be common.

DIET Bottom fishes, squid and shrimp. This species has a distinctive hunting technique of spitting water to scare small fishes into shallow water.

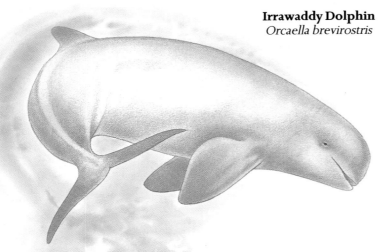

31

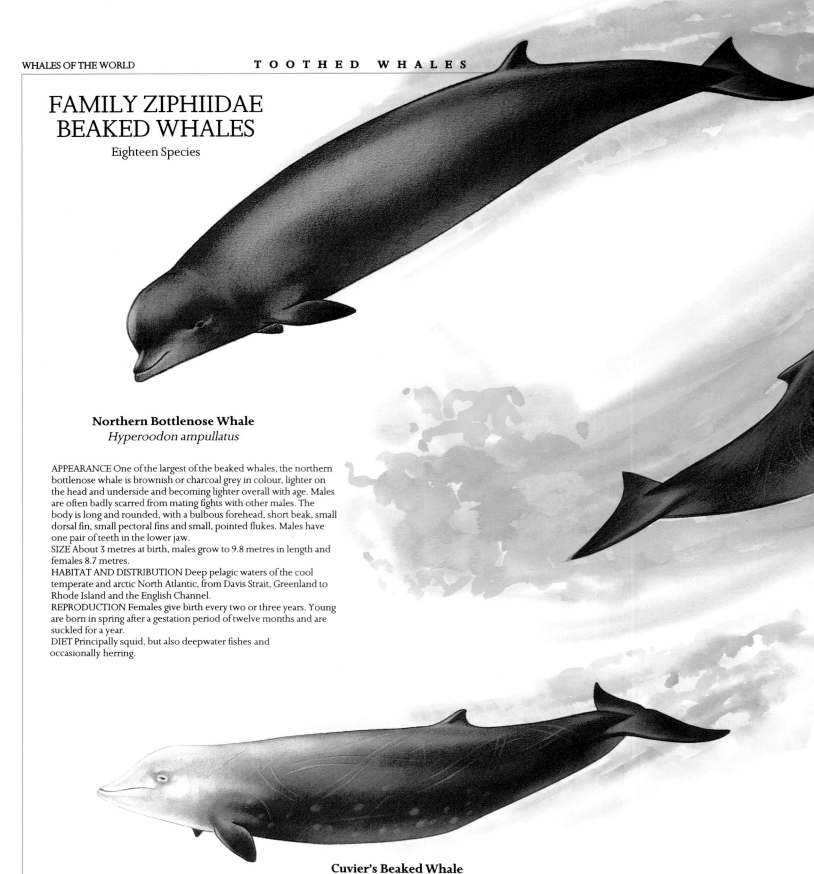

FAMILY ZIPHIIDAE
BEAKED WHALES
Eighteen Species

Northern Bottlenose Whale
Hyperoodon ampullatus

APPEARANCE One of the largest of the beaked whales, the northern bottlenose whale is brownish or charcoal grey in colour, lighter on the head and underside and becoming lighter overall with age. Males are often badly scarred from mating fights with other males. The body is long and rounded, with a bulbous forehead, short beak, small dorsal fin, small pectoral fins and small, pointed flukes. Males have one pair of teeth in the lower jaw.
SIZE About 3 metres at birth, males grow to 9.8 metres in length and females 8.7 metres.
HABITAT AND DISTRIBUTION Deep pelagic waters of the cool temperate and arctic North Atlantic, from Davis Strait, Greenland to Rhode Island and the English Channel.
REPRODUCTION Females give birth every two or three years. Young are born in spring after a gestation period of twelve months and are suckled for a year.
DIET Principally squid, but also deepwater fishes and occasionally herring.

Cuvier's Beaked Whale
Ziphius cavirostris

APPEARANCE Also known as the goose-beaked whale, this is one of the most commonly sighted members of a rare family. Colouration ranges from brown to grey or purplish black with a lighter belly and very often pale in the region of the face. Overall colour fades with age. Scars are common in males, which have a single pair of teeth in the lower jaw only. Cuvier's beaked whale has small, rounded pectoral fins and large, tapered flukes.

SIZE Between 2.5 and 3 metres at birth, reaching 7 metres (males) to 7.5 metres (females).
HABITAT AND DISTRIBUTION Temperate and tropical waters around the world.
REPRODUCTION Young are born in late summer to early autumn after a gestation period of about twelve months. Males are sexually mature at 5.5 metres, females at 6 metres.
DIET Deepwater fishes and squid.

Baird's Beaked Whale
Berardius bairdii

APPEARANCE This species' alternative common name of giant bottlenose whale describes its most distinctive feature — it is more than 2 metres longer than the next largest beaked whale and up to twice as long as some species. Colouration is slate grey with irregular whitish patches on the belly, and fighting scars are common. The dorsal fin is small, the pectoral fins are broad and rounded, and the flukes are relatively small. Males have two pairs of teeth in the lower jaw only with one pair protruding visibly from the tip of the jaws.
SIZE About 4.8 metres at birth (the adult length of some other beaked whales), males grow to 11.9 metres and females to 12.8 metres.
HABITAT AND DISTRIBUTION A temperate and subarctic species of the North Pacific, from Japan and southern California to the Bering Sea. It is usually seen in open ocean waters and dives to more than 1000 metres.
REPRODUCTION Mating takes place in October and November, and young are born after a relatively long gestation period of seventeen months. Males reach sexual maturity at 10 to 11 metres but there is no information for females.
DIET Deep-sea squid and fishes, with sea-cucumbers and crustaceans taken occasionally.

Strap-toothed Whale
Mesoplodon layardii

APPEARANCE The strap-toothed whale has a long, muscular body that tapers sharply behind the small, dorsal fin. The pectoral fins are small and rounded, and the flukes are broad and pointed. Colouration is bronze to purple or dark bluish black, with white areas on the beak, throat and genital area. Adults are greyish on the back, shoulders and head. Males can be identified by the two long, strap-like teeth in the lower jaw and, in older animals, these teeth may grow so long that their tips touch and prevent the mouth opening fully.
SIZE Calves are 76 centimetres or more at birth. Adult females reach 6.2 metres and males 5.8 metres in length.

HABITAT AND DISTRIBUTION Known primarily from strandings in the Southern Hemisphere, from New Zealand and Australia to South America and southern Africa.
REPRODUCTION Nothing known though one female stranded in New Zealand in September had recently given birth.
DIET Almost exclusively squid. It is believed that males use their tongues and throat grooves in a piston-like action to suck squid into the mouth when their teeth grow so long that they cannot open their mouth.

Sowerby's Beaked Whale
Mesoplodon bidens

APPEARANCE Only occasionally seen and sometimes probably confused with other beaked whales, Sowerby's beaked whale is undistinguished in appearance, with an elongated body, a more or less noticeable bulge in front of the blowhole and a longish beak. The dorsal and pectoral fins are relatively long and pointed, and the flukes are slender and pointed. Colour is usually mottled charcoal or bluish grey. Males have a single tooth halfway along each side of the lower jaw.
SIZE From about 2.4 metres at birth to 5 metres at maturity.

HABITAT AND DISTRIBUTION Despite its alternative name of North Sea beaked whale, this species is by no means confined to the North Sea and is apparently widespread (though nowhere common) in cool pelagic waters of the North Atlantic from Newfoundland to southern Norway and the Bay of Biscay.
REPRODUCTION Young are apparently born in late winter and early spring after a one-year gestation period, and are suckled for about a year.
DIET Squid and deepwater fishes.

FAMILY DELPHINIDAE
DOLPHINS AND OTHER SMALL TOOTHED WHALES
Thirty-one Species

Orca
Orcinus orca

APPEARANCE Unmistakable, the orca is the largest of the dolphins, with a robust and graceful body boldly marked in glossy black and white. The back and sides are black except for a teardrop-shaped patch of white behind and above the eye and a variably shaped 'saddle' behind and below the distinctive tall, elongated triangle of the dorsal fin, which is much larger in males than females. The head is rounded with no distinct beak, the pectoral fins are large, rounded and paddle-like, and the flukes are broad with a deep central notch. There are ten to twelve large, conical teeth in each side of the upper and lower jaws.

SIZE Orcas are about 2.4 metres long at birth and females grow to 8.2 metres and males to 9.4 metres.

HABITAT AND DISTRIBUTION Orcas are found in tropical, temperate and polar waters. They appear to prefer cooler coastal areas where their selected prey species are abundant.

REPRODUCTION The breeding season lasts all year. Calves are born after thirteen to sixteen months' gestation and are suckled for at least a year. Females reach sexual maturity at about 5 metres (males at 6.7 metres) and give birth every three to ten years.

DIET The orca resembles the great white shark in its predatory skill and range of food. This species eats seabirds, turtles, fishes (including sharks, even great white sharks), whales, dolphins, porpoises, seals and sea lions. Orcas are highly efficient co-operative hunters, feeding in groups of two to twenty animals, and will harry and kill baleen whales much larger than themselves.

False Killer Whale
Pseudorca crassidens

APPEARANCE The false killer whale is typically dolphin-like in shape and colouration (glossy black to dark grey) but lacks any sign of a beak. The body is long and torpedo-shaped, with an extended tail stock. The pectoral fins have a distinctive hump on their leading edge, the flukes are slender and pointed, and the dorsal fin is relatively large. The upper jaw overhangs the lower jaw and there are eight to eleven large, conical teeth in each side of both upper and lower jaws.

SIZE About 1.8 metres at birth, reaching 5 metres (females) or 6 metres (males) at maturity.

HABITAT AND DISTRIBUTION Highly social and sometimes forming herds of several hundred animals, the false killer whale is found in all tropical and temperate seas. The species is typically oceanic and is rarely found in shallow waters, where it strands occasionally.

REPRODUCTION Although the false killer whale is responsive and playful in captivity, little has been learned of its reproductive biology. Calves seem to be born at all times of the year.

DIET False killer whales feed almost exclusively on squid and fishes up to 60 centimetres in length, but they have been observed attacking other dolphins and sick or young humpback whales.

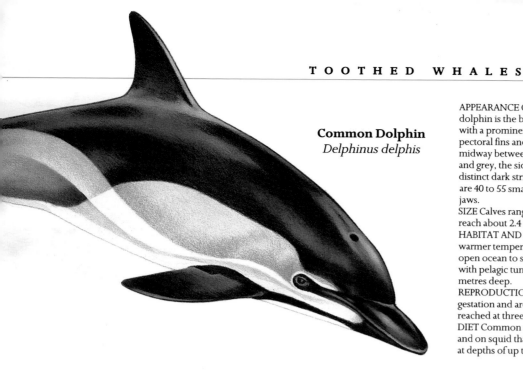

Common Dolphin
Delphinus delphis

APPEARANCE Celebrated in art since ancient times, the common dolphin is the best known of the small whales. The body is robust, with a prominent, sickle-shaped dorsal fin, long, slender and pointed pectoral fins and powerful flukes. The back is black from the beak to midway between the dorsal fin and the flukes, the flanks are ochre and grey, the sides of the tail stock are greyish white and there is a distinct dark stripe from the black beak to and around the eye. There are 40 to 55 small, pointed teeth in each side of the upper and lower jaws.
SIZE Calves range in length from 76 to 86 centimetres. Adult females reach about 2.4 metres and males 2.6 metres.
HABITAT AND DISTRIBUTION The common dolphin lives in warmer temperate and tropical waters around the world, from deep open ocean to shallow coastal seas. It is often found in association with pelagic tuna schools, but will also hunt in water only a few metres deep.
REPRODUCTION Calves are born in spring after eleven months' gestation and are suckled for five to six months. Sexual maturity is reached at three to four years of age or 1.7 to 1.8 metres in length.
DIET Common dolphins feed on anchovies, herring and sardines, and on squid that are hunted in the late afternoon and early evening at depths of up to 280 metres.

Indo-Pacific Humpback Dolphin
Sousa chinensis

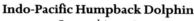
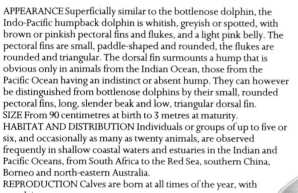

APPEARANCE Superficially similar to the bottlenose dolphin, the Indo-Pacific humpback dolphin is whitish, greyish or spotted, with brown or pinkish pectoral fins and flukes, and a light pink belly. The pectoral fins are small, paddle-shaped and rounded, the flukes are rounded and triangular. The dorsal fin surmounts a hump that is obvious only in animals from the Indian Ocean, those from the Pacific Ocean having an indistinct or absent hump. They can however be distinguished from bottlenose dolphins by their small, rounded pectoral fins, long, slender beak and low, triangular dorsal fin.
SIZE From 90 centimetres at birth to 3 metres at maturity.
HABITAT AND DISTRIBUTION Individuals or groups of up to five or six, and occasionally as many as twenty animals, are observed frequently in shallow coastal waters and estuaries in the Indian and Pacific Oceans, from South Africa to the Red Sea, southern China, Borneo and north-eastern Australia.
REPRODUCTION Calves are born at all times of the year, with a peak in summer.
DIET Reef-dwelling fishes and possibly crustaceans. This species may cross mudbanks in search of prey and has been observed hunting with bottlenose dolphins and finless porpoises.

Melon-Headed Whale
Peponocephala electra

APPEARANCE Similar in shape and behaviour to the pygmy killer whale, the melon-headed whale is dark grey over the entire body, with a thin white strip on the lips and a white anchor-shaped pattern on the upper chest. The prominent dorsal fin is large and sickle-shaped and the pectoral fins and flukes are well developed. There are between forty and fifty small, pointed teeth in each jaw.
SIZE Known to grow to at least 2.8 metres.

HABITAT AND DISTRIBUTION Like the pygmy killer whale, the melon-headed whale is found in the tropical and temperate Atlantic, Indian and Pacific Oceans.
REPRODUCTION Late winter breeding is suggested by sightings of newborn calves in the Southern Hemisphere in July and August.
DIET This species is known to feed on squid and small fishes.

FAMILY DELPHINIDAE
(continued)

White-Beaked Dolphin
Lagenorhynchus albirostris

APPEARANCE Despite its scientific and common names, this species can have a white, grey or dark beak. The back is dark grey, fading to grey on the flanks and white on the belly. The dorsal fin is sickle-shaped and prominent, the pectorals are pointed and the flukes are pointed with a distinct central notch. There are twenty-two to twenty-eight small, conical teeth in each side of the upper and lower jaws.
SIZE From 0.95 metres at birth to a maximum adult size of 3 metres.
HABITAT AND DISTRIBUTION Restricted to coastal regions of the North Atlantic, from the north-eastern United States to Greenland and the North Sea.
REPRODUCTION Calves are born between June and September, weighing around 40 kilograms. Their large size and weight are probably adaptations to birth in cold arctic waters. Sexual maturity is reached at about 2 metres.
DIET Squid, cod, herring, octopus and bottom-dwelling crustaceans.

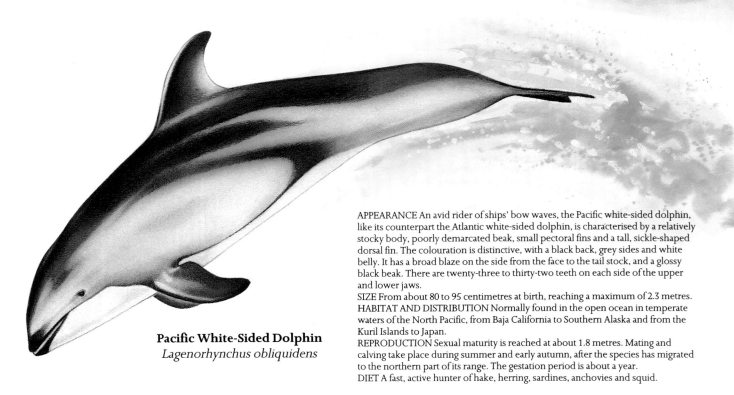

Pacific White-Sided Dolphin
Lagenorhynchus obliquidens

APPEARANCE An avid rider of ships' bow waves, the Pacific white-sided dolphin, like its counterpart the Atlantic white-sided dolphin, is characterised by a relatively stocky body, poorly demarcated beak, small pectoral fins and a tall, sickle-shaped dorsal fin. The colouration is distinctive, with a black back, grey sides and white belly. It has a broad blaze on the side from the face to the tail stock, and a glossy black beak. There are twenty-three to thirty-two teeth on each side of the upper and lower jaws.
SIZE From about 80 to 95 centimetres at birth, reaching a maximum of 2.3 metres.
HABITAT AND DISTRIBUTION Normally found in the open ocean in temperate waters of the North Pacific, from Baja California to Southern Alaska and from the Kuril Islands to Japan.
REPRODUCTION Sexual maturity is reached at about 1.8 metres. Mating and calving take place during summer and early autumn, after the species has migrated to the northern part of its range. The gestation period is about a year.
DIET A fast, active hunter of hake, herring, sardines, anchovies and squid.

Fraser's Dolphin
Lagenodelphis hosei

APPEARANCE Also known as the short-snouted whitebelly, this medium-sized species is bluish grey on the back with a dark eye patch, a greyish yellow patch on the flanks and pale pink to white on the belly. The colouration on the flanks is complicated by bands of white and there is a dark line from the mouth to the very small, narrow pectoral fins. The dark grey dorsal fin is small, as are the pointed flukes, and the beak is short but well defined. There are forty to forty-four teeth in each side of the upper and lower jaws.

SIZE Known to reach at least 2.4 metres at maturity, the length at birth is not known.
HABITAT AND DISTRIBUTION Tropical and warm temperate waters of the Indian and Pacific Oceans, with recent sightings in the tropical Atlantic. Fraser's dolphin is an open-ocean species and so wary of boats that it was known until 1979, only from a skeleton collected in 1895. In 1979, several were caught in tuna nets in the eastern Pacific and groups of more than 500 have since been observed.
REPRODUCTION Nothing known.
DIET Deep-sea fishes, squid and shrimp.

Bottlenose Dolphin
Tursiops truncatus

APPEARANCE Well known because of its ready adaptability to captivity, the bottlenose is the largest of the beaked dolphins, with a long, robust body, relatively small, pointed pectoral fins and flukes, and a short, stout beak marked by a crease where it meets the forehead. Colouration is usually dark grey above, fading on the sides to a pinkish white belly, but wholly pinkish brown specimens have been recorded. There are many (about forty) small, sharp, conical teeth in each of the upper and lower jaws.
SIZE Calves range in length from 90 to 130 centimetres at birth and grow to a maximum of 4 metres. Bottlenose dolphins have been known to live for thirty-seven years.
HABITAT AND DISTRIBUTION Worldwide in temperate and tropical waters, usually in coastal areas but often encountered in mid-ocean.
REPRODUCTION Sexual maturity is reached at 2.2 to 2.6 metres or between five and twelve years of age (variable) for females and males. Mating and calving vary geographically, but usually occur between spring and autumn. The gestation period is one year and calves suckle for up to eighteen months. The reproductive cycle for most females is two to three years.
DIET Small fishes, eels, catfish, mullet, squid, and shrimp. Bottlenose dolphins have been observed chasing fish on to mudflats, then sliding out of the water to seize their prey.

Hourglass Dolphin
Lagenorhynchus cruciger

APPEARANCE This remarkably attractive, fast-swimming dolphin has a stout body with a high, curved dorsal fin, long, curved pectorals and flukes, and a very short beak. Its colouration is striking — black from the beak along the back and pectoral fins to the flukes, white on the belly from the chin to the tail stock. The distinctive hourglass shape is created by a white blaze from the eye to below the dorsal fin, with a second blaze from the dorsal fin to the sides of the tail. There are about twenty-eight teeth in each side of the upper and lower jaws.
SIZE Little is known, but a 1.6 metre male and a 1.8 metre female have been recorded.
HABITAT AND DISTRIBUTION Cold subantarctic and antarctic offshore waters on both sides of the Atlantic Convergence.
REPRODUCTION Nothing known.
DIET Nothing known.

FAMILY DELPHINIDAE (continued)

Pantropical Spotted Dolphin
Stenella attenuata

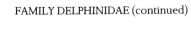

APPEARANCE A long, slender and typically delphinid body with a sickle-shaped dorsal fin, small, pointed pectoral fins and flukes, and a beak like that of the bottlenose dolphin but more slender. Although colouration is variable, it is generally steel grey with a dark stripe from the pectoral fins to the beak, the tip of which is usually white. The upper body and flanks are covered with dense grey spots, extending to the belly with age. There are many (about eighty) small, conical teeth in each of the upper and lower jaws.

SIZE Calves are about 80 centimetres long at birth and grow to a maximum of 2.5 metres, with males slightly larger and heavier than females. Individuals can live to forty-five years.

HABITAT AND DISTRIBUTION In coastal waters and open ocean in tropical and some subtropical regions throughout the world.

REPRODUCTION Males reach sexual maturity at around fourteen years, females at ten to twelve years. The gestation period is about eleven months and calves suckle for a further year.

DIET Squid, midwater and surface-dwelling fishes such as flying fish. This species is often sighted in association with yellowfin tuna.

Risso's Dolphin
Grampus griseus

APPEARANCE The grey grampus or Risso's dolphin is a stout-bodied species with a deep chest and a bulbous head without a beak. The dorsal fin is high and sickle-shaped, the pectoral fins are long and the flukes are wide and pointed. The body is generally mid to dark grey, lighter on the belly, with males becoming increasingly scarred with age. There are no teeth in the upper jaw and the lower jaw has three to seven conical teeth on each side.

SIZE About 1.5 metres at birth, growing to 4.3 metres.

HABITAT AND DISTRIBUTION Worldwide in tropical to cool temperate zones, almost always in the open ocean.

REPRODUCTION Risso's dolphins become sexually mature at about 3 metres but little else is known about their reproductive biology.

DIET Principally, if not exclusively, squid and octopus.

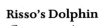

Hector's Dolphin
Cephalorhynchus hectori

APPEARANCE A particularly beautiful small dolphin. The tip of the lower jaw and the sides of the head are black, the back and sides are light brown to light grey and the belly is white. There is a hooked expansion of the white belly colour on the tail stock and a somewhat darker stripe along the sides from the eye to below the dorsal fin. The beak is barely discernible, the dorsal and pectoral fins are rounded and the flukes are very long and pointed. There are twenty-seven to thirty-two small, conical teeth in each side of the upper and lower jaws.

SIZE From about 50 centimetres at birth to a maximum of 1.8 metres at maturity.

HABITAT AND DISTRIBUTION Hector's dolphins prefer turbid, cloudy coastal and estuarine waters. The species is known definitely only from New Zealand but there have been unconfirmed reports from Australia and Borneo.

REPRODUCTION Calves are believed to be born during the summer migration from the South Island to the North Island of New Zealand.

DIET Bottom-dwelling fishes, anchovies, crustaceans, and squid.

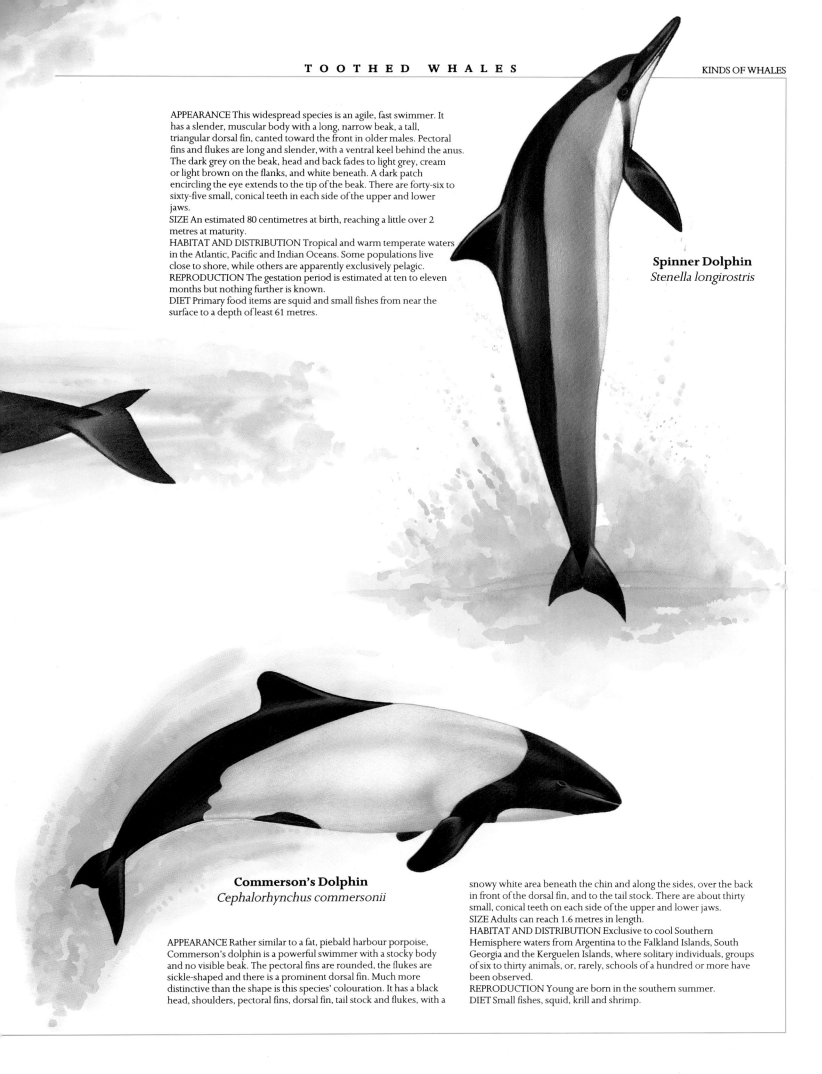

APPEARANCE This widespread species is an agile, fast swimmer. It has a slender, muscular body with a long, narrow beak, a tall, triangular dorsal fin, canted toward the front in older males. Pectoral fins and flukes are long and slender, with a ventral keel behind the anus. The dark grey on the beak, head and back fades to light grey, cream or light brown on the flanks, and white beneath. A dark patch encircling the eye extends to the tip of the beak. There are forty-six to sixty-five small, conical teeth in each side of the upper and lower jaws.
SIZE An estimated 80 centimetres at birth, reaching a little over 2 metres at maturity.
HABITAT AND DISTRIBUTION Tropical and warm temperate waters in the Atlantic, Pacific and Indian Oceans. Some populations live close to shore, while others are apparently exclusively pelagic.
REPRODUCTION The gestation period is estimated at ten to eleven months but nothing further is known.
DIET Primary food items are squid and small fishes from near the surface to a depth of least 61 metres.

Spinner Dolphin
Stenella longirostris

Commerson's Dolphin
Cephalorhynchus commersonii

APPEARANCE Rather similar to a fat, piebald harbour porpoise, Commerson's dolphin is a powerful swimmer with a stocky body and no visible beak. The pectoral fins are rounded, the flukes are sickle-shaped and there is a prominent dorsal fin. Much more distinctive than the shape is this species' colouration. It has a black head, shoulders, pectoral fins, dorsal fin, tail stock and flukes, with a snowy white area beneath the chin and along the sides, over the back in front of the dorsal fin, and to the tail stock. There are about thirty small, conical teeth on each side of the upper and lower jaws.
SIZE Adults can reach 1.6 metres in length.
HABITAT AND DISTRIBUTION Exclusive to cool Southern Hemisphere waters from Argentina to the Falkland Islands, South Georgia and the Kerguelen Islands, where solitary individuals, groups of six to thirty animals, or, rarely, schools of a hundred or more have been observed.
REPRODUCTION Young are born in the southern summer.
DIET Small fishes, squid, krill and shrimp.

FAMILY PHOCOENIDAE
PORPOISES
Six Species

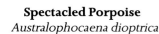

Spectacled Porpoise
Australophocaena dioptrica

APPEARANCE Larger than the three species in the genus *Phocoena,* the spectacled porpoise is known from very few specimens. The body is stocky, short, rounded pectoral fins, triangular dorsal fin, short triangular flukes. There is no trace of a beak but the small, rounded head has a well-defined 'forehead'. Colouration is distinctive, glossy black above with a white belly (extending to midway up the flanks). There is a grey 'saddle' on the sides of the tail stock, but the most distinctive feature is the white-circled eye that gives this species its common name. There are about forty small, spade shaped teeth in each of the upper and lower jaws.

SIZE One foetus, collected in 1912, measured 46 centimetres. Adult females average 1.8 metres and males 2 metres have been recorded.
HABITAT AND DISTRIBUTION Although most reports are from the western South Atlantic Ocean, there are records from New Zealand waters and subantarctic islands, suggesting it may have a circumpolar distribution in subantarctic latitudes. Observed near offshore islands of Argentina, Uruguay, the Falkland Islands and South Georgia.
REPRODUCTION Nothing is known but spectacled porpoises may breed in spring.
DIET Fish and squid.

Dall's Porpoise
Phocoenoides dalli

APPEARANCE With an almost perfectly hydrodynamic shape, Dall's porpoise is perhaps best known for its astonishing bursts of speed — so rapidly can it accelerate that it produces 'rooster tails' of spray behind it. The body is extremely chunky, with a small head, pectoral fins and flukes, and a prominent, triangular dorsal fin. There is a pronounced dorsal ridge behind the dorsal fin, and the tail stock, though deep, is narrow and tapering and especially in old males bears distinct keels above and below, just in front of the flukes. Colouration is black and white. There are nineteen to twenty-eight small, spade-shaped teeth on each side of the upper and lower jaws.

SIZE About 1 metre at birth; adult males reach 2.2 metres and weigh 200 kilograms.
HABITAT AND DISTRIBUTION Cold waters of the North Pacific, from Japan and California to the Bering Sea. Mainly found in inshore waters, but sometimes captured by tuna fishermen up to 1000 km offshore.
REPRODUCTION Males become sexually mature at 1.8 metres, females at 1.7 metres. Calves are born in July and August after a twelve months or less gestation period.
DIET Lanternfish, squid and small schooling fishes.

Finless Porpoise
Neophocaena phocaenoides

APPEARANCE Similar in many features to the belukha, the finless porpoise is also known as the black finless porpoise. Though black individuals have been recorded in Japanese waters, the general colour is pale grey on the back and white below. The body is rather stocky, with a blunt, rounded head that is given the suggestion of a beak by slightly protuberant jaws. Many individuals have pink eyes. The pectoral fins are long, tapered and pointed. The flukes are long and thin and the dorsal fin is reduced to a low ridge from the middle of the back to the tail. There are thirteen to twenty-two short, compressed, spade-like teeth on each side of the upper and lower jaws.
SIZE Young are 60 to 98 centimetres at birth and grow to 1.8 metres.
HABITAT AND DISTRIBUTION Warm coastal waters (rarely more than 5 kilometres from land) in Asia, from Pakistan to Korea, Japan and south to Borneo and Java.
REPRODUCTION Young are born in the summer after eleven to twelve months' gestation and suckle for at least a year, often riding on their mothers' backs.
DIET Small fishes, shrimp and squid.

Harbour Porpoise
Phocoena phocoena

APPEARANCE The harbour or common porpoise of the Northern Hemisphere is neither common nor seen often in harbours. It has no beak, small pectoral fins rounded at the tips, small flukes and a low, blunt dorsal fin. The stocky body is brown or dark grey on the back, often distinguished sharply from the light grey belly along the flanks. There are 23 to 28 small, spade-shaped teeth in each side of the upper jaw and 22-26 in each side of the lower jaw.
SIZE From 70 to 90 centimetres at birth, adults reaching 1.8 metres. Females are slightly larger and heavier than males.
HABITAT AND DISTRIBUTION Coastal waters of the North Atlantic from West Africa to Davis Strait and Iceland, with a separate population in the Black Sea — and also in the North Pacific from Alaska South to Baja California.

REPRODUCTION Harbour porpoises reach sexual maturity at four years and mate at two year intervals. Mating takes place in summer, there is a ten-month gestation period and the young suckle for at least six months.
DIET Herring, cod and other small schooling fishes, sole and bottom fishes (to a maximum of 90 metres), squid and shrimp.

FAMILY PLATANISTIDAE
RIVER DOLPHINS

Two Species

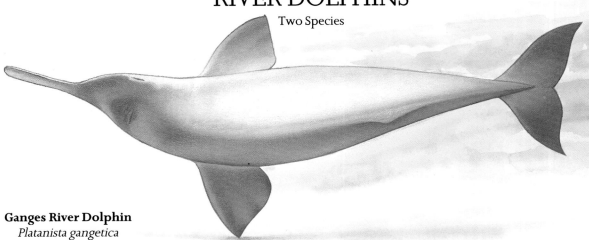

Ganges River Dolphin
Platanista gangetica

APPEARANCE The Ganges River dolphin or Ganges susu is also known as the side-swimming dolphin from its habit of swimming on its side to allow the leading edges of its large, rounded pectoral fins to comb the bottom. The eyes, which are capable only of distinguishing light from dark, are tiny and effectively non-functional — this species moves and feeds using only echolocation. The body is dark grey on the back, fading to light grey on the belly. The dorsal ridge culminates in a vestigial dorsal fin, the flukes are pointed and the beak is long and thin, bulging at its forward end. There are twenty-seven to thirty-three thin teeth on each side of the upper and lower jaws, increasing in size from the back of the jaw to the front.

SIZE Calves are about 75 centimetres long at birth, growing to a maximum of 2.4 metres.
HABITAT AND DISTRIBUTION The Ganges River dolphin is widespread along most of the Ganges, Brahmaputra and Karnaphuli Rivers of India and Bangladesh. The Indus River dolphin of Pakistan is separated geographically and is classified in a different species. But is essentially the same animal.
REPRODUCTION Calves are born in the spring after eight to nine months' gestation and are weaned within a year. Sexual maturity is reached at ten years and a length of 1.7 metres in males and around 2 metres in females.
DIET Includes shrimp, catfish, carp.

FAMILY INIIDAE
AMAZON RIVER DOLPHIN

One Species

Amazon River Dolphin
Inia geoffrensis

APPEARANCE Largest of the freshwater dolphins, the bouto or Amazon River dolphin has many unusual features. Pink overall or grey on the back merging to pink on the belly, it lacks a distinct dorsal fin, though its paddle-shaped pectoral fins are well developed and the flukes (often serrated on the trailing edge) are wide and pointed. The eyes are small but functional. The beak is very long and powerful, and there are twenty-five to thirty-five large teeth on each side of the upper and lower jaws. Most bouto have a few hairs on the beak at birth, but these usually disappear with age.
SIZE From 75 centimetres at birth to 2.5 metres or 3 metres and 90

kilograms in weight at adulthood. Males are generally slightly larger than females.
HABITAT AND DISTRIBUTION Main rivers of the Amazon and Orinoco River systems of tropical South America. There are three geographically distinct varieties, separated by mountain ranges but these are not sufficiently different to be classified as separate species.
REPRODUCTION Calves are born between July and September after a nine- to twelve-month gestation period and sexual maturity is reached at 2 metres (males) or 1.7 metres (females).
DIET Crustaceans, catfish and small freshwater fishes.

FAMILY LIPOTIDAE
CHINESE RIVER DOLPHIN
One Species

Chinese River Dolphin
Lipotes vexillifer

APPEARANCE The rare and endangered baiji or Chinese river dolphin has a low, triangular dorsal fin, which is often all that is seen of this shy animal. The body is stocky, with a bulbous melon, the beak is long, thin and tilted slightly upward. The pectoral fins are small and broad, and the flukes are well developed. The body is light to dark bluish grey on the back, fading to white on the belly. There are thirty-one to thirty-six relatively broad, wrinkled teeth on each side of the upper and lower jaws.

SIZE Fully developed foetuses have been found measuring 57 centimetres. Adult males reach about 2.1 metres and females about 2.4 metres.

HABITAT AND DISTRIBUTION Now restricted to the middle and lower reaches of the Yangtze River of China, the Chinese river dolphin's highly developed echolocation faculty is a response to the very silty waters of its habitat.

REPRODUCTION Males reach sexual maturity at around four years and females at around six years. The gestation period is very short.

DIET Eel-like, bottom-dwelling catfishes and other freshwater fishes have been found in the stomachs of animals accidentally hooked by fishermen.

FAMILY PONTOPORIIDAE
FRANCISCANA
One Species

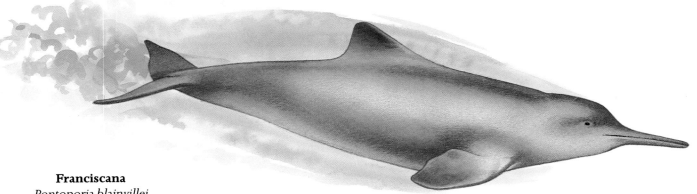

Franciscana
Pontoporia blainvillei

APPEARANCE The franciscana is an obscure, uncommon species that lives in shallow coastal waters along the Atlantic coast of South America. It is relatively stocky, with an exceedingly small head and a long, slender beak. The dorsal fin is triangular and extends as a ridge to the tailstock. The pectoral fins are paddle-shaped and the flukes are large and pointed. Colouration is pale brown above, fading to light brown below, and there are fifty or more small, very sharp teeth on each side of the upper and lower jaws.

SIZE Calves are about 70 centimetres long at birth and reach 1.5 metres and 32 kilograms (males) or 1.7 metres and 40 kilograms (females) at maturity.

HABITAT AND DISTRIBUTION Seen rarely in shallow coastal waters of the South Atlantic from Valdés Peninsula and La Plata delta of Argentina to near Rio de Janiero, Brazil.

REPRODUCTION Calves are born after ten months' gestation in October to February and are suckled for at least nine months. Sexual maturity is reached at two to three years of age, and calving occurs every two years.

DIET At least nineteen species of fishes, three species of shrimps and one species of squid. Franciscana are primarily bottom feeders.

BALEEN WHALES

WILLIAM H. DAWBIN

Baleen whales are filter feeders, using baleen (often referred to as whalebone) for sieving out small planktonic organisms. The group is sometimes also referred to as the 'great whales'. This term, however, while certainly applicable to all the larger members of the group, seems less appropriate to the smallest species, which are in fact exceeded in size by some of the toothed whales, for example, the orca (*Orcinus orca*), some bottlenose whales and, above all, by the great sperm whale (*Physeter catodon*). However, the largest of the baleen whales, the blue whale (*Balaenoptera musculus*), is not only the largest of all living animals but the largest ever known to have existed, greatly exceeding the size of the largest dinosaurs. This is even more impressive when one considers that it, and the other baleen whales, feed on the smallest organisms of any cetacean.

Paul Ensor

▲ The feature that separates baleen whales from their toothed cousins is whalebone: bristly plates that range in length from less than a metre in the minke whale to 4.5 metres in the bowhead. Straining some of the sea's smallest prey through their baleen, these whales have grown to enormous size.

The special adaptation for this feeding are horny plates arranged along either side of the upper jaw, more or less like the leaves of a book with the inner portion (facing the inside of the mouth) frayed out into bristle-like fibres, which may be coarse or almost silky depending on the type of animal being preyed upon. Baleen is a horny material related to keratin and therefore it is similar to human finger nails or the outer portion of the horns in cows, but totally different from bone. For this reason, the term whalebone can be rather misleading.

All the baleen whales depend on searching out massive concentrations of the very small organisms on which they feed, and the method of filtration used by each group differs according to diet. Since dense swarms of suitable plankton occur in the upper layers of the sea, baleen whales tend to travel mainly in the top 100 metres of the water and to be more shallow in both their cruising and feeding movements than the deep-diving sperm or bottlenose whales. They therefore do not need to spend as much time on each dive, so there is a shorter interval between 'blows', which are the visible condensations of moisture in the breath expelled under pressure when the animal surfaces. The shape and height of a blow is often distinctive enough to identify the species of whale. The dive interval varies from 4 or 5 minutes to 20 minutes, although longer intervals and deep dives can occur in special circumstances, for example, after harpooning. However, the dives of 90 minutes to depths of 2000 metres recorded for sperm whales are unknown for baleen whales.

The families within the baleen whale group (Suborder Mysticeti) can be described popularly, as the right whales, the pygmy right whale, the grey whale and rorquals, the latter term being used here in the broad sense to include the humpback.

RIGHT WHALES
Right whales are distinguished from the other baleen whales mainly by their very long baleen, with an almost silky texture to the bristles. They feed on small planktonic crustaceans, mainly copepods.

Right whales are large, heavy-bodied animals with thick blubber, and it was the combination of the high oil yield obtained from the blubber layer together with the great value that was placed on the very fine silky baleen that gave them the name of right whales. meaning the 'right' whales to catch.

Because of the nature of their feeding — a skimming motion that involves ploughing through the water with the mouth partly open, the water

Francois Gohier/Auscape International

streaming out from the inside through the baleen plates with the tiny organisms being trapped on the silky bristles — there is no need for expansion of the throat, and ventral grooves or large pleats in the throat region are absent in this family. They have no dorsal fin and the mouth is greatly arched to contain the long baleen.

There are three species in the right whale family; the northern right whale (*Eubalaena glacialis*), the southern right whale (*Eubalaena australis*) and the bowhead (*Balaena mysticetus*).

The first species to become generally known was the northern right whale, which was first hunted in the Bay of Biscay by the Basques in the tenth century, and for several centuries thereafter. Basque operations extended to the North Atlantic right across to Newfoundland. They were joined by whalers from Holland and Britain, and catches over a period of several centuries finally decreased right whale numbers to the stage where they had become extremely rare throughout the region and are only now starting to show signs of recovery in some areas, particularly along the east coast of North America.

Northern right whales reach a maximum length of 17–18 metres. They have a limited cyclical

movement through the seasons, going into warmer waters in winter and cooler waters, where most of the feeding occurs, during the summer months.

Past migration limits for northern right whales were largely deduced from the history of catches, which showed that they did not travel as far north into arctic waters as the bowhead but that they travelled much further south along the east coast of the United States to Florida and to the Cintra Bay region of North Africa. In the Pacific Ocean, they entered Japanese waters and were caught from the Gulf of Alaska to British Columbia and occasionally to California, with only a few taken in the Bering Sea, where the main bowhead catches occurred.

The southern right whale is so similar in overall appearance that many whale biologists retain the same specific name, although at a recent International Whaling Commission Symposium, the decision was made to retain separate identities for northern and southern stocks, which appear to be geographically quite separate, since there is a big gap across equatorial and tropical regions between the northern and southern animals.

Southern right whales were hunted later than the northern stocks, with the entry of the whalers

▲ The first of the great whales to be commercially hunted, the 18-metre-long northern right whale earned its name because it swims slowly, floats when dead and yields an unusual amount of baleen and oil, and was therefore considered the 'right' whale to hunt. This species was hunted to the edge of extinction.

DIFFERENCES BETWEEN BALEEN AND TOOTHED WHALES

MICHAEL BRYDEN

The characteristics that separate Cetacea into the two suborders baleen or whalebone whales (Mysticeti) and toothed whales (Odontoceti) are the presence or absence of baleen plates and teeth. However, there are other differences between the suborders; namely the shape of the skull, the appearance of the blowhole and the form of the ribs and the sternum.

The skull of odontocetes, when viewed from above, is markedly asymmetrical, but the significance of this is not understood. Possibly related to this asymmetry is the presence of a single opening at the blowhole.

One end of the rib of a land mammal usually bears two articular processes. One (the head) forms a joint with the vertebral body, while the other (the tubercle) forms a joint with the transverse process of the vertebra. Most ribs in mysticetes bear a tubercle, but no head.

Ribs that articulate with the sternum are known as sternal ribs, as opposed to floating ribs, which have no connection with the sternum.

The distinguishing features of the two suborders of Cetacea are as follows:

Mysticeti	Odontoceti
Teeth lacking (except as embryonic vestiges)	Teeth present (although in some species they do not emerge through the gum)
Baleen plates present	No baleen plates
Skull symmetrical	Skull asymmetrical
External nasal openings paired	Single external nasal opening
One to three ribs have heads	Four to eight ribs have heads
Sternal ribs absent	Sternal ribs present
Sternum composed of a single bone, which articulates with the first pair of ribs only	Sternum composed of three or more bones, which articulate with three or more pairs of the ribs

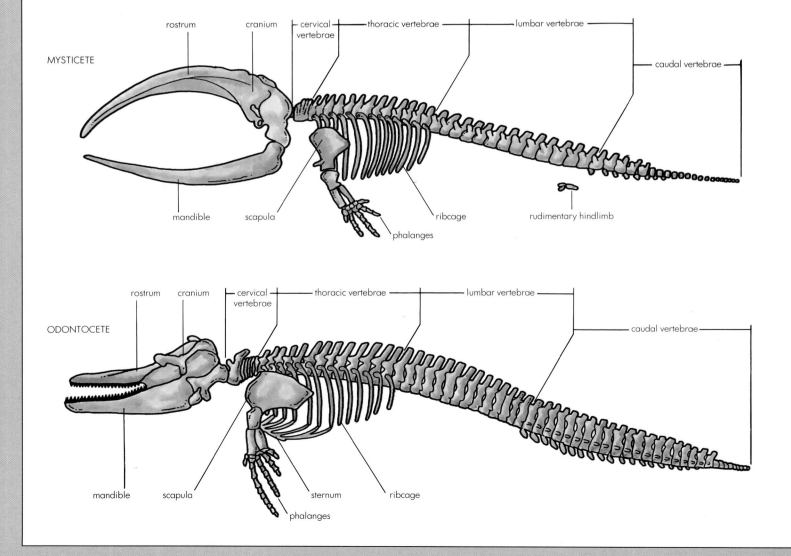

MYSTICETE — rostrum, cranium, cervical vertebrae, thoracic vertebrae, lumbar vertebrae, caudal vertebrae, mandible, scapula, phalanges, ribcage, rudimentary hindlimb

ODONTOCETE — rostrum, cranium, cervical vertebrae, thoracic vertebrae, lumbar vertebrae, caudal vertebrae, mandible, scapula, phalanges, sternum, ribcage

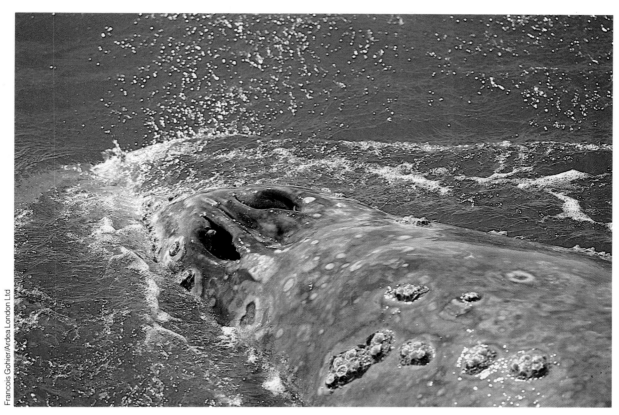

Francois Gohier/Ardea London Ltd

Apart from significant internal differences that suggest the two suborders of whales evolved independently, there are obvious external differences. Great size is one: few species of toothed whales approach the length of the smallest baleen whales, and whereas toothed whales have a single nasal opening or blowhole, baleen whales have two of roughly equal size.

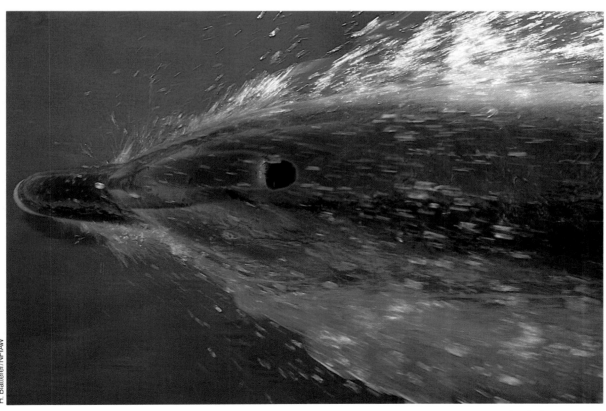

H. Blatterer/NPIAW

Toothed whales range in length from 1.5 metres to almost 20 metres and are generally faster swimmers than baleen whales, since they must actively hunt their prey: feeding is not simply a matter of swimming through a 'soup' of food. As well as having only one blowhole, toothed whales have skeletal structures that differ in detail from those of baleen whales.

Dave Watts/Australasian Nature Transparencies

▲ Classified as a distinct species largely because of its geographical separation from the northern right whale, the southern right whale was hunted unmercifully in the nineteenth century.

into the South Atlantic during the late eighteenth century and into the Pacific mainly at the very end of the eighteenth century, expanding rapidly through the nineteenth century. Stocks, as located, were attacked on the high seas by pelagic sailing vessels that put over long boats on sighting prospective catch. Peak activity was carried out by the Yankee whaling fleet (mainly from the New England ports of Nantucket and New Bedford). Because breeding animals usually come close to shore, a great many shore stations were established on different land masses, such as South Africa, Australia, particularly Tasmania and around the coast of New Zealand.

The combined result from all these activities occurring simultaneously was that in the Australasian region alone, for example, more than 12 000 southern right whales were taken in the five-year period, from 1835 to 1839 inclusive, with a further 7000 during the next five years. Within this decade, more than three-quarters of all Australasian catches occurred and the stocks were

depleted to such small numbers that most operations ceased. Southern right whales have remained a vary rare animal throughout the Southern Ocean for more than a hundred years. Some recovery was first noted off South America during aerial observations and off South Africa, and later off Western Australia, then southern Australia and New Zealand, but still with only isolated individuals being observed off eastern Australia or Tasmania.

Despite the long history of catching, very little of their biology was known until studies were carried out this century, long after whaling for this species had ceased. A great deal of this information was first unravelled from studies by Roger Payne off peninsula Valdés in Argentina where monitoring of animals, identified by photos of their individual markings, showed that in coastal areas some southern right whales come relatively close to shore to calve. It was some time before it was realised that nearly all the animals close to shorelines were in fact pregnant females, and calving can occur as close as a matter of some hundreds of metres behind the surfline. It soon became apparent that animals that calved in one year were not seen for the next two years. New crops appeared in these successive years, showing that the great majority of right whales calved at an interval of three years, and this has been confirmed repeatedly by known animals that have returned. The situation of immature animals and mature males is less clear, but they do appear to be further away from the shoreline. The fact that females and calves are the ones close to shore has contributed greatly to their history of destruction, particularly by operations from shore stations. Whalers had no compunction in killing the calves to make it easier to attack the mother, and the combination of these two mortalities along with catches on the high seas proved devastating.

Southern right whales do not migrate as far south as the rorquals, so were not part of the catch of modern whaling in the area where krill is the predominant food. Southern right whale movements, as confirmed by recent systematic sighting surveys, appear to end at the Antarctic Convergence — the invisible southern line of temperature change from coolish subantarctic waters to the truly cold antarctic krill-bearing waters. Southern right whales therefore are rarely encountered among the swarms of krill, and in fact feed on much smaller crustaceans, mainly copepods. Their migration is therefore more limited in that they do not go so far south and nor do they travel so far north on their return to warmer waters for calving.

Characteristically both northern and southern right whales are slow swimmers that do not normally expose large amounts of the body and breaching or leaping clear of the water is infrequent in adult animals but it can sometimes be seen as long sequences in the possibly more playful juveniles and young.

The largest, least known and, in its day, the most commercially valuable of the right whale family is the bowhead. Confined entirely to arctic and subarctic waters, this animal reaches about 18 metres in length and has an enormous head that can be up to 40 per cent of total body length. The upper jaw is arched, giving a mouth capacity that allows the baleen plates to reach such extraordinary lengths as 4.5 metres, that is, more than double the length of the baleen of northern or southern right whales. This made their baleen by far the most valuable of any whale's, and they, like their cousins, were also massive producers of oil.

Bowheads are slow-moving, confined very much to cold waters. They were originally known in particular around Spitzbergen, where they were hunted from the 1700s onwards until stocks were drastically depleted, then off Greenland, Baffin Island and Hudson Bay, and later still in the North

Bruce Krogman/National Marine Fisheries Service

◄ Confined to far northern waters, the bowhead readily swims beneath broad sheets of ice from one 'lead' of permanently ice-free water to another. Like the northern right whale, the bowhead sometimes swims upside down. It can then be identified from the air by its white chin and belly markings.

Don Croll

Pacific in the Bering and Okhotsk seas. The inevitable overfishing reduced stocks to such low levels that possible extinction was once feared and all catching prohibited, except for a controversial small quota (about 20–30), allowed by the United States to Eskimo whalers to maintain this aspect of their cultural heritage. The fact that this catch has continued has prompted intense investigation of stocks by aerial surveys, by sightings from ice and land plus monitoring by underwater hydrophones to record whale sounds and movements. Fortunately, this effort has suggested that stocks are not as desperately endangered as was once thought and the population of at least 3000 or 4000, although not large, may be relatively secure.

PYGMY RIGHT WHALE

This small (up to 6 metres) whale has long baleen with fine bristles like the larger right whales, but there are enough anatomical differences including such things as the rib cage and the presence of a

▲ Yielding even more oil and baleen than the other right whales, the bowhead has a huge head and an arched upper jaw, with baleen plates up to 4.5 metres in length. It is a strong, if slow swimmer: a harpooned bowhead once towed a fully rigged whaling ship for more than thirty hours at a steady two knots.

dorsal fin to warrant separating it from the larger right whales as a distinct family.

The pygmy right whale (*Caperea marginata*) is entirely Southern Hemisphere in distribution and, until recent years, had been known almost solely from strandings, about 40 in all, from Australia, especially Tasmania, New Zealand and South Africa. It is assumed that these coastlines are somewhere near the northern end of the range, and that they possibly migrate into subantarctic waters, like the large right whales, and also feed on small crustaceans, such as copepods. This has been partly confirmed from the examination of stomach contents of a few taken for scientific purposes off Tristan da Cunha.

Until recently, their sounds were unknown, but hydrophones adjacent to a solitary animal in Victoria, Australia, picked up on several occasions double thumps like the bang of a large drum but no other sound was recorded.

When swimming, the fin of the pygmy right projects in much the same position and appears similar to that of the minke whale (*Balaenoptera acutorostrata*). In fact, unless the distinctive head of the pygmy right is exposed, and this is seldom seen, the back has almost certainly been misidentified on a number of occasions as minke. For this reason, it may well be that this species is not as rare as has been believed.

GREY WHALE

This 14-metre long whale has some features that are sufficiently distinctive to justify separation of the single species into a family of its own. Like right whales, the grey whale (*Eschrichtius robustus*) has no dorsal fin but there are a series of humps (up to 10) along the top of the tail stock. The head has a curved upper jaw, but the mouth is not as markedly arched as in right whales and the baleen plates suspended from it are therefore shorter. The baleen also has coarser bristles and the animal follows a different feeding regime. There is a single pair (rarely, two pairs) of short throat grooves, compared with none in right whales and 20–90 long pleats in rorquals. The colouration is basically grey, as the name indicates, but this is usually broken by mottling to give a somewhat blotched effect.

Grey whales have a more rugged, less streamlined appearance than the rorquals and their moderate swimming speeds are closer to those of right whales although they are capable of short, high-speed bursts in aggressive displays. They undertake long-distance seasonal migrations from coastal warm-water calving areas visited in winter to cold, temperate or subarctic feeding areas in summer; the routes determined by the geography of the stock locations, all of which are in the Northern Hemisphere.

The grey whale is the only baleen whale to feed on bottom-living organisms, which it stirs up

Francois Gohier/Ardea London Ltd

by using the snout to bring gammarids (related to sandhoppers) and other material free from the bottom. The turbid water is then actively sucked into the mouth, filtered through the baleen and finally sucked back into the throat. Usually the grey whale is a 'right-sided' feeder, that is, it goes down and stirs up the bottom on its right side so that the baleen on that side is worn away. Some 'left-sided' animals have been seen with the left baleen plates worn away in a similar fashion.

Grey whales occurred in North Atlantic seas in prehistoric times, as shown by subfossil remains in Sweden, Holland and East Anglia in the United Kingdom. There are descriptions of sightings that seem to apply to this species at sea or in occasional catches into the early part of the eighteenth century. There have been no records in the North Atlantic since that time and its extinction in the region would seem to be from causes other than whaling, since it was never a major quarry in this part of the world.

In the North Pacific, grey whales were a relatively common animal in the nineteenth century with two main stocks, one of which migrated seasonally along Asian coastlines from the Sea of Japan past Korea to the southwest portion of the Bering Sea and the other along the western United States from the Gulf of Alaska down to lagoons in Baja California, Mexico. The Asian stock was probably the smaller of the two and it was hunted to extinction by about 1930–40.

▶ Just as the industrial revolution created a host of new uses for whale oil, from wool processing to machine lubrication, new uses were found for baleen. It was employed in the making of corsets, umbrella staves, venetian blinds, window gratings and riding crops — even furniture springing and portable sheep pens.

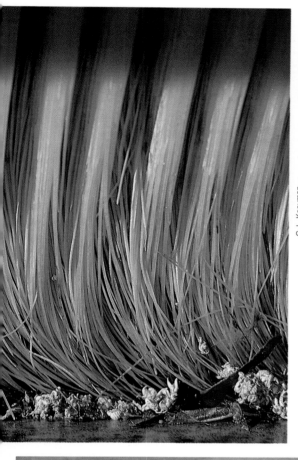

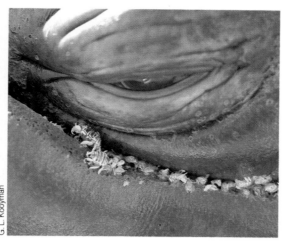

G. L. Kooyman

◄ The grey whale's eye, a little larger than that of an ox, is almost lost in the huge head. Nevertheless, it is fully functional both in water and in air, and can distinguish objects at some distance as well as at close range in the mud stirred up by this species' feeding habits. Whale 'lice' inhabit skin folds around the eye and throat grooves.

The stock off western United States was pursued in breeding areas, notably Scammon's lagoon from 1846 and became greatly reduced and endangered. Total protection (except for some small-scale aboriginal catches) was applied from 1946 and stock recovery has been carefully monitored ever since to show steady increases with a stock now stabilising at about 11 000 animals. These provide great delight to many whale spotters and are the object of intense study along the northwest coastline of the United States.

▼ Grey whales feed primarily by stirring up bottom sediments, 'ploughing' the sea bed for small organisms and fish, but they also take mouthfuls of kelp from which they strain small creatures. Most greys are 'right-sided' feeders, swimming on their sides to feed and wearing down the baleen plates on the right side of the mouth.

Gerard Wellington/Earthviews

RORQUALS

This family of six species contains several of the largest of all whales, but also includes the minke, which is considerably smaller than some cetaceans in other families. All, however, share a number of features. Their overall shape is very streamlined with pointed head, a distinctive fin, relatively small compact flippers and, above all, a large series of longitudinal throat grooves extending from immediately under the chin to well posterior to the line of flippers. These grooves or pleats are numerous, ranging from about 50 in sei whales (*Balaenoptera borealis*) to 90 in blue whales. They function in allowing the expansion of the throat like the unfolding of a concertina, increasing the mouth capacity during feeding. The amount of food required for the growth and maintenance of the huge rorquals, such as the fin whale (*Balaenoptera physalus*) and the blue whale, necessitates the ingestion of vast amounts of seawater from which to filter the relatively tiny krill. In recent years, some magnificent aerial shots have been taken, mainly in the Northern Hemisphere, showing the mouth open to 45° or more and full extension of the throat grooves to form an enormous pouch-like sac, like a greatly magnified pelican. It is clear that many tonnes of seawater are filtered per mouthful.

All rorquals are active, relatively fast swimmers and most undergo extensive migrations from polar waters, where they feed, to warm temperate or subtropical waters for breeding. There are differences in colouration detail and small differences in shape, but the overall impression is one of remarkable uniformity in appearance, except for the great differences in size between the largest and smallest.

The largest species is of course the blue whale, reaching maximum lengths of nearly 31 metres,

▶ Celebrated by Herman Melville as the most 'gamesome' of the great whales, the humpback breaches more often than other baleen whales and can leap almost clear of the water. This behaviour is most common on breeding grounds, but solitary humpbacks have been observed breaching by themselves, apparently for enjoyment.

▼ The humpback's large head, gigantic flippers fins and stocky body are in sharp contrast to the sleek, streamlined appearance of other rorquals. Like them, however, it has throat grooves that allow it to take in extraordinary amounts of water and it often 'lunge feeds', engulfing schools of fish or shrimp by surfacing with its mouth agape.

Rosemary Chastney/Ocean Images, Inc./Planet Earth Pictures

Rosemary Chastney/Ocean Images, Inc./Planet Earth Pictures

Francois Gohier/Auscape International

▲ Unrivalled in its grace and dreadnought size, the blue whale was held in awe by open-boat whalers who could not keep pace with it, much less carry the line needed to harpoon and capture it. Leviathans succumbed to Norwegian Svend Foyn in 1876 with the introduction of the grenade harpoon and steam catcher, and may never recover from the exploitation that saw 30 000 killed in a single year.

▶ Paradoxically, the cold and often light-poor arctic and antarctic waters are rich in nutrients and support a far greater mass of animal life than tropical oceans. Small euphausiid shrimps called krill are exploited directly by the largest animals in these — and any other — regions.

and one has been weighed, piece by piece, to give a total of 180 tonnes. These huge animals could produce up to 30 tonnes of oil and, after the whale hunters' technology improved sufficiently, they became the prime target of the twentieth-century whalers, particularly in waters surrounding Antarctica. Much of their biology has been deduced from the more detailed measurements and records maintained by twentieth-century whaling inspectors and from the collection of reproductive organs, foetuses and other material in a way that did not occur during the earlier hunting of species such as the right whales, bowheads and, to a lesser extent, the grey whale. The final conclusions were that mating occurs in warm waters, gestation lasts 10–12 months, followed by a lactation period of something less than a year. Rapid growth has produced sexual maturity at somewhere between about 7 and 12 years. The exact age of maturity seems to depend a good deal on the availability of food and there is substantial evidence that as whale numbers declined due to overhunting — and presumably more food became available to the survivors — the age of maturity was reduced. Calves are probably produced at two-year, or sometimes three-year, intervals.

The blue whale in southern waters feeds almost exclusively on krill (*Euphausia superba*), and it was the feeding grounds, where the animals were fattening up, that was the location of most hunting. Northern Hemisphere stocks do occur in subarctic waters where they must feed on a mix of other crustaceans, since true krill does not occur in these waters.

In both hemispheres the animals migrate to warmer waters for mating and calving, but it appears that during this migration they actively avoid close proximity to major shorelines since

Flip Nicklin

catching from shore never produced large blue whale catches. Off Australia and New Zealand, for example, only three blue whales have been caught among many thousands of humpbacks (*Megaptera novaeangliae*). No major concentrations representing a homogeneous circumscribed breeding area have been identified, so it is assumed that the animals must be fairly widely dispersed across the oceans during the breeding phase. Humpbacks were the main antarctic whaling catches during the early part of this century, due to the location of onshore factories in the South Atlantic or factory ships adjacent to bays and sheltered waters, combined with the much greater ease of catching this species. However, the development of the catchers' equipment combined with wide-ranging pelagic floating factories enabled the much more valuable blue whale to become the main quarry later in the century. This developed to the stage where in 1930, the peak year, nearly 30 000 blue whales were taken. This was vastly more than the stocks

could sustain and from that period onwards there was a steadily declining proportion of blue whales in the catch as whalers turned to the next species, the fin whale.

The fin whale reaches a maximum size of about 26 metres and produces about half as much oil as the largest of the blue whales. As the name suggests, it has a slightly more prominent fin than the blue whale and is a darker, more uniform grey than the bluish or mottled blue colour of its larger cousin. It reached a major peak in catches under

the onslaught of the whalers followed by progressive decline. Attempts to regulate this exploitation were made seriously in postwar years, commencing with the International Whaling Commission in 1946, which set overall quotas for all species that could be caught in antarctic waters.

However, the quotas were not set species by species, and could be made up of any mix in the ratio of: 1 blue whale = 2 fin whales = 2.5 humpbacks = 6 sei whales. Thus pressure from the whalers was maintained on the larger animals

▲ Similar in appearance to the blue and sei whales, the fin whale is distinguished by a falcate dorsal fin and by the astonishing speeds at which it can swim. A cruising speed of 16 to 20 kilometres per hour can be reached during migrations by this 26-metre-long 'greyhound of the sea'.

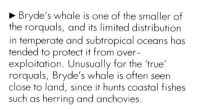

▲ Ignoring the lessons of early open-boat and mechanised whaling, in which overfishing led to the disappearance of their livelihood, whalers turned from the gigantic blue to ever smaller species. The medium-sized (15 metres) sei whale was a poor substitute for blues and fins, but was pursued until numbers were greatly reduced.

and the smaller species were only turned to progressively as the stocks of larger whales declined. This led to the well-known sequence of a major onslaught on blue whales, followed by the peak catch being made up of fin whales, which were in turn followed by a sei whale peak as the fin whales also declined. Finally, an animal that was not even included in the original quotas, the small minke, originally regarded as too small and unimportant for catching, became the target, not so much for its oil, but for the value of its meat, particularly to the customers of Japan.

The sei whale reaches a length of about 15 metres, has a very distinctive falcate fin and the standard rorqual overall shape, but the bristles on the inside of the baleen plates are considerably finer than those of its larger cousins. There is evidence that sei whales feed mainly on food similar to that taken by right whales and that they do not penetrate so far south into the waters of the krill. Sei whales migrate, therefore, from a position not so far into cold polar waters as the blue and fin whales, but they also migrate into warmer waters to calve, and calving and mating appear to occur mainly away from immediate shorelines.

The minke whale is the smallest of the 'true' rorquals, reaching a maximum length of about 8–9 metres. It is distributed right into the pack ice and individuals have often been observed pushing their quite sharp pointed heads up through cracks between the ice floes — providing considerable entertainment for scientists and travellers in those areas. They leave the ice during the breeding season, but as with the larger rorquals, there do not seem to be major coastal assemblages in the

breeding season. In some waters, for example, off eastern Australia and across to New Zealand, minke whales can be seen irregularly throughout the year and their colour pattern of white usually extending from across the flipper right up into the shoulder region is distinctive. The animals in the region appear not to reach such large sizes as the better known cold-water minkes and it may be that they are a separate warmer water subspecies.

Bryde's whale (*Balaenoptera edeni*), unlike the other rorquals, does not penetrate into polar waters but appears to be largely a temperate subtropical water whale with rather limited migration since it seems to feed all the year round on a diet including small herring and pilchard-like fish. They have quite often been observed feeding close to shore off eastern Australia and northern New Zealand and, at the latter locality, a limited number were caught over a brief period in the 1950s, when they were tentatively identified as sei whales, which superficially they closely resemble. However, baleen saved from the catches was much coarser in texture and quite different from the fine fibres of the sei whale's baleen. Bryde's whales have not formed a major component of catches in any of the world's oceans although occasional specimens have been taken.

For a number of reasons, the highly distinctive humpback has become the best known and most intensively studied of all the large species. While it belongs to the same family as the rorquals, it is sufficiently distinctive in a number of features to justify separation into the separate genus (*Megaptera*). Its very large flippers, which are larger than those of blue whales of more than

▶ Bryde's whale is one of the smaller of the rorquals, and its limited distribution in temperate and subtropical oceans has tended to protect it from over-exploitation. Unusually for the 'true' rorquals, Bryde's whale is often seen close to land, since it hunts coastal fishes such as herring and anchovies.

twice the length, are perhaps the most distinctive feature. The flippers are so prominent that they can often be seen from considerable distances from the air, especially in breaching whales, which carry out back-somersaults and other manoeuvres to expose the whole body above water. Humpbacks will also, on occasion, protrude the whole flipper above water while the animal itself is lying on its side, and this solitary, gently waved structure, up to 4.5 metres in length, may be raised for up to one hour at a time. While this seems to occur in or near breeding areas, its real meaning is not understood.

Humpbacks reach a maximum length of about 15 metres for females, slightly less for males, although a few larger animals have been reported. Sexual maturity occurs at a length of about 13 metres for females, 12 metres for males — at the age of about 8–12 years, as is the case with other rorquals. Mating occurs in waters that are warmer than those frequented by other rorquals but, since humpbacks are also found almost to the pack ice

during feeding, they must undertake longer migrations to cover the distance between breeding and feeding areas.

In antarctic waters humpbacks feed on krill, but early South Atlantic captures showed that in subantarctic waters some also fed on a different organism, the lobster krill. Observations of feeding in antarctic waters are not abundant although animals have been noted lying more or less on their sides, swimming round in fairly tight circles with the mouth partly open so that water flows out through the baleen as they swim and periodic closing of the mouth forces out remaining water to capture material within. The throat, although containing considerably fewer throat grooves (about 20) than other rorquals, seems to be able to expand in a similar way to the throats of blue and fin whales. Many observations of different modes of feeding have been made in the Northern Hemisphere, in the area from about Cape Cod to Newfoundland and at Glacier Bay, Alaska. Here, animals are sometimes seen circling with their

▲ *Megaptera novaeangliae*, the humpback whale, was once named *Megaptera nodosa* in recognition of its great wing-like flippers (up to 4.5 metres and a third of the animal's total length) and the relatively regular protuberances around the edge of the upper jaw.

THE BLOW

SIR RICHARD HARRISON

A whale, being a mammal, has to breathe and must come to the surface to carry out the respiratory act. On surfacing, sometimes just before, the whale breathes out or 'blows' — thus the cry from the masthead — 'There she blows' at the sight of the whale spouting. Early whalers thought the animal actually sent up a spout of water but it is a cloud of vapour or steam blown off as a result of the whale emptying its lungs. This forceful exhalation is followed by inspiration and then there is a short pause until the cycle is repeated, often five or six times each minute, until the whale dives.

Ancient mariners have warned against touching the blow. The outer part was acrid, made the skin smart and caused peeling as if it had been burnt. Should it enter the eyes, blindness could result; it was wisest to leave the deadly, poisonous spout alone. Herman Melville, author of *Moby Dick or The Whale,* observing a mist above his head while composing a little treatise on Eternity, postulated that as with all profound thinkers a 'certain semi-visible steam' emanates from the head on deep thoughts!

The blow is composed of moist exhaled air which is undergoing adiabatic cooling together with some condensation of water vapour; it also contains an emulsion of fine oil droplets from cells lining the air sinuses, mucus from the abundant tracheal glands and surfactant from the lungs. Surfactant is a mixture of lipoproteins which reduces surface tension in pulmonary fluids and aids the rapid ventilation of the whale's lungs. The blow does leave a greasy film on what it touches, and it smells of a mixture of bad fish and sump oil. An old text claimed that the breath of a whale is so insupportably smelly that it brings on disorders of the brain.

The blow varies in its characteristics depending on climate and weather, size of the animal, and the type of whale, so that skilled captains could identify in good weather what they were chasing. The blow is whiter and more obvious in cold weather but is badly disturbed by high winds. The height of the blow is greatest (5–8m) in sperm, blue and fin whales, moderate (2–3m) in right, sei, grey and humpback whales, low (1m) in bottlenose and minke whales. The blow is difficult to discern or is only momentary in the smaller toothed whales. It is double in right whales due to their two blowholes, single and directed forwards in sperm whales, and tall and single in blue, fin and sei whales.

The frequency of the blow is related to what the whale is doing. When unmolested and cruising on its way, a large whale will blow and take in a regular series of breaths at one or more per minute and then sound for a long period. On surfacing once more, the same pattern of repeated breaths occurs; this was known to the old whalers as *having his spoutings out* and it indicates the need for repeated blows to rid the circulation of lactic acid and carbon dioxide accumulated during the long dive. At the same time the oxygen stores, such as the myoglobin in muscles, are replenished and it is probable that some of the venous blood retains a higher oxygen content for use later in a dive.

Experienced whalemen thought that a whale needed to make so many spoutings out before diving deep and if molested before completion of that number would 'always be dodging up again to make good his regular allowance of air'. Thus if encountered before ready to sound to the depths, a whale was much more easily pursued and struck. There are several accounts of whales, especially sperm whales, turning on their hunters and in great fury smashing the boats — perhaps they were molested too early in their spoutings out.

One final reflection on a whale's breathing; so seldom does it draw breath, especially when hunted, that one has to reckon that it only breathes on the equivalent of every Sunday, if it were not so molested perhaps it might be able to breathe every Monday as well.

► The size, shape and direction of the blow can help to identify some species of whales from a distance in good weather. The blow of this humpback whale, like that of all species, is composed of moist exhaled air, together with some condensation of water vapour and secretions from the air sinuses, windpipe and lungs.

Ben Osborne/Oxford Scientific Films

Al Giddings/Ocean Images Inc./Planet Earth Pictures

mouth partly open, while others travel more or less in line with the surface, again with their mouth partly open, in a method somewhat resembling the skimming of right whales. Others, in what is called lunge feeding, come up from deep water at a marked angle towards the surface with their mouth partly open, sometimes emerging almost vertically before closing the mouth and forcing out the contained volume of water. The most fascinating feeding technique, however, is 'bubble netting'. Here the animal appears to circle below the concentration of food organisms and, as it circles slowly while rising towards the surface, the humpback gently expels air, which rises as bubbles to the surface. Due to the whale's simultaneous swimming, this chain of bubbles gradually forms almost a screen or net that may act as a deterrent or barrier to the dispersal of the animals 'trapped' within. After a suitable interval, the humpback simply emerges vertically within this screen, with its mouth open, engulfing the food contained in that body of water. All these forms of feeding occur almost exclusively in cold waters whether of the Northern Hemisphere or the krill-dominated regions in the Southern Hemisphere. Of the many thousands of humpbacks caught during whaling days on migration towards the breeding area,

almost none contained food and there is very little evidence of feeding on the warm-water breeding areas. Relatively few humpbacks were caught by whalers during migration towards the colder waters, but of those that were, most still had empty stomachs. A few, however, did contain full stomachs, indicating that feeding may well resume some time before complete return to polar waters.

Humpback migrations, unlike those of other rorquals, which seem to avoid land masses, follow relatively close to the shores of the mainland masses of both Northern and Southern hemispheres. In fact, it is this characteristic that made them particularly vulnerable to hunting, since they could just as easily be attacked by shore-based operations as from factory ships on the high seas. Their coastal distribution made them vulnerable as early as the 1830s, when right whales were the main quarry and other rorquals could not be hunted because of their greater speed and the lack of technology to catch them. Humpbacks were caught in the Southern Hemisphere at points along the coast of all the land masses, for example, Angola and the Congo (West Africa), Mozambique and Madagascar (East Africa), the northwest shelf (Western Australia), the Coral Sea (off northeast Australia), Tonga and New Zealand. Small

▲ Humpbacks employ a far greater number of feeding strategies than other rorquals, including co-operative hunting in which schools of fish or shrimp are herded by as many as four to six whales: the humpbacks then take turns diving and lunging upward, mouths wide open, through their densely packed prey.

Duncan Murrell/Seaphot Limited/Planet Earth Pictures

▲ At least partly because intensive hunting of humpbacks coincided with scientific and public concern over whale conservation, more is known about this species than any other rorqual. Observation and tagging studies have revealed a remarkable degree of separation between stocks, even when different populations meet on feeding grounds.

Mike Osmond/Pacific Whale Foundation

▲ The commercial exploitation of humpbacks ended by international agreement in the 1960s. Discoveries about the species' complex social system, fascinating songs and not least the fact that its migration routes pass close to populated coastal areas combined to enlist popular and political support for protection.

numbers were also caught from Norfolk Island and the New Hebrides up almost to the equator, off western South America right up to the Equator, and along parts of the east coast of South America up to Brazil. They were the first species hunted in large numbers in antarctic waters, mainly in the southwest Atlantic where they were speedily depleted and have still not recovered to former numbers, despite negligible catches in this area for almost 80 years. In the Northern Hemisphere during the nineteenth century there are no records of humpbacks being caught or even sighted around Hawaii, which has now become the best-known assembly point and research centre for humpbacks in the entire North Pacific. This is one of the only cases where, with almost complete certainty, a migration route has changed but there is no indication of the reason for the change.

While the maximum length of humpbacks is similar to that of the sei whales, they are much more rotund and heavily built with more than double the oil yield for comparable length. They are also slower swimming than any of the other rorquals, with a cruising speed of only about 4 or 5 knots. They could be caught by hand harpoon and usually did not sink. Although the many land-based catch areas had provided a great deal of information on seasonal occurrences, it was not until the commencement of the systematic campaign of whale marking that the degree of intermixing between stocks could be assessed.

Originally, whale marking was carried out by using numbered, stainless steel tubes with a conical lead head. These were fired from modified twelve-bore shotguns into undersized whales or those excluded from catch quotas, in addition to the campaigns designed solely for tagging whales. Over a period of years, nearly a thousand whales were tagged in antarctic waters by several nations, a similar number along the east and west coasts of Australia and a further 960 in the southwest Pacific from islands in the warm-water calving grounds near Tonga, Fiji, Norfolk Island and New Hebrides to a number of locations from the north to the south of New Zealand. The combined returns from all these programs demonstrated very clearly that whales that bred for example on one side of a continent, such as the west coast of Australia, could mix in the feeding areas with those that had come there from the east coast in at least some degree of overlap, but that the great majority returned to the same breeding/calving areas in which they were marked. In fact, out of more than 100 recaptures in the Australasian area, only two transferred from one major area to another, in this case from the east coast of Australia round to the west coast. There was even a fairly significant amount of segregation between stocks passing New Zealand as compared to those passing eastern Australia, but there was also a degree of intermixing.

The migratory habits of the humpback

contributed to the devastation of stocks, because of catching at breeding and feeding areas as well as from parts of the migratory pathways within reach of shore-based land stations. Perhaps the clearest example of this is Western Australia, where stocks had been hunted several times prior to World War II, showed recovery from each, but were exploited again between 1949 and 1962 when more than 12 000 animals were taken at the same time as nearly 6000 were captured in the corresponding antarctic feeding areas. Over the same period, catches off the east coast of Australia combined with those off Norfolk Island and New Zealand amounted to more than 10 000. At the same time more than 5000 were taken from the corresponding antarctic feeding area. In both regions, the combined attack reduced stocks to such a level that the industry ceased in 1962 through lack of whales, and humpbacks were, ironically, given complete protection worldwide the following year.

Since the end of humpback whaling, there has been monitoring off both east and west coasts of Australia for evidence of recovery of stocks. Several groups of shore observers have monitored them annually on the east coast, especially off Stradbroke Island, Byron Bay and Coffs Harbour, supplemented by periodic intensive aerial surveys. Off the west coast, periodic aerial surveys covering as near as possible the same route that aerial spotters used to follow during whaling days, have been carried out. Closer to the whales, it is frequently possible to photograph the underside of the tail flukes when the whale dives. The colour patterns here have proved to be individual so it is now possible to identify and track particular animals as they move between different locations. This method of identification is currently being used off the Caribbean, Hawaiian and Australian coasts and has great potential since the animal can be resighted many times. It is only in the last year or so that it has been possible to say with some confidence that stocks really are increasing and may now indeed be two or three times as large as they were at the end of whaling. However, it must be remembered that humpback numbers had been reduced to very low levels on both coasts and, at this rate, it will take many decades before stocks even approximate their pre-whaling abundance.

PARASITES

Several types of organisms attach to the skin of whales. Many are commensals (rather than true parasites) in that they gain no nourishment from the host but, for convenience, they are all often referred to as parasites. Most noticeable among these must be the large barnacle encrustations that occur on all humpbacks, particularly under the chin and along the leading edges of the flippers, although some may be present on other parts of

the body as well. These barnacles can become very large (specimens up to 6 centimetres in diameter being known) and are certainly prominently visible on any close approach to a whale. Observers have speculated that one of the behaviours often recorded for humpbacks — rubbing themselves against rocks — could be an effort to dislodge these barnacles. However, this seems highly unlikely since it takes very considerable effort with hooked metal implements to draw them off by force on the flensing platform. It seems far more likely that loss of barnacles is a natural phenomenon brought about by changes in water temperature during the animals' migration. Large barnacles, in particular, appear to have high mortality and spontaneously drop off in warm waters, to be replaced by very rapidly growing juveniles, which presumably attach somewhere in these same waters. Barnacles attached to or embedded in the skin often have a further crop of stalked forms growing out from them.

Whale 'lice', which are not related to the lice of land animals but are in fact crustaceans, are present on the skin of most species of whales, being conspicuous on humpbacks but, above all, on right whales where they aggregate on the large wart-like callosities. Since the lice are very light in colour, these accumulations make the callosities very much more visible than they would otherwise be. In fact, their presence has made it much easier for whale observers to photograph the callosities and demonstrate the individual nature of their distribution pattern.

On rorquals, an infrequent but sometimes conspicuous parasite is a modified copepod called *Penella* that shows up as a rope-like or tassel-like structure dangling from the side of the body of the host.

Evidence suggests that the lesser known internal parasites are normal inhabitants and rarely if ever a cause of mortality. They include roundworms in the stomach, tapeworms and thorn-headed worms in the intestine and flukes, sometimes present in lungs and other regions.

◄ Parasites and commensals commonly evolve in concert with their hosts: each of the great whales has its own population of specialised barnacles. These barnacles filter small plankton and the whale's scraps from water passing around the whale, which gives them free rides to rich food.

▲ 'Whale lice' — actually crustaceans rather than terrestrial spider-like animals — are found in folds around eyes, flippers, throat grooves and commonly infest barnacle accretions and wart-like callosities. They apparently cause little damage to their hosts, and unlike barnacles seem not to be affected by changes in water temperature.

Francois Gohier/Ardea London Ltd

Jeff Foott/Bruce Coleman Ltd

WHALE SONGS

Sound production by baleen whales was known and formed the subject of anecdotes for the old time open-boat whalers but was largely discounted by biologists since the anatomists had shown that none of the whales possessed vocal chords and it was therefore wrongly assumed that they were mute. The earliest recordings of large whales were made by accident through underwater military listening off Bermuda and Hawaii, when long underwater moans and complicated sounds were recorded in the early 1950s but could not at that time be identified. William Schevill, who has done so much in the pioneering of recording of toothed whales, both in the field and in studies in captivity, identified one such set of field recordings as being of humpback whales. Now that sound recordings of whale sounds have become more feasible with the development of the necessary technology, they are used as a method of monitoring whales.

The main results of intensive sound recording studies are that the echolocation-type clicks, so well known and documented for toothed whales, do not exist in that form in baleen whales although there is still some speculation that certain pulsed signals reported for several species may have a less elaborate, partial echolocating function. More typical sounds appear to be largely communicative, whether for display, or definition of territory or other behaviour. The loudest are the long moans of the blue whale that may last up to half a minute or more at very low frequencies and with strengths of up to 188 decibels, which makes it the loudest sustained sound of any living animal. Fin whales also produce long moans and a very characteristic 20-Hz signal so constant that, for a long time, it was doubted that this could be biological. However, it was finally established that these very low notes, produced in pulses, occur in many seas where fin whales are known. It is speculated that these may be reproductive displays and, from their power, the signals can certainly carry for hundreds of kilometres. It is also suggested that, in special thermoclime conditions, these signals can travel for thousands of kilometres. Minke whales also produce a variety of very loud notes, including some that are pulsed. Sounds from sei whales are so far not known with certainty. Right whales produce long, low moans, among a number of other signals, and the sounds of bowheads have been used in recent years as a supplement to visual and other surveys in an attempt to estimate population numbers.

The best known of all whale sound producers is the humpback, which produces the longest, most complex sequences of any whale or possibly of any animal. The word 'song' is used since it is a distinct sequence of different sounds — varying from moans, groans, roars and sighs to high-pitched squeaks and chirps — changing for periods of up to 10 minutes or more and then the entire sequence is repeated intact. This repetition possibly continues for many hours at a time. Each song is made up of subdivisions, major elements being called

Al Giddings/Seaphot Limited/Planet Earth Pictures

themes that are subdivided into smaller components known as phrases.

In any one area and time *all* animals produce the same sound sequences but these change through the seasons gradually and simultaneously in all animals. Each year's song is therefore slightly (sometimes substantially) different from the song of the year before. Major stocks, semi-isolated into separate geographic areas have their own local song sequence so, for example, sounds of humpbacks in the Caribbean differ from those off Hawaii, which in turn differ from those off Australia.

It seems that all the singers are males and the songs may

well be used as a warning to others in defining territory, in aggression and in courtship of the females — the best or most powerful singer possibly has selective advantage. There appear to be no recordings of humpback cows 'talking' to calves although recordings have been made of cow-calf sounds in right whales.

While humpback singing is most evident in the warm-water breeding areas, there is accumulating evidence of complete song repertoires over substantial distances of the migration routes. It appears, however, that only isolated segments of sound are typically used in the cold-water feeding areas.

Signal patterns or codas are used by a number of toothed whales, especially the sperm whale, as individual identifiers but similar acoustic markers, which would identify individuals, have not been established for baleen whales. Discovery of such identifying signal patterns would be of enormous value for future behavioural and migration studies in baleen whales. There is hope that further studies of the sounds made by baleen whales will contribute, along with other methods, to the identification of specific stocks and considerable work is currently being carried out in many parts of the world to this end.

TOOTHED WHALES

LAWRENCE G. BARNES

The feature that unites all of the toothed whales is the possession of teeth. Unlike baleen whales, which have developed whalebone to sieve animals from the water, toothed whales have perpetuated what was apparently the feeding mode employed by the earliest whales more than 45 million years ago: selecting and capturing individual prey. In more highly evolved toothed whales the trend has been toward simplification of all the teeth to single roots and conical crowns as well as an increase in the number of teeth. However, some highly evolved species of toothed whales have lost most of their teeth or developed specialised teeth. The narwhal (*Monodon monoceros*) has even developed a tusk. Some of the species that have undergone tooth loss have developed horny thickenings on the palate or the gums instead.

It is interesting that the same specialised changes in dentition have occurred independently in several different families of toothed whales. Thus we see reduction or loss of the upper jaw teeth in species as different as the sperm whale (*Physeter catodon*), the beaked whales (family Ziphiidae) and Risso's dolphin (*Grampus griseus*). In each case the change in dentition is associated with a diet of squid.

▼ Separated from the baleen whales by the obvious distinction of possessing teeth, the odontocetes or toothed whales are generally fast swimmers after fishes and squid. They are widespread in a great variety of habitats, from freshwater rivers to deep oceans.

Paul Ensor/Hedgehog House, New Zealand

Indeed, the most remarkable thing about toothed whales is their diversity. They demonstrate an incredible range of forms, behaviour and lifestyles that reflect their long evolutionary history and the variety of environments in which they live. There are toothed whales that are exclusively marine, some that are exclusively fresh water, and some that can move between the two.

Interestingly, the habit of living in fresh water has evolved independently in four different groups. First the river dolphins — four species in three closely related families — are exclusively freshwater-dwelling. Second, the Irrawaddy dolphin (*Orcaella brevirostris*), a member of the white whale family, which is at home both in rivers and in the ocean. Third, the finless porpoise (*Neophocaena phocaenoides*) likes mangroves and estuaries, but has a strictly freshwater population in the Yangtze River. Last, there are the two members of the dolphin family, the Indo-Pacific humpback dolphin (*Sousa chinensis*), which moves between salt and fresh water, and the tucuxi (*Sotalia fluviatilis*), which has

both marine and exclusively freshwater populations. It is remarkable that so many of these species are able to live in both salt and fresh water, and even move between them, because living in these different environments poses different physiological problems for an animal.

The diversity of the toothed whales extends to every facet of their biology. Reproductive strategies, migration patterns and even daily activities vary greatly among species. These factors allow different species to occupy the same territory and to minimise competition for resources.

Nevertheless, a rich source of food will attract many species of toothed whales, especially dolphins. It is possible to see massive feeding aggregations out at sea that may include the bottlenose dolphin (*Tursiops truncatus*), the pilot whale, Risso's dolphin, the rough-toothed dolphin (*Steno bredanensis*), the pantropical spotted dolphin (*Stenella attenuata*), the striped dolphin (*Stenella coeruleoalba*), the common dolphin (*Delphinus delphis*), the false killer whale

▲ A typically active open-ocean inhabitant of southern temperate and cool waters, the dusky dolphin has up to 144 simple, conical teeth with which to grasp its prey, which includes fast-swimming surface fishes such as anchovies and midwater squid, hunted in the early morning and late afternoon.

SPERM WHALES (FAMILY PHYSETERIDAE)

WILLIAM H. DAWBIN

There are only three species in this family — the 'great' sperm whale (*Physeter catodon*), the pygmy sperm whale (*Kogia breviceps*) and the dwarf sperm whale (*Kogia simus*). The two smaller species are rarely seen at sea and are known mainly from infrequent strandings. They are among the least known whales.

The three species of sperm whales differ greatly in size, ranging from the 18-metre male and 12-metre female great sperm whale to the 3-metre pygmy sperm whale and the 2.5-metre dwarf sperm whale but they share a number of features that do not occur in other cetaceans. The top of the head projects well beyond the tip of a narrow lower jaw that fits into a groove-like channel above and carries the only functional teeth. In the front of the head, above the upper jaw there is a spermaceti organ containing a specialised wax-like substance that differs from the oils of baleen whales and this probably plays a role in adjusting buoyancy during the changing pressures encountered in deep dives. The spermaceti organ in the pygmy and wharf sperm whales is smaller in scale but of similar chemical structure to that of the great sperm whale.

Unlike the great sperm whale, however, the two smaller species have a small fin, there is no size difference between the sexes and they do not form polygynous schools but seem to be solitary or form small groups. They are deep divers and almost certainly feed on squid.

Because of the special properties of the sperm oil and the wax-like spermaceti in the huge head of the great sperm whale, it has been a special target in all oceans since the first was caught

in 1714 until it was given protection in 1981. Despite the greater toll than for any other whale species, it was never reduced to the critically low levels of most of the baleen species and it is still present in fairly substantial numbers in all oceans.

Sperm whales emit a series of rapid clicks. Recent research has shown that the clicks communicate complex behavioural information and coded identification.

Bulls become sexually mature at 10–12 years but it is not until their early twenties that they are able to compete for harems and oust other bulls to become reproductively effective. Gestation lasts about 15 months and suckling continues for 2–3 years so that the interval between calves is 3–4 years.

Although not their only food, deepwater giant squid form a major part of the diet. The largest recorded squid was 19.5 metres but the size of tentacle fragments found in stomach contents suggests that even larger squid are consumed. To get to their main food source, sperm whales routinely dive to 800 metres but there is good evidence that dives to over 3 kilometres have been made. This means that, in tropical waters, a dive will range from 25°C in sparkling daylight to just above freezing and total darkness with extreme pressure. The longest recorded dive lasted 2 hours 18 minutes.

The tremendous physiological resilience the great sperm whale shows in very deep dives and its adaptability to many oceanic conditions is paralleled by its reproductive resilience against all odds.

One of the greatest dangers to small toothed whales is commercial tuna netting, which every year accounts for the deaths of tens of thousands of animals in the economically important Pacific tuna fishery alone.

▲ Spotted dolphins gather in herds of up to several thousand animals and commonly associate with yellowfin tuna. In the mid-1970s, before efforts were made to limit 'incidental' kills, as many as 300 000 dolphins were killed each year by tuna fishermen.

(*Pseudorca crassidens*) and the sperm whale.

The numerous and diverse adaptations of toothed whales have not helped them to escape the threat posed by humans. Fishing for commercial gain or for food is the most obvious threat. Species such as the sperm whale, the belukha (*Delphinapterus leucas*), the pilot whale and the beaked whales (family Ziphiidae) have all attracted the attention of whalers in the past, and some countries continue to hunt them; they provide such products as oil and animal food. Species such as the narwhal in the Arctic and many dolphins and porpoises in Japan and Turkey are hunted for human consumption. The shore-drive technique is often used for dolphins and porpoises. Some species have been hunted for more unusual but often valuable products: the narwhal for ivory, and the dried eyes and reproductive organs of the Amazon River Dolphin (*Inia geoffrensis*) in South America (and even Europe) for their supposed ability to make the human owner sexually irresistible!

Fishermen are also responsible for many toothed whale mortalities. Large numbers of the spinner dolphin (*Stenella longirostris*) and pantropical spotted dolphin are caught 'incidentally' by tuna fishermen engaged in purse seining or by other fishermen using gill nets (shark nets) set to protect beaches. In various places dolphins are killed by fishermen because they eat the fish species that the fishermen net and are, therefore, regarded as competition. Finally, in Chile, dolphins of various species are killed illegally by crab fishermen who use the dolphin meat as bait for the crabs. The population of Commerson's dolphin (*Cephalorhynchus commersonii*) in the Strait of Magellan has been greatly reduced in less than ten years by this activity.

ENVIRONMENTAL IMPACT

Populations (especially in inland seas) have been severely depleted or eradicated by pollution. River-dwelling species such as the Chinese river dolphin (*Lipotes vexillifer*) and the Bornean populations of the Irrawaddy dolphin have suffered greatly from environmental disturbance. In addition to development and pollution of their vulnerable habitat, they have had to contend with the effects of damming, which has restricted their movements and divided their population. River species are also threatened by collison with boats, and undersea naval detonations are thought to have claimed the lives of dolphins. Some of the faster swimming dolphins have even been hunted simply for 'sport'.

Not all human interactions with toothed whales are hostile. Fishermen in various tropical countries enlist the co-operation of dolphins to drive fish into their nets; the dolphins are rewarded with a share of the catch. At Monkey Mia in Western Australia a group of wild bottlenose dolphins have become a tourist attraction because they come into the shallows and allow humans to stroke and feed them.

BEAKED WHALES

The beaked whales (family Ziphiidae) are medium-sized pelagic whales that feed primarily on squid. Most species are rare and little is known about their biology and population sizes. Unlike other cetaceans, they usually lack the notch in the tail. The general evolutionary trend in beaked whales has been to reduce or lose all the teeth in the upper jaw and most of the teeth in the lower, except for one or two pairs at the front end that have become greatly enlarged. In some species these front teeth are developed as tusks, sometimes extending upward beside the beak. Most fossil species and some living species retain small conical, 'dolphin-like' teeth in both jaws, indicating that beaked whales evolved from animals that were there much like dolphins. Except for the northern and southern bottlenose whales and a few other species, female beaked whales are generally larger than males. Beaked whales characteristically have scars inflicted by the teeth of large male members of their own species. Mass strandings are extremely rare. The most primitive of the living beaked whales is the very rare Shepherd's beaked whale (*Tasmacetus shepherdi*).

Baird's beaked whale (*Berardius bairdii*) is one of the better-known species. These whales form organised herds comprising 3 to 30 animals, including adults of both sexes and their young, and appear to have a degree of social organisation. It takes eight to ten years for one of these whales to reach sexual maturity, but they are not physically mature until they reach 20 or more years of age, and they live for up to 70 years. They can dive to 2400 metres, and while they usually stay submerged for about 15 to 20 minutes, they can remain below the surface for up to an hour. This species has been hunted systematically by whalers and is still taken in small numbers around Japan. Baird's beaked whale is confined to the North Pacific; in the Southern Hemisphere Arnoux's beaked whale (*B. arnuxii*) occurs. The first two pairs of teeth in the lower jaw are enlarged in both species.

The largest genus of beaked whales is *Mesoplodon:* it has 11 species, most of which are rare and little known. The male of Blainville's beaked whale (*M. densirostris*) has a prominent upward-curved lower jaw with a forward-projecting flat, broad tooth protruding on each side from the highest point; barnacles often form on these teeth. These whales have been observed in herds of 5 to 12, and sometimes dive for 45 minutes or more.

The most prominent feature of the aptly named strap-toothed whale (*M. layardii*) is a pair of strap-like teeth, up to 30 centimetres long, projecting upward and backward from the lower jaw. In older animals, these prevent complete opening of the mouth. Gray's beaked whale (*M. grayi*) is less rare than most species of *Mesoplodon*. Evidence from strandings suggests it forms small herds. A single stranding occurred off the coast of the Netherlands, but all other strandings have been from the cool waters of the Southern Hemisphere. Hector's beaked whale (*M. hectori*) is the smallest of all living beaked whales, and is extremely rare, known only by 15 beach-stranded specimens. Longman's beaked whale (*Indopacetus pacificus*) is the rarest of all the beaked whales, and indeed of all whales. It is known only from two beached skulls, one found in Australia and the other in Somalia.

There are two species of bottlenose whale. The northern bottlenose whale (*Hyperoodon ampullatus*) is the better known of the two; its counterpart in the colder waters of the Southern Hemisphere is the rare southern bottlenose whale (*H. planifrons*). Northern bottlenose whales form small mixed herds numbering 5 to 15, but segregate according to sex at various times of the year, for migration. Females become sexually mature about 8 to 12 years of age, males about a year earlier, and animals have been known to live for at least 37 years. Males are often badly scarred from fights. These whales make a complex range of calls, and tend to remain around a companion that is in distress. Apparently they can stay submerged longer than any other whale — more than one hour, and perhaps as much as two. They are curious about ships, and will boldly approach them. The northern bottlenose is officially classified as 'vulnerable'. The entire population has been greatly reduced by intense whaling,

principally by Norwegians up to 1972. Even the southern bottlenose has been taken by whalers, despite its rarity.

Cuvier's beaked whale (*Ziphius cavirostris*) is found in schools numbering fewer than 20 and up to 40, and it seems to exhibit social organisation while swimming and feeding. Some older males

become solitary. Characteristically, just before they dive, Cuvier's beaked whales elevate their tail flukes straight out of the water. They can breach and clear the water's surface entirely, as well as dive to great depths, remaining submerged for at least half an hour. Whalers from Japan, Taiwan, the Lesser Antilles and elsewhere have been known to kill these whales, but the species is too scarce to hunt systematically.

▲ Largest of the eighteen species of beaked whales, the Baird's or giant bottlenose whale swims in groups of up to 30 animals in the North Pacific. It has a Southern Hemisphere relative, the somewhat smaller Arnoux's beaked whale.

▲ Reaching almost 10 metres in length at maturity, the northern bottlenose whale was greatly depleted by commercial whaling — which was made easier by this species' intense interest in ships and its habit of remaining close to injured or distressed companions, leading to many herd members being killed at one time.

▼ One of the most frequently seen beaked whales, the Cuvier's or goose-beaked whale is nevertheless sparsely distributed and is subject only to light hunting pressure. However, very little is known about its biology, and the effects of hunting cannot be assessed with any degree of accuracy.

Pat Morris/Ardea London Ltd

▲ The belukha or white whale is widespread in arctic waters, although hunting and environmental damage have reduced its numbers and there are no signs of recovery from depletion in the past decade or so. Native arctic peoples alone take at least 6000 belukhas each year in traps and shore drives.

WHITE WHALES

The family Monodontidae includes the narwhal, the belukha and the tropical Irrawaddy dolphin. It was formerly regarded as being strictly arctic in distribution, but this has changed since the Irrawaddy dolphin has been recognised as a member and fossil belukhas have been found in the temperate latitudes of California and Mexico. Whales in this family have blunt heads, no beak, and relatively long neck bones (allowing movement of the head), and they have a visible external neck. They are related to the porpoises (family Phocoenidae) and the dolphins (family Delphinidae).

The whale that gives the family its common name is the belukha or white whale (*Delphinapterus leucas*). The seasonal movements of belukhas are highly variable, depending on the population and on biological and environmental conditions. In winter they tend to form small groups, but in summer they gather in bays in large herds (numbering in the thousands) and swim hundreds of kilometres up major rivers. Their diverse range of sounds includes loud clicks, yelps, squeaks and shrill whistles (they are sometimes

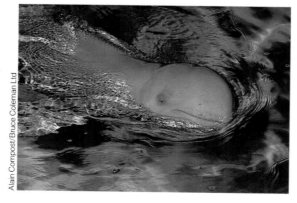

Alain Compost/Bruce Coleman Ltd

▶ Despite its coastal, estuarine and riverine distribution, little is known about the biology and population dynamics of the Irrawaddy dolphin. It is regarded as locally common, but pollution — especially from logging operations — is destroying its habitat and food resources in many parts of Southeast Asia.

called 'sea canaries'), and they commonly swim upside down while calling. Belukhas swim slowly, but are known to reach speeds of up to 22 kilometres per hour. They have unusually flexible bodies, which reflect their unusual bone structure. They can rotate their flippers and heads, twist their bodies around while swimming, and scull backwards using the flukes. Belukhas usually dive for up to 5 minutes, but can remain underwater for as long as 15 minutes and can travel 2 to 3 kilometres before surfacing. This ability, like their sophisticated echolocation system, is an obvious benefit in an environment that has frozen sea ice.

The total world population is estimated to be between 62 000 and 88 000 animals. There are several separate populations, most of which have been depleted. The Cumberland Sound population, for example, has declined to about 600 animals, only 12 per cent of its estimated total in 1922, and the population of the St Lawrence River has similarly declined; neither population is recovering. Despite warning signs such as these, belukhas are still hunted by native arctic peoples, and are killed commercially by whalers from Norway and the USSR. The species is also threatened by pollution, not to mention its natural enemies the orca (*Orcinus orca*) and the polar bear.

The other arctic species is the narwhal. The famous tusk of the male narwhal is apparently used in fights to establish dominance, and about one-third of adult males have broken or damaged tusks. Narwhals form small family pods of 3 to 20 individuals, and larger aggregations of up to 2000 move seasonally with the spread of sea ice. Their range of sounds appears to be nearly as diverse as that of belukhas. They can dive to depths of 370 metres and remain submerged for up to 15 minutes. The forehead is used to break through sea ice and form breathing holes. The narwhal is threatened by native hunting, commerce and construction.

Narwhals are killed by orcas, polar bears and by becoming trapped under the ice, but their greatest threat is people. Native peoples of the Arctic hunt narwhals throughout their range — both legally and illegally. The tusks are carved and sold for ivory and souvenirs, the meat is eaten, and the sinews and hide are used for various purposes. Narwhals in the Canadian Arctic region have been hunted since the tenth century. There may be more than 10 000 narwhals along the northwest Greenland coast, but the kill in Canada and Greenland in the 1970s exceeded the birthrate. Hunting together with increasing commerce and industry in the Arctic threatens the species.

Different in habitat from these two sea-dwelling arctic species is the tropical estuarine Irrawaddy dolphin. It swims sluggishly and occasionally spy hops from the water. When it surfaces to breathe, every 1 to 1.5 minutes, only the

Fred Bruemmer

top of the head and back break the water's surface. Like the belukha, this animal has a very flexible body and its flippers and neck are mobile. Irrawaddy dolphins form small schools of up to ten individuals, but little is known about their behaviour.

The total population size is unknown, but the species is described locally as being 'fairly common'. Irrawaddy dolphins often drown when caught in anti-shark nets set off the coast of northern Australia, and in fishing nets elsewhere.

In the Pela and Mahakam rivers of Kalimantan (Borneo) a population of about 100 dolphins has been extirpated by logging operations in the nearby rainforests that have clogged the rivers with silt and debris. In other areas, fishermen have enticed the dolphins to co-operate in fishing expeditions attracting them by tapping oars on the sides of the boats. As the dolphins approach, they reputedly herd the fish into the waiting nets, and the fishermen then share their resulting catch with them.

▲ The narwhal's bizarre anatomy has inspired steady hunting pressure since the Middle Ages, when narwhal tusks were sold at exorbitant prices as genuine unicorn horns. The species is still threatened, especially by unscrupulous poachers in search of trophies and items for the souvenir trade.

PORPOISES

Porpoises (family Phocoenidae) are a distinctive group with a long evolutionary history. They are different enough from dolphins (family Delphinidae) to warrant a separate family. Porpoises have no distinct beak, and the forehead slopes almost uniformly forward to the tip of the snout. They also share various anatomical features, including a particularly well-developed air sinus system in the head, which is probably related to pressure adjustment during dives and/or to insulation of the brain and/or ear from the animal's own echolocation signals and other sounds.

One of the most highly evolved members of the family is the rather striking black and white Dall's porpoise (*Phocoenoides dalli*). Its skull and air sinuses are very complex, and its diminutive teeth are recessed among horny 'gum teeth', which serve the functions of the once larger teeth. Its vertebral column is one of the most highly evolved of any cetacean, being comprised of numerous vertebrae that are extremely compressed front to rear with exceptionally long spines. This increase in the number of vertebrae is commensurate with increased trunk muscle mass, and undoubtedly explains why the Dall's porpoise is probably the fastest, strongest swimmer of all the cetaceans. These porpoises bow ride, and commonly swim so quickly (up to 50 kilometres per hour) at the water's surface that they splash up a plume of water in their wake.

Dall's porpoises are found in small schools from 2 to 20, and occasionally in larger feeding aggregations of up to several hundred. They eat squid and small schooling fish, commonly at great depths — 180 metres or more.

The population of Dall's porpoises is estimated to be about 920 000, but it has been severely depleted during the past 25 years, as a direct result of various Japanese, Taiwanese and South Korean fishing operations. Hundreds of thousands of these porpoises have been killed. Perhaps 20 000 a year are killed incidentally in the North Pacific in salmon and squid nets, and more than 10 000 a year are killed off the east coast of Japan for human consumption.

The harbour porpoise (*Phocoena phocoena*) is seen singly, in pairs or in small groups. It generally avoids boats and swims slowly, but can if necessary reach speeds of up to 22 kilometres per hour. It rarely leaps out of the water, and usually only exposes its back briefly, diving for up to four minutes. The dead bodies of harbour porpoises frequently wash ashore, and because of this relatively constant source of specimens during the past 200 years it has been possible to study their anatomy in detail. Since the harbour porpoise has been hunted for meat and oil, especially in the Black Sea, and has been caught incidentally in gill nets its population in many areas has begun to decline.

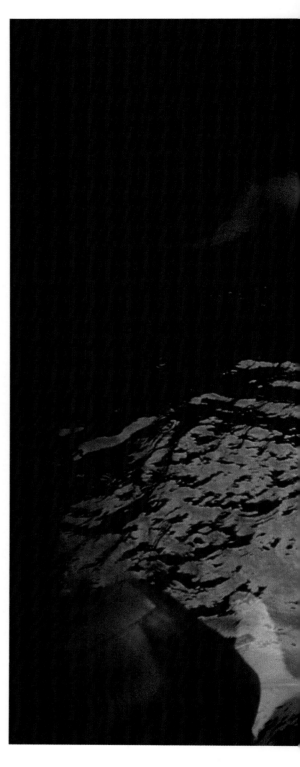

▲ Strikingly marked, the Dall's porpoise has a vertebral column extensively modified to give it extraordinary speed: this Northern Hemisphere species can reach speeds of 27 knots (50 kilometres per hour) over considerable distances.

Two relatives of the harbour porpoise are Burmeister's porpoise (*Phocoena spinipinnis*) and the vaquita (*P. sinus*). Burmeister's porpoise, found off the east and west coasts of South America, is a shy and little-known animal. It is, nevertheless, seriously threatened by human fishing activities: it is hunted for human food and illegally for crab bait, and is caught incidentally in gill nets. The vaquita is under greater threat and is considered an endangered species. This rare porpoise is restricted to part of the Gulf of California. Its population is declining as a result

Ken Balcomb/Earthviews

of incidental catches in gill nets, and changes to the ecology of the gulf as a result of damming of rivers.

The finless porpoise inhabits warm to temperate coastal waters in the Indian Ocean and off the coast of southwest Asia and some estuaries and rivers around their shores, particularly mangrove swamps. It can be found singly, in mated or cow-calf pairs, or in small schools of up to ten individuals. These small groups may aggregate into larger groups, apparently for co-operative feeding. The finless porpoise is also

found in the Yangtze River, where it associates with Chinese river dolphins. The population in the Yangtze River is apparently restricted to fresh water, never migrating to the sea. The population around Japan migrates seasonally between the Inland Sea and the Pacific Ocean.

Although the current size and status of the world population is not known, this species has suffered from the effects of pollution in bays and in Japan's Inland Sea, and has been caught incidentally in fishing nets. In Japan it is also killed for meat.

▲ The finless porpoise is a relatively slow-moving species which is rarely seen more than 5 kilometres from shore and often penetrates fresh water. As a result it has been killed for meat, as a competitor of fishermen and by pollution.

Nicholas Tapp/Seaphot Limited/Planet Earth Pictures

DOLPHINS AND OTHER SMALL TOOTHED WHALES

The delphinidae, the largest and most diverse living cetacean family, includes the various dolphins as well as killer whales, pilot whales and their relatives. It has a fossil record extending to at least 11 million years ago. Some living species feed exclusively on either fishes or cephalopods (squid, cuttlefish), while others are generalists, feeding on a variety of animals, including crustaceans. The most primitive living delphinids are generalists and (like primitive fossil types) have snouts of intermediate length and width. Among the modern species there are to be found a variety of skull, dental and body adaptations reflecting the varying diets and methods of locomotion. Broad-headed delphinids, such as the pilot whale and Risso's dolphin, eat cuttlefish; narrow-headed delphinids, such as the common dolphin and the spinner dolphin, eat mostly fishes; and animals

with intermediate-width skulls, such as the bottlenose dolphin and striped and white-sided dolphins, are usually the more generalised feeders. Some extreme anatomical adaptations have evolved in members of this family. The orca (*Orcinus orca*) has a relatively robust body with a long dorsal fin, while the right whale dolphins have long, slender bodies with no dorsal fin; the false killer whale (*Pseudora crassidens*) has only a few large teeth, while the common dolphin has many small teeth, and Risso's dolphin has totally lost its upper teeth. The rough-toothed dolphin (*Steno bredanensis*) has developed wrinkled enamel on its teeth.

The Indo-Pacific humpback dolphin can attract attention through its behaviour. It can ride waves, and sometimes leaps acrobatically from the water. Characteristically it swims back and forth in

▲ A more northern cousin of the closely related white-beaked dolphin, the Atlantic white-sided dolphin is a generalised feeder with fairly unspecialised teeth. Deliberate or accidental killing by humans is negligible, but mass strandings along the US coast may be a factor in control of its population size.

shallow waters while pursuing and eating reef-dwelling fish. It is able to travel between salt and fresh water, and sometimes lives in estuaries and mouths of rivers. The related Atlantic humpback dolphin (*S. teuszii*) lives in the waters off the west coast of Africa and is said to chase fish into nearshore nets tended by fishermen. The dolphin apparently responds to sounds made when fishermen slap sticks against the water and moves toward the sound, helping to drive the fish toward the nets. There are no data on the population status or numbers of either species of humpback dolphin.

The tucuxi has adopted the freshwater habitat even more exclusively than the Indo-Pacific humpback. While populations of the tucuxi are found in salt water, other populations are found in various South American rivers that are exclusively freshwater — the only case of this in the Delphinidae — and penetrate the Amazon and its tributaries right up to the foothills of the Andes. These freshwater tucuxis are found with Amazon river dolphins; and the two species use entirely different sorts of echolocation signals.

Tucuxis do not swim actively and rarely leap out of the water. They congregate in small schools of 10 to 25, and eat small fish and occasionally shrimp. They roll gently at the surface of the water when they breathe, and animals in the same group tend to swim and surface in unison. They are characteristically most active early and late in the day. The status of the population is unknown, but these dolphins are fairly common in some parts of the Amazon River system. They too are threatened by fishermen and are also killed for bait and caught in fishing nets.

Perhaps the best-known dolphin is the bottlenose dolphin. Trained bottlenose dolphins are often seen in oceanaria and are used by military to locate mines. These dolphins are mostly found in small schools of up to 30, and occasionally in schools of up to several hundred. They are fairly active swimmers, occasionally leaping wildly from the water, and are frequently seen riding the bow waves of ships and in waves near the surf zone. At Monkey Mia, Western Australia, bottlenose dolphins come into shallow waters and allow humans to pet and feed them. Other examples of 'friendly' behaviour have been reported elsewhere. Bottlenose dolphins are said to help chase fish into the nearshore nets of native fishermen in Mauritania, Africa (along with Atlantic humpback dolphins) and, in the past, in Queensland, Australia.

Offshore schools often swim and feed with other members of the dolphin family, sperm whales, grey whales (*Eschrichtius robustus*) and right whales. Individuals are known to live up to 37 years. Bottlenose dolphins have hybridised with Risso's dolphins, rough-toothed dolphins and humpback dolphins, in captivity as well as in the wild.

The size of the world population is unknown. Great numbers of these dolphins have been killed in Japanese waters. The usual method is to drive herds into shallow waters, where the animals are slaughtered. Japanese fishermen kill them because they regard them as competitors for fish, but many of these dolphins are killed for human consumption. They are also eaten in many other parts of the world, and are caught incidentally in the netting of fish.

Risso's dolphin is found in all oceans of the world, from the tropics to the cool-temperate

▲ Largest of the 'typical' dolphins, the widely distributed bottlenose is generally found in coastal waters, and in many parts of the world it is regarded as the epitome of the 'friendly' dolphin. However, large numbers are killed as competitors of commercial and subsistence fishermen and for human consumption.

USE AND MISUSE OF THE TERMS 'WHALE', 'DOLPHIN' AND 'PORPOISE'

MICHAEL BRYDEN

Whales, dolphins and porpoises are all included in the order Cetacea. How are they distinguished from each other?

The order Cetacea is divided into three suborders: Archaeoceti (which became extinct during the Oligocene), the Mysticeti (whalebone or baleen whales), and the Odontoceti (toothed whales). Within each suborder are families that are made up of genera and species.

All members of the suborder Mysticeti are referred to as whales; for example, blue whale, minke whale, Bryde's whale, grey whale. Among the Odontoceti, however, different names arise, and the term 'whale' is used to indicate size rather than any zoological affinity. The killer whale, the pilot whale and the white whale are all close relatives of the common dolphin, the Irrawaddy dolphin and the bottlenose dolphin, but, in relation to them, they are usually much bigger.

Likewise, there is no precise definition of the terms 'dolphin' and 'porpoise'. Members of the family Platanistidae (river dolphins) and smaller delphinids are referred to as 'dolphins'. In the past, particularly in the United States of America, there has been a tendency to refer to all small odontocetes as 'porpoises', to avoid confusion with the dolphin-fish or dorado (*Coryphaena* sp). It is becoming the convention, however, to restrict the term 'porpoise' to members of the family Phocoenidae.

latitudes. It is unusual because it has no functional upper teeth and only a few lower teeth in the front end of the jaw. Instead, it has corrugations on the palate to help hold its slippery prey, usually squid, cuttlefish or octopus. The species has cross-bred with bottlenose dolphins and rough-toothed dolphins in captivity yielding unusual-looking offspring.

Three species in the family Delphinidae are interesting for the size of the groups they form. The white-beaked dolphin (*Lagenorhynchus albirostris*), the Atlantic white-sided dolphin (*L. acutus*) and the related Pacific white-sided dolphin (*L. obliquidens*) are usually seen travelling in very large schools sometimes numbering in the thousands. The pantropical spotted dolphin forms even larger schools — up to several thousand animals. In some areas they associate closely with other dolphins, seabirds and yellowfin tuna in massive feeding aggregations. Unfortunately, their association with yellowfin tuna makes them vulnerable to 'incidental' capture by fishermen while purse-seining. The fishermen set the nets where they see dolphins, knowing the tuna will be close by. In the early days of purse-seining (which began in the 1950s) many thousands of the dolphins caught in the nets died. By 1974 more than 300 000 dolphins a year were being netted by the US alone. This number has now dropped to about 15 000 a year as a result of improvements to the design of the nets, but other countries, using

▼ Named for its spectacular spinning leaps, the spinner dolphin hunts small fish and squid in the tropical and temperate Atlantic, Pacific and Indian Oceans. Unfortunately, it seeks the same prey as yellowfin and skipjack tuna, and many thousands are trapped each year by purse-seiners.

Bernd Würsig

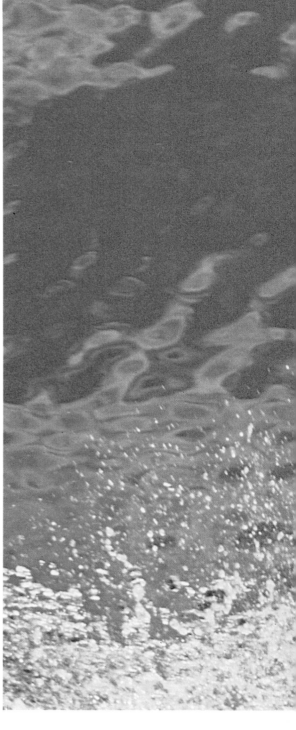

the older-style net, are expanding their tuna fisheries and so the slaughter continues.

Similar numbers of the spinner dolphin die in the same way. The spinner dolphin is very fast and an agile swimmer. It frequently leaps clear of the water while swimming, and its name derives from the characteristic behaviour of spinning around rapidly when it leaps in the air. Spinner dolphins

Marc Webber/Earthviews

congregate in pods of up to several hundred individuals, and frequently school with feeding pantropical spotted dolphins. The much less common clymene dolphin (*Stenella clymene*) also 'spins', but less spectacularly.

Another striking acrobat is the striped dolphin (*Stenella coeruleoalba*). This dolphin breaches, porpoises upside down, performs cartwheels, flips

around when leaping from the water, and occasionally bow rides. It travels in schools of several hundred individuals and is the subject of an intensive shore-drive fishery in Japan, which began in the 1940s. By 1974 the Japanese population of striped dolphins had been reduced to half of its original 400 000. Fortunately, the species is fairly widespread.

▲ In 1972 a conservatively estimated 380 000 dolphins were killed in tuna netting operations; and the majority of these were pantropical spotted dolphins. However, the species is so widespread and abundant that it appears to be recovering from such losses, especially as supervision and new tuna-netting techniques reduce the number of 'incidental' kills.

Francois Gohier/Ardea London Ltd

▲ Abundant and with a high rate of reproduction, common dolphins appear able to weather the pressures of deaths from pollution, commercial fishing and limited hunting. They are efficient group hunters of open-ocean and midwater fishes and squid, and form herds of up to several hundred animals.

The common dolphin is even more widespread and shows some variation from population to population. It forms herds of tens to many hundred and is highly visible when it swims rapidly at the surface, sometimes leaping clear of the water. Common dolphins often bow ride, like the spotted and spinner dolphins, they associate with tuna, and are captured incidentally in purse seine nets, although in lesser numbers than other species. They have also been the subject of direct fisheries; for example, up to 120 000 a year were killed in the Black Sea, so that, by the mid-1960s, the population was almost eradicated. The hunting finally stopped, although the Turkish government did not ban killing of common dolphins until 1983.

The northern right whale dolphin (*Lissodelphis borealis*) is a streamlined animal remarkable for its speed: individuals can swim at speeds exceeding 45 kilometres per hour and can leap simultaneously as they swim, turning the surface of the sea to froth. They are shy of boats, but are known to ride the pressure waves from the grey whale and the fin whale (*Balaenoptera physalus*). Schools of right whale dolphins sometimes number more than 2000, and migrate seasonally. One of their main foods is squid, and tens of thousands of dolphins are being caught incidentally in drift net fisheries while feeding on these molluscs. The temperate waters of the Southern Hemisphere are inhabited by the southern right whale dolphin (*L. peronii*).

Among the largest members of the dolphin family are the long-finned and the short-finned pilot whales (*Globicephala melaena* and *G. macrorhynchus*). The short-finned pilot whale forms schools of a few to many hundreds of individuals, while herds of the long-finned species range from a few hundred to many thousands. Pilot whales have a complex social organisation and hunt co-operatively; this high degree of social organisation makes them prone to mass stranding, and also highly vulnerable to shore-drive hunting. The long-finned pilot whale can attain speeds of up to 40 kilometres per hour, but pilot whales usually swim quite slowly. During the day they commonly laze at the water surface, while at night they hunt for squid and fishes. Short-finned pilot whales have been known to live for up to 63 years.

Another dolphin notorious for its mass

Ken Balcomb/Earthviews

strandings (sometimes numbering in the hundreds) is the false killer whale (*Pseudorca crassidens*). These animals are highly social, sometimes forming herds of more than 800 animals. They are known to breach and jump free of the water's surface, and also ride the bow waves of ships. Like short-finned pilot whales, they sometimes swim with bottlenose dolphins. They are hunted for food and also killed by fishermen who regard them as a nuisance or as competitors.

▲ Narrow, tapered and streamlined with no vestige of a dorsal fin, the medium-sized northern right whale dolphin is a migratory species whose most often remarked characteristic is its astonishing speed: it can attain 24 knots (45 kilometres per hour) in schools of as many as 2000 animals, all moving in perfect synchrony.

Eric M. Le Feuvre

◄ Representing the line of delphinid evolution that includes the orca, the false killer whale is a more sociable species found in groups of several hundred animals. Like its close relatives the pilot whales, the open-ocean false killer whale is notorious for mass strandings, which may be a factor in its population size and density.

Rosemary Chastney/Ocean Images Inc./Planet Earth Pictures

▲ Distinctive in size and appearance, the orca is an efficient predator of virtually all marine vertebrates from seabirds to baleen whales. Orcas are skilled co-operative hunters with a complex social system and are popular additions to oceanaria, where they adapt readily to captivity.

Largest and perhaps most striking of the dolphin family is the orca or killer whale. Orcas hunt and feed co-operatively in schools of 2 to 50, and have a complex social structure. They swim (usually at speeds of 10 to 13 kilometres per hour, but occasionally up to 45 kilometres per hour) by porpoising, and they occasionally lobtail and leap vertically or obliquely from the water. In various countries they are viewed as competitors by fishermen and killed or caught incidentally in fishing nets. They have also been hunted by fisheries around the world, which have been criticised by the International Whaling Commission. Being friendly, quick to learn and hardy in captivity, orcas have become a valuable commodity in oceanarium shows.

RIVER DOLPHINS

There are five species of river dolphins belonging to three or four related families whose members have invaded freshwater habitats. Today, apart from the franciscana (*Pontoporia blainvillei*) they are found only in rivers, although fossils of marine relatives have been found.

The Amazon River dolphin (*Inia geoffrensis*) swims relatively slowly, rolls gently at the surface to breathe, and only occasionally makes small leaps from the water. Its eyes are very small but still functional, and they probe muddy river bottoms for small fish. It has large teeth with wrinkled enamel.

Amazon dolphins are found in groups of one to twenty. They inhabit silty and stagnant water and range widely through various river systems in South America. During floods they move outward among the flooded forests, and are then commonly at risk of being stranded in ponds and cut off when the flood waters recede. They are also threatened by pollution, dams, motorboat traffic, hunting for fat, skins and 'sport', and other sorts of human activities (including fishing).

The Chinese river dolphin is one of the most endangered species of toothed whales and is represented by a mere 250 to 300 individuals in the Yangtze River. It is sometimes considered a relative of the Amazon River dolphin, and shares the wrinkled teeth of that animal. Chinese river dolphins usually occur in pairs and sometimes form small schools. They dive only briefly.

The Chinese river dolphin is threatened by the effects of damming, by increased boat traffic, by the hazards of fishing lines and by occasional hunting. Fortunately, biologists and politicians in China are aware of the problem, and the dolphin has become more widely known with the public. But its preservation will require a concerted effort,

and instigation of safeguarded sections of the river. Transplanting the dolphins to other, less impacted rivers, or the introduction of deflectors around boat propellers must also be considered.

A primitive marine relative of the Chinese river dolphin is the franciscana. Unlike the others, it does not inhabit rivers but shallow nearshore ocean waters. Franciscana dolphins feed near the bottom of the ocean and do not form schools. They are rarely seen alive, but — like most of the South American toothed whales — are all too often seen dead, when they are caught in nets set for sharks or smaller fish.

In contrast to the primitive franciscana, the Asiatic freshwater dolphins or susus (family Platanistidae) are highly evolved. They have extensive and complex air sinuses in the skull, which also has a large crest on each side over the eyes, giving the animal a distinctive bulbous forehead. There are two very closely related species: the Ganges River dolphin (*Platanista gangetica*) found in the rivers of India and Bangladesh, and the Indus River dolphin (*P. minor*) found in the Indus River system of Pakistan. Virtually sightless, these creatures live in muddy waters where they use echolocation and probing with their snouts to find food on the bottom.

Susus are slow breeders and are under considerable threat in their vulnerable habitat, which has largely been destroyed by environmental degradation and damming. Although it is illegal, hunting also continues despite legislation. There may be as few as 400 Indus River dolphins in existence — split into small populations by damming — and the Ganges River dolphin population in Nepal may be a mere 40 animals.

Institute of Hydrology, Academia Sinica Wuhan, P.R. China

▲ Once regarded as primitive, river dolphins such as the baiji or Chinese river dolphin (*Lipotes vexillifer*) have been recognised as highly specialised animals, superbly adapted to life in turbid, silty water and thus vulnerable not only to floods but also to pollution, over-fishing of their prey and predation by humans.

Marineland of Florida

◄ Largest of the freshwater dolphins, the bouto or Amazon river dolphin is widely distributed in the Amazon and Orinoco River systems. It is an efficient predator, using its small but functional eyes and its well-developed echolocation sense to detect prey in muddy water. The bouto is especially vulnerable to pollution of its habitat.

► In an effort to stimulate public awareness of an endangered species and to encourage support for conservation, the Chinese Government has issued stamps showing the baiji and even markets Baiji brand beer.

► The riverside city of Tongling has adopted the baiji as its municipal mascot and is constructing a semicaptive holding facility to breed and conserve the species, which is also honoured by a sculpture outside the city guest house.

THE BAIJI

KAIYA ZHOU

Like the giant panda, the Chinese river dolphin or baiji (*Lipotes vexillifer*) is a national treasure of China, deserving worldwide recognition. This rarest of river dolphins is a graceful animal with a very long and narrow snout. It can easily be identified by the low triangle of its dorsal fin.

In China, it is known by the name baiji meaning white dolphin. The name dates from classical times and is to be found in the ancient dictionary, *Erh Ya* (Anonymous), published as long ago as 200 BC.

The Chinese river dolphin has previously been classified in the same family as the Amazon River dolphin, but because it is substantially different from the Amazon dolphin, it should be placed in a separate family.

The baiji's closest relative is a fossil, *Prolipotes yujiangensis*, about 15 million years old from the bank of the Yujiang River in southern China. The ridges on the crowns of the teeth show a similar pattern in both the living species and the fossil.

The baiji was recognised by the Species Survival Commission of the International Union for Conservation of Nature and Natural Resources in 1986 as one of the 12 most endangered animals in the world. There are only about 300 left in the Yangtze River, and the population appears to be declining. The range of distribution of the baiji in the Yangtze in the 1940s was similar to that at the end of the nineteenth century, but since 1970 it has become extinct in the upper end of the middle reaches of the river, partly as a result of hydro-electric development. Recently, it has only been seen downstream from Yidu.

This endangered species faces many threats, including entanglement in fishing gear, collision with boat propellers and general habitat degradation, especially sluices built on the river courses connecting the Yangtze with its tributaries and lakes, which blocked pathways of migratory fishes. About half the dead baijis found have been killed accidentally by multiple-hook lines and other illegal fishing gear. Some of the individuals entangled on multiple-hook lines manage to free themselves and escape with wounds, but others are killed. The escaped dolphins can be identified by hook wounds on their body surface. One critically ill female taken from the river in 1982 had a total of 103 hook scars of different sizes, two large ulcers (6.5 by 3 centimetres and 7 by 6.6 centimetres) and three smaller ulcers on its skin.

Occasionally the dolphins are killed or injured by ship propellers, particularly in the lower reaches of the Yangtze, where freight volume is much higher than in the middle reaches. In the past 30 years, the river traffic in the lower reaches has doubled every ten years and will soon double again under a new program of economic expansion. Plans for further development in shipping will make life for the baiji even more hazardous.

The baiji is a protected animal in China. But in practice it is difficult to prohibit fishing in certain parts of the Yangtze and impossible to forbid or diminish navigation on the river. Accidental death still occurs frequently — at least 18 baiji died in this way in 1984. There is general agreement that the animal's habitat is rapidly deteriorating, and that the best hope of saving the species is to develop semicaptive breeding colonies until their habitat has been restored. The construction of the first of a series of seminatural reserves has already started at Tongling, a city that has adopted the baiji as its mascot. (There is a sculpture of five in front of the city guest house, and there is even a brand of beer named after the animal — the bottle cap shows a jumping dolphin and carries the words '*Lipotes vexillifer*'. The reserve consists of a 1.5 kilometre channel between two islands, and serves both as a dolphin sanctuary and as a scientific research station. Initially, the number of dolphins kept will be between five and ten.

The survival of the baiji can only be ensured by establishing safe sections of the river and creating more seminatural reserves, and perhaps by installing deflectors around boat propellers.

► Now restricted to perhaps 300 animals in the wild, the baiji has disappeared from most stretches of the Yangtze River in the face of pollution, competition for food, accidental capture by fishermen and injury from boat propellers.

Kaiya Zhou

DISTRIBUTION AND ECOLOGY

PETER CORKERON

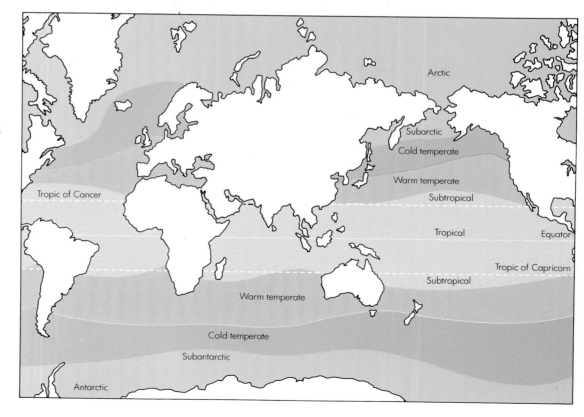
Stephen Leatherwood/Earthviews

▲ Insulated by thick blubber, bowhead whales can take full advantage of the incredibly rich food resources of the Arctic Ocean. Although they do not move beyond polar waters to breed, bowheads migrate with their calves as the ice cap fluctuates.

Where are different cetacean species found? Why are some species found worldwide, while others have restricted ranges? Why do some species engage in regular seasonal movements? These are some of the questions that the study of distribution and ecology attempts to answer.

On an evolutionary time scale, historical zoogeography (the study of how species distributions have changed with time) is affected by the history of climatic change, continental drift and the evolutionary response to these abiotic (non-biological) factors by animal groups. However, to understand patterns of distribution we also need to examine the ecological factors that can affect distribution. These factors include water temperature, depth, salinity and the topography of the sea floor, as well as the availability and abundance of food.

Whales are found in various types of waters situated right around the globe. Areas in high latitudes (that is, near the poles) are classed as arctic or antarctic. Moving towards the equator from these waters, we have subarctic (or subantarctic), cold temperate, warm temperate, subtropical and finally tropical waters. Waters are also defined according to their oceanographic type. Offshore, in the deep ocean basins, are the pelagic waters, and moving towards a continent, the waters of the continental slope and shelf. Nearshore are the coastal and inshore waters.

Most baleen whales are found in all oceans, and most undertake extensive migrations. Toothed whales are found in a variety of habitats, but many are restricted to relatively small areas. Among the dolphins, for example, there are some species found only in rivers, some that are found only in inshore waters and others that are found only in the open ocean. Some whole families of toothed whales are found only in the open ocean, such as the sperm whales (family Physeteridae) and the beaked whales (family Ziphiidae), while some species, such as the bottlenose dolphin and the orca, are seen in both inshore and deep ocean waters.

► Although the divisions between isothermal ocean regions are not always well defined — subtropical waters, for example, vary in extent according to season and currents, often merging with warmer and cooler water masses — the distribution of many cetaceans follows a pattern similar to water temperatures.

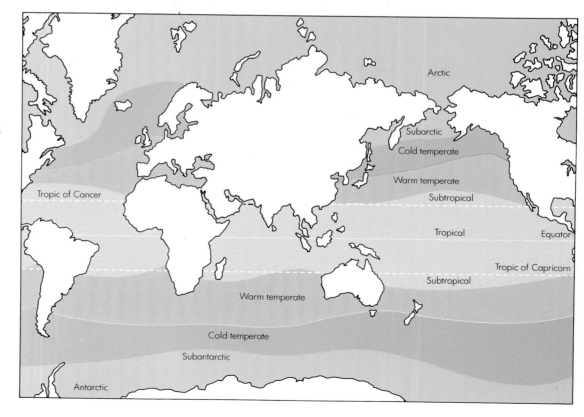

Paul Ensor

DISTRIBUTION OF BALEEN WHALES

Most rorquals are found in all the ocean basins of the world. The blue whale is found at the edge of continental shelves and the sei whale also tends to be found in oceanic waters. Fin and minke whales may be found in both nearshore and pelagic waters. The exception is Bryde's whale, which is found only in temperate and tropical waters in both inshore and offshore areas.

Humpback whales are also found in all oceans. These whales undertake extensive migrations, when they tend to inhabit coastal waters.

The northern right whale is found in the North Pacific and Atlantic oceans, while the southern right whale lives in the South Pacific,

Indian and Atlantic oceans. Neither species moves into tropical waters, although both migrate annually from high latitudes to temperate waters.

The related bowhead whale lives in arctic waters. Its migration patterns are closely associated with the seasonal changes of the arctic ice cap.

Very little is known about the pygmy right whale, but it seems to be found in the temperate waters of the Southern Hemisphere. There are records of this animal in both pelagic and inshore waters.

Grey whales are found only in the waters of the North Pacific, virtually all in the eastern North Pacific. These whales migrate along the west coast of North America to calving lagoons in Mexico.

▲ The open ocean may seem a featureless and barren place to humans, but to the minke whale, smallest and most 'playful' of the rorquals, it is a rich and varied environment of underwater prairies and mountain ranges stretching from the tropics to polar regions.

DISTRIBUTION OF TOOTHED WHALES

As there are so many species of toothed whales, they have been divided here into species with worldwide distributions, related species that together have a wide distribution, and species with restricted distributions.

SPECIES WITH WORLDWIDE DISTRIBUTIONS

Common species of dolphin, Risso's dolphin and the false killer whale occur in tropical and warm temperate waters, where they are found in pelagic to coastal areas. The rough-toothed dolphin, the melon-headed whale, the pigmy killer whale and Fraser's dolphin are all found in tropical and subtropical pelagic waters.

The bottlenose dolphin is found in all waters, from inshore to pelagic, and from tropical to cold temperate areas. The orca is found in all oceans from inshore to pelagic waters. Cuvier's beaked whale is found from cold temperate to tropical waters in both hemispheres, and tends to prefer pelagic waters. The sperm whale is also truly cosmopolitan, and inhabits pelagic waters and those of the continental slopes and shelves; it is a migratory species.

The pygmy sperm whale and the dwarf sperm whale are found worldwide in temperate to tropical waters. Both species are found offshore in deep waters, but it appears that the dwarf sperm whale may also inhabit waters slightly nearer shore, probably on the continental shelf and slope.

RELATED SPECIES THAT TOGETHER HAVE A WIDE DISTRIBUTION

The second type of distribution pattern is where a genus as a whole is widely distributed, but its individual species have restricted distributions that overlap to varying extents. Particularly interesting are the genera with just two species whose distributions complement each other without overlapping (a pattern also seen in the right whales). These probably represent the result of recent evolution: a single ancestral species has developed two geographically separated populations that have finally become separate species. For example, the short-finned pilot whale lives in all oceans in tropical and warm temperate waters, while the long-finned pilot whale is found in the cold temperate waters of both the Northern and Southern hemispheres.

Three genera of toothed whales have one of their species in the Northern Hemisphere and one in the Southern. These include the northern and southern right whale dolphins, the northern and southern bottlenose whales, and Baird's (northern) and Arnoux's (southern) beaked whales. All these species are found in either cold temperate or polar waters, and all inhabit pelagic areas. The southern representatives of these

▶ The common dolphin is one of the most widespread and abundant small cetaceans and inhabits virtually all tropical and warm temperate seas from the Mediterranean and Black Sea to the equatorial Pacific, Indian and Atlantic Oceans.

Jacki Kilbride/Earthviews

Paul Ensor

▲ Closely related species may have overlapping or complementary distributions. Short-finned pilot whales (top) are restricted to tropical and warm temperate waters, while the physically similar long-finned pilot whale (bottom) hunts similar prey — principally squid — in cool temperate waters.

Don Croll

▲ Resident in temperate offshore waters of the North Pacific, the Pacific white-sided dolphin is separated from the Atlantic white-sided dolphin by the continent of America.

▶ Like its relative the Peale's dolphin, the dusky dolphin is found fairly close to shore in cool temperate waters of the Southern Hemisphere though it has a far more widespread distribution.

species are circumpolar in distribution, but the northern bottlenose whale is found only in the North Atlantic and arctic waters, while the northern right whale dolphin and Baird's beaked whale are found only in the North Pacific Ocean.

One genus of beaked whales, *Mesoplodon*, contains 11 different species, all found in pelagic waters. In the Southern Hemisphere the strap-toothed whale has a circumpolar distribution, while Andrews' beaked whale is found in the Indian and South Pacific oceans. Hector's beaked whale inhabits temperate waters of the southern oceans, where it appears to be circumpolar, but it is also found in the temperate North Pacific Ocean. Several other *Mesoplodon* species also inhabit the North Pacific. These include the ginkgo-toothed beaked whale in warm temperate to tropical waters, also in the northern Indian Ocean; Hubbs' beaked whale in cold temperate waters, and Stejneger's beaked whale in subarctic to cold temperate waters. In the North Atlantic, Sowerby's beaked whale inhabits subarctic to cold temperate waters and Gervais' beaked whale is found in warm temperate to tropical waters. True's beaked whale has a curious distribution, having been found in the temperate North Atlantic and also off the southern coast of South Africa. It is quite possible that this species' range is greater than is known at present. Another unusual distribution pattern is demonstrated by Gray's beaked whale, which is found in all the ocean basins of the Southern Hemisphere, yet has also been found on the North Sea coast of Holland. Finally, Blainville's beaked whale is found in the tropical and warm temperate waters of all oceans.

Longman's beaked whale is considered by

some taxonomists to be a member of the genus *Mesoplodon* while others consider that it should have its own genus, *Indopacetus*. As the species is known from only two skulls, one collected on the east coast of Australia and the other from the east coast of Africa, very little is known about the species, or its distribution. Recently, sightings of an unknown species of beaked whale have been reported from the pelagic areas of the eastern tropical Pacific. These whales may prove to be the elusive Longman's beaked whale, or they may be an entirely new species.

Among the dolphins, the genus *Lagenorhynchus* contains the greatest number of species, which range from the waters of the subarctic North Atlantic to the Antarctic. The hourglass dolphin inhabits the pelagic waters of the subantarctic and Antarctic, and is circumpolar in distribution. Peale's dolphin is found in the coastal waters of southern South America, on both Pacific and Atlantic coasts. The dusky dolphin is circumpolar, living in temperate coastal waters around most of the continents, and around several islands of the Southern Hemisphere. In the Northern Hemisphere, both the white-beaked dolphin and the Atlantic white-sided dolphin live in the North Atlantic. The white-beaked dolphin inhabits more northern waters, ranging to the subarctic, while the Atlantic white-sided dolphin lives in temperate waters. Their ranges overlap. The Pacific white-sided dolphin is found in the offshore waters of the temperate North Pacific.

Members of the genus *Stenella* tend to be found in much warmer waters. The striped dolphin is found in all oceans in temperate to tropical areas, generally in offshore waters. The

DISTRIBUTION OF GENUS *Mesoplodon*

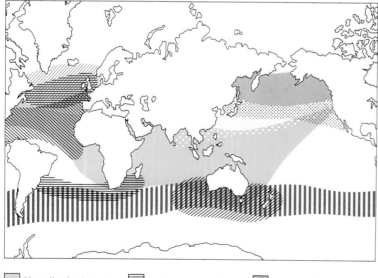

Blainville's beaked whale	True's beaked whale	Stejneger's beaked whale
Sowerby's beaked whale	Gray's, strap-toothed & Hector's beaked whales	Ginkgo-toothed beaked whale
Gervais' beaked whale	Andrew's beaked whale	Hubbs' beaked whale

DISTRIBUTION OF GENUS *Lagenorhynchus*

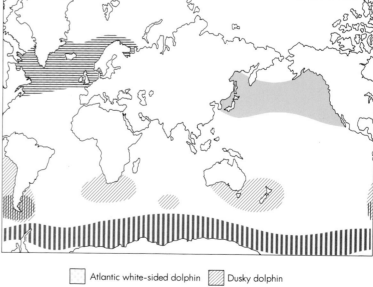

Atlantic white-sided dolphin		Dusky dolphin
White-beaked dolphin		Hourglass dolphin
Pacific white-sided dolphin		Peale's dolphin

► Small and distinctively marked, Commerson's dolphin is found only in the cold temperate waters of southern South America and off the Kerguelen Islands in the Indian Ocean. It feeds on small fish, squid and shrimp and shallow coastal waters, harbours and kelp beds.

Francisco Erizo/Bruce Coleman Limited

Stephen Leatherwood/Earthviews

▲ Similar in shape and size to the unrelated Commerson's dolphin, Dall's porpoise also feeds on small fish and squid, though its range encompasses pelagic waters and it is restricted to the cold temperate waters of the North Pacific.

clymene dolphin inhabits the tropical and subtropical waters of the deep Atlantic. The spinner dolphin lives in tropical to warm temperate waters of all the oceans, and is generally pelagic, although it may move into coastal areas. The pantropical spotted dolphin is distributed worldwide in tropical and subtropical waters. It is found in the open ocean and also in coastal areas. The Atlantic spotted dolphin occurs in the tropical to warm temperate waters of the Atlantic Ocean. It is also known to live in the waters of the continental shelf to fairly close to shore, but its offshore distribution is unknown.

The genus *Cephalorhynchus* comprises four species of small dolphins, all of which inhabit coastal waters in the Southern Hemisphere. Hector's dolphin is found around the coast of New Zealand, while Heaviside's dolphin inhabits the waters of southwestern Africa, from the Cape of Good Hope to approximately 18° South. The

southern coastal waters of South America are home to the other two species: the black dolphin, found off the west coast from Chile to Cape Horn, and Commerson's dolphin, found off the Chilean coast south from about 50 degrees, off the Argentinian coast north to about 42 degrees, and around the Falkland Islands, South Georgia and Kerguelen Island.

The harbour porpoise (family Phocoenidae) probably represents the northern ecological counterpart of these southern *Cephalorhynchus* species. It is a coastal animal, found in cold temperate and subarctic waters of western Europe, North America, the Pacific coast of Asia and the Black Sea. The vaquita is found in the Gulf of California and Burmeister's porpoise is found in temperate inshore waters of South America. Its range may be much more extensive than this — recently, a skull was reported from Heard Island. The spectacled porpoise is probably circumpolar in pelagic subantarctic waters, but records other than those of stranded animals are rare.

SPECIES WITH RESTRICTED DISTRIBUTIONS

Other members of family Phocoenidae have restricted distributions. Dall's porpoise inhabits northern Pacific pelagic waters, in subarctic to cold temperate areas, although it is seen in coastal waters less frequently. The finless porpoise is found in shallow inshore waters of the northern Indian Ocean, from Pakistan eastwards to the South-West Pacific, and north to Japan. This porpoise also lives in rivers and lakes in these areas.

Another inhabitant of the inshore waters of the tropical Indo-Pacific region is the Irrawaddy dolphin. This dolphin is found from northern

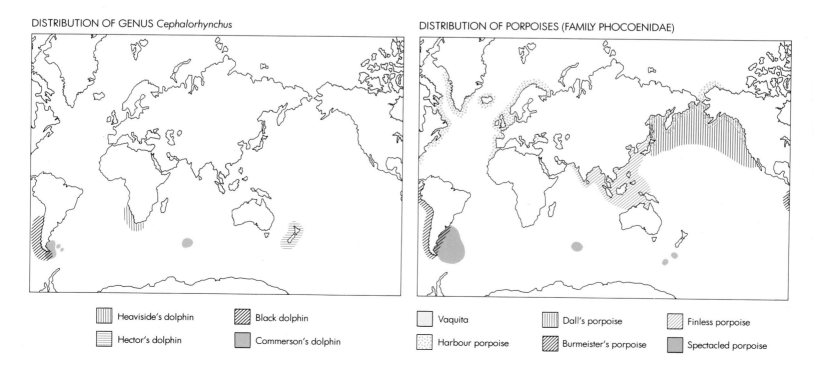

DISTRIBUTION OF GENUS *Cephalorhynchus*

DISTRIBUTION OF PORPOISES (FAMILY PHOCOENIDAE)

| | Heaviside's dolphin | | Black dolphin |
| Hector's dolphin | | Commerson's dolphin |

| | Vaquita | | Dall's porpoise | | Finless porpoise |
| Harbour porpoise | | Burmeister's porpoise | | Spectacled porpoise |

Fred Bruemmer

◄ Evolution and ecology appear to have worked hand-in-hand in shaping the almost exclusively pelagic distribution of the narwhal — its unique spiral tusk is unsuited for feeding in shallow waters, and it feeds on squid, fish, crabs and shrimp in the open Arctic Ocean.

▼ The belukha has a complementary distribution to the narwhal, being exclusively Arctic but, unlike the narwhal, it is found only in shallow continental seas, estuaries, bays and rivers. In summer it may be seen hundreds of kilometres up major rivers, in fresh water.

Fred Bruemmer

Australia in the east, through the Indonesian archipelago and Indochina to the Bay of Bengal in the west. It may also be found in rivers. The humpback dolphins (*Sousa* species) are also found in rivers and inshore waters of this region, from eastern Australia north to southern China and west along the coasts of India and Pakistan, along the Indian Ocean coast of Africa and up the Atlantic coast of Africa to Mauritania.

Related to the humpback dolphins, the tucuxi lives in tropical to warm temperate inshore waters on both coasts of South America, as well as in the large river systems of the continent. Also occupying the coastal waters of eastern South America is the unrelated franciscana. Although the northern limit of its range overlaps with the southern limit of the tucuxi's, it is an animal of more temperate waters.

There are several species of river dolphins — small toothed whales related to the franciscana — that are entirely restricted to river systems. These include the Amazon River dolphin in the Amazon and Orinoco river systems of South America and the Chinese river dolphin, found in the Yangtze River system of China. The Chinese river dolphin and the finless porpoise happily overlap in the middle and lower reaches of the Yangtze River, sharing the available food. This is unusual since other rivers only have one resident cetacean. The Indus River system is home to the Indus River

dolphin, while the Ganges, Meghna and Brahmaputra systems are the home of the Ganges River dolphin.

Finally, the white whale of the Northern Hemisphere, the belukha, is restricted to arctic and subarctic waters, where it is circumpolar. Its relative, the narwhal, lives in the high arctic, and is also circumpolar.

These distributions reflect species' responses to ecological conditions that prevail today.

ECOLOGY OF THE HARBOUR PORPOISE IN THE BAY OF FUNDY

Extensive surveys of the harbour porpoise in the Bay of Fundy, Canada, have taught us much about the ecological factors that can affect the distribution of a species on a local scale. The distribution of porpoise mothers and calves was determined through carefully designed surveys and compared with a variety of physical and biological factors. These factors included water temperature, current speed, water depth and the availability of food. It was found that female porpoises and their calves seek out areas of warm, stable water with concentrations of plankton that create a rich marine food web. Further research on the distribution and abundance of all harbour porpoises (not just mother–calf pairs) showed that their density was correlated with physiographic factors that concentrated prey (herring), and with water depth. Herring tend to be in deep water during the day, which explains why porpoises tend to be found in deep water. Another possible explanation is that the porpoises are avoiding the turbulence found in shallow water in the Bay of Fundy, where the enormous tidal changes create very strong tidal currents. Still further research

within restricted areas of the bay has shown that the number of porpoises peaks at the time when the largest catches of herring are made. Porpoises are also more common during times of small tidal changes, and when the wind is blowing onshore. Individual porpoises have regular home ranges, and regular patterns of traversing their range.

Because harbour porpoises are small for cetaceans and live in quite cold waters, they have to be metabolically very active, and need to eat up to 10 per cent of their body weight every day. Therefore, they seem to spend most of their time feeding. Also, herring is a relatively unpredictable food source, which means these porpoises are likely to be restricted to areas where the concentration of prey is greatest, and so their range is fairly narrow compared with other inshore toothed whales.

ECOLOGICAL SEPARATION OF TWO SPECIES FOUND IN THE SAME AREA

Many areas are home, permanently or temporarily, to more than one cetacean species. In most cases, the species have little or no effect on each other, for example, when migrating baleen whales pass through the ranges of coastal dolphins. However, where two similar species reside in the same general area, we need to ask how they can coexist; ecological theory asserts that to be able to coexist, the two species must have different ecological requirements. One example of this is the mixed

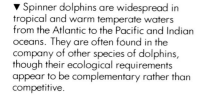

▼ Spinner dolphins are widespread in tropical and warm temperate waters from the Atlantic to the Pacific and Indian oceans. They are often found in the company of other species of dolphins, though their ecological requirements appear to be complementary rather than competitive.

schools of spinner and spotted dolphins found in the eastern tropical Pacific.

There have been a number of studies of inshore or nearshore populations of bottlenose dolphins in recent years. However, only in a few instances has it been possible to compare their ecology with that of other dolphin species in the same area.

In a study of dolphins in a bay off the Patagonian coast of Argentina, bottlenose dolphins were found in shallower water than were dusky dolphins. The two species did not mix regularly, yet both interacted with other marine mammals — both whales and seals. It was unclear whether the two dolphin species competed for food, for although both fed in the same area they did so at different times of day.

Two studies have compared aspects of the ecology of bottlenose and humpback dolphins. The first, off the southeast coast of South Africa, found that humpback dolphins occurred in smaller groups than bottlenose dolphins and were located close to shore, while bottlenose dolphins inhabited both nearshore and offshore waters. Food preferences of the two species varied: the humpback dolphins apparently took mostly reef fish while the bottlenose dolphins fed on both reef-dwelling and open-water fishes. The two species interacted occasionally, and sometimes they appeared to play together.

In the second study, in a bay in southeast Queensland, humpback dolphins were found in shallower water than bottlenoses and tended to be located on the mainland side of the bay. The humpback dolphins appeared to be less perturbed by human activities and were found in shipping lanes, in small boat harbours and also in the vicinity of a major sewerage outlet. Both species fed behind fishing boats, and groups contained both bottlenose and humpback dolphins. However, within these groups the two species did not seem to mingle, and no amicable social behaviour was observed.

These two studies revealed quite different patterns of interaction between the two species. In one area the bottlenose and humpback dolphins shared a food source (fish discarded by the fishing boats), yet did not appear to interact socially and in the other, the two species interacted but fed on different types of prey.

ECOLOGY OF PELAGIC DOLPHINS

The ocean appears to us to be a uniform environment. However, dolphins living in the deep oceans show patterns of distribution that can be correlated with oceanographic conditions, and with the topography of the ocean floor. Extensive surveys of the waters of the eastern tropical Pacific Ocean have been undertaken as part of the United States Government's research on the dolphin stocks affected by tuna purse-seining. These

Peter Corkeron

◄ Bottlenose dolphins form distinct populations according to habitat, with shallow-water bottlenoses being smaller than offshore populations. Both, however, are often seen with other species of dolphins, though they may or may not interact.

surveys have shown that two communities, both consisting of several dolphin species, can be found in the area, and that these communities are associated with two quite different water masses. In one water mass, where tuna fishing occurs, there is relatively little variation in the temperature of the surface water, and spotted and spinner dolphins predominate. In the other water mass there is a much greater variation in the surface water temperature, and striped and common dolphins predominate. Both communities contain several other dolphin species.

Detailed analysis of the distribution and abundance of dolphins in the area where tuna fishing occurs has demonstrated further division of dolphin groupings. In oceanic waters relatively close to shore, pilot whales, bottlenose and Risso's dolphins (and, to a lesser degree, common dolphins) predominate. Further offshore, spotted and spinner dolphins are the main species found. These groupings can be divided further into

▼ Striped dolphins are highly social animals. They pursue a variety of prey in pelagic tropical, subtropical and warm temperate waters of the Atlantic, Pacific and Indian oceans, and the Mediterranean. They prefer areas where surface water temperatures are highly variable.

Robert Pitman/Earthviews

TUNA NETTING

Throughout the waters of the eastern tropical Pacific Ocean, yellowfin tuna (*Thunnus albacares*) and skipjack tuna (*Katsuwonus pelamis*) are found in association with groups of dolphins, generally spotted dolphins (*Stenella attentuata*), spinner dolphins (*S. longirostris*) and, less frequently, common dolphins (*Delphinus delphis*). The reasons for this phenomenon is not well understood, but it is thought that the tuna probably follow the dolphins to prey patches, as the dolphins are probably much better at finding prey than the tuna. However, the tuna are preyed upon by humans. Fishing boats catch tuna by setting huge nets, called purse seines, around tuna schools. These nets are from 900 to 1400 metres long and up to 130 metres deep. The tuna netting industry was established by the United States in the 1950s, and several other American countries also have large purse-seining operations underway.

The fishing vessels exploit the natural association of the tuna and dolphins. Schools of fifty to several thousand dolphins are chased by speedboats for an average of 20 to 30 minutes, although chases may last up to one and a half hours. The dolphins are then herded together and encircled by the seine net. The bottom of the net is drawn together and the net is pulled gradually to the mother ship. The tuna, following the dolphins, are also caught.

While this fishing method is extremely efficient, it has led to incredibly high dolphin mortalities. The United States National Marine Fisheries Service (NMFS) has been studying many aspects of this fishery, looking at the effects of the kills on the dolphin populations, and researching methods of reducing dolphin mortalities.

By placing observers aboard tuna vessels, the NMFS has been able to estimate the number of dolphins killed by the entire United States fishing fleet. The numbers are staggering. Between 1959 and 1972, an estimated 4.8 million dolphins were killed by United States registered vessels. The greatest number estimated to have been killed in one season was 534 000 in 1961. But further research has shown that placing an observer aboard a boat reduces the number of dolphins killed, presumably because the crew put greater effort into getting all dolphins out of their nets. This 'observer effect' means that the dolphin mortality estimates are all underestimates, but we have no idea by how much. To put these numbers in some perspective, about 42 500 great whales (fin, sei, Bryde's, minke and sperm whales) were killed by whalers in the 1972–73 whaling season, but an (under)estimated 380 000 dolphins were killed

'incidentally' in the 1972 tuna fishing season!

The introduction of marine mammal protection legislation by the United States government led to annual quotas being introduced; if the quotas were exceeded, tuna fishing had to stop. These quotas have been generally in the order of 20 000 dolphins a year. Vessels from other American countries are 'controlled' by the Inter-American Tropical Tuna Commission (IATTC).

In 1984, the IATTC estimated that 32 000–39 000 dolphins were killed; in 1985, 55 000; and in 1986, 125 000–129 000. There seems to be little hope for international management of the problem, as the IATTC sets no quotas on dolphin catches, and its other member nations do not enforce quota restrictions on vessels flying their flags.

Research has been conducted into ways of altering fishing gear so that dolphin mortalities can be reduced. Changes have been made to portions of the nets so that dolphins can escape more easily, and the way the nets are pulled in has been modified as well. Small boats are deployed at the area where dolphins leave the net, and crew assist dolphins if they become entangled.

The dolphins have altered their behaviour around fishing boats, also resulting in a reduction in mortalities. In areas where fishing effort has been heavy for many years, dolphins flee from approaching boats, and have become difficult to set nets around. When entrapped, experienced dolphins wait, apparently calmly, near the section of the net where they will be released.

The dolphins of the eastern tropical Pacific can be divided into separate stocks, and these have been affected to differing degrees by tuna fishing. The most heavily exploited stock, the eastern stock of the spinner dolphin, has been reduced to approximately 17 per cent of its initial (pre-1959) numbers, and an estimated 15 000–16 000 of these dolphins were killed in 1986. One school of thought suggests that when the size of a stock of large mammals drops precipitously, the rate at which they reproduce should increase. Contrary to these expectations, the most heavily exploited stocks of both spinner and spotted dolphins show no evidence of such effects. The effects of tuna fishing on other dolphin species caught less frequently — including bottlenose dolphins (*Tursiops truncatus*), rough-toothed dolphins (*Steno bredanensis*), striped dolphins (*Stenella coeruleoalba*) and short-finned pilot whales (*Globicephala macrorhynchus*) are less well known, but appear to be far less severe.

▶ Dolphins are often used as reliable indicators of the presence of tuna schools. Several species of dolphins die in large numbers by drowning when they are trapped inside purse seine nets. American tuna fishing associations and fisheries authorities are attempting to reduce losses, often by manual rescue of trapped dolphins.

Robert Pitman/Earthviews

separate stocks, as discussed below.

In the waters of the California Bight, the distribution and abundance of pilot whales and common dolphins have been linked to the topography of the sea floor. Pilot whales feed primarily on squid, while common dolphins eat a variety of food types, including several fish species. Both cetacean species, but particularly the pilot whales, are more likely to be found over areas where the sea floor is mountainous rather than flat. Unfortunately, little is known about the distribution and abundance of the prey of these two species, but it seems likely that the restricted distribution of pilot whales reflects their more restricted food choice.

Further research has shown that the number of common dolphins in the area increases in the summer and autumn, and that they enter from the south and move through the Bight in an anticlockwise pattern.

DISTRIBUTION, STOCKS AND SPECIATION

While many cetacean species are found over large ocean areas, an individual whale would not necessarily cover the entire area. In general, a species can be divided into stocks; a stock is a large group of whales (generally numbering in the thousands) found in a geographically definable area.

For example, humpback dolphins have generally been considered to comprise two species, the Indo-Pacific humpback dolphin and the Atlantic humpback dolphin. However, 'Indo-Pacific' humpback dolphins found on the east coast of South Africa differ in general body form from those found on the eastern edge of the species' range (for example, those in Australian waters). The South African dolphins have the pronounced hump that gives the species its name, but Australian animals lack this hump and appear similar to the 'Atlantic' humpback dolphins.

▲ Predators adapt to the abundance and distribution of their prey. Thus, relatively deep-diving pilot whales usually gather near underwater mountain ranges where their preferred prey of squid is most often found.

Michael Bryden

▲ The abundance and distribution of prey also lead to the isolation of 'stocks' or populations of predators, which may become physically different over time. Humpback dolphins from the Atlantic and from Southeast Asia lack the dorsal hump found in members of the South African population.

Bottlenose dolphins provide another good example of stock separation. Inshore and offshore populations in the same general area tend to differ in body form, with inshore animals generally being smaller. Bottlenose dolphins found in enclosed seas tend to be smaller than those of the open ocean. Taxonomists still debate the number of species of bottlenose dolphin, in particular, whether some stocks are different enough to be considered separate species.

In the eastern tropical Pacific ocean, regional differences in the body shape and colouration of spinner dolphins allow them to be divided into stocks. These dolphin populations demonstrate the necessity to recognise that species exist in discrete stocks. Different stocks have been variously affected by the tuna purse-seining industry. In the past 20 years, some stocks have been reduced dramatically, while others have been less affected.

The best-known examples of cetacean stocks are those of the baleen whales. Blue, fin, sei, Bryde's, minke and humpback whales are found in both hemispheres. Their migrations are timed so that whales from the Northern Hemisphere are in the breeding grounds at different times to whales from the Southern Hemisphere, so that the two groups never meet. Because of this separation, whales from stocks in the two hemispheres are different in size and shape. Right whales are considered sufficiently different to classify the northern and southern types as two distinct species, although this has been disputed.

In the Southern Hemisphere, the waters of the Antarctic have been divided into six zones for the purpose of defining stocks for whaling management. While the populations of whales of each species within these zones are generally from the one stock, some interchange between stocks occurs. Recent research in the North Atlantic has confirmed the existence of three separate feeding stocks of humpback whales (off Greenland, off Newfoundland and Labrador, and in the Gulf of Maine), which intermingle on their breeding grounds off the West Indies. Whether a similar pattern exists in Southern Hemisphere waters remains to be examined. Data collected during whaling operations off the east coast of Australia and New Zealand indicate that, while the whales hunted in both places were supposedly of the one stock, and there was some interchange, the New Zealand subpopulation appeared to be separate from that off Australia.

Much is still to be learned about the ecology and distribution of cetaceans. Even species that are thought to be well studied, such as the grey and humpback whales or the bottlenose dolphin, still retain their secrets. Many aspects of cetacean ecology will remain poorly understood until general knowledge of the marine environment improves.

◄ 'Spy hopping' by southern right whales in antarctic waters is also seen in northern right whales in arctic waters. Virtually identical, these separate 'species' may be no more than geographically isolated populations.

WHALE MIGRATION

BALEEN WHALES

Baleen whales undertake some of the longest migrations in the animal kingdom. The distribution and abundance of food, and the availability of sites for reproduction are the factors that motivate these migrations.

In polar waters, summer brings huge increases in the populations of small organisms on which baleen whales feed called krill, so these baleen whales migrate to the areas where prey are most abundant. In the Southern Hemisphere, blue, fin, humpback and minke whales feed entirely on krill, while right whales eat a wider variety of crustaceans. Sei and Bryde's whales feed on other crustacean species and also on fish. Because of their different food preferences, sei, Bryde's and right whales are not found as far south as the other species. In the Northern Hemisphere, only the blue whale feeds entirely on krill; the other baleen whales feed on a variety of crustaceans and fish.

Humpback and grey whales have been studied intensively on their winter calving grounds. Both these species migrate close to the coastlines of continents and so are relatively easy to study. Their calving grounds are distinguished by sheltered, warm and fairly shallow water. Right whale calving grounds are also in coastal waters. Other baleen whales appear to calve in the open ocean, and their calving grounds are not easily identifiable.

Whale migrations are not necessarily a well-defined procession of animals moving north or southwards at an exact time of year. Bryde's whales live in tropical or warm temperate waters in all seasons; presumably their diet is sufficiently varied and they can find enough areas of high productivity (for example, around oceanic upwellings) to meet their food requirements. Sei whale migrations are also fairly diffuse and, if ecological conditions are suitable, these whales may invade areas where they are infrequently seen. Bowhead whale migrations depend on the conditions of the arctic pack ice, which varies from year to year.

Humpback and grey whales engage in regular migrations from their polar feeding grounds to their tropical breeding grounds through coastal waters. The migratory patterns of humpback and grey whales are predictable. However, anomalous sightings of these whales have also been recorded. Small numbers of grey whales feed in the summer in cold temperate waters, well south of the main feeding aggregations. Humpback whales have been reported remaining on feeding grounds in the North Atlantic in the winter, and on breeding grounds in the summer. In the Indian Ocean humpback song has been recorded in the summer, while in the Pacific Ocean off the coast of Australia, humpbacks have been seen in the summer in tropical waters north of the subtropical winter breeding grounds.

SPERM WHALES

Of the large pelagic toothed whales, only the sperm whale's migrations are reasonably well understood. Sperm whales are found in a variety of types of groupings — nursery groups, composed of females, juveniles and occasionally adult males; bachelor groups of several young males; and small groups of very large males. Nursery groups and groups of small bachelor males move towards the equator in the autumn, then back to warm temperate waters in the spring. Medium-sized bachelors travel to lower latitudes in the warmer months while harem masters, the largest bulls, feed in polar waters in the summer. The further towards the pole a male travels, the later it arrives in the equatorial waters in the breeding season and the sooner it leaves to return to its feeding grounds. There is some suggestion that large males may not leave their polar feeding grounds every year. The reasons for this complex migration pattern are discussed further in the chapter on social behaviour.

▶ Humpback whales undergo extensive and complex migrations from their winter breeding grounds in tropical and subtropical waters to their summer feeding grounds in polar waters. Some individuals may, however, remain at the feeding grounds throughout the winter.

MIGRATION OF HUMPBACKS

MIGRATION OF GREY WHALE

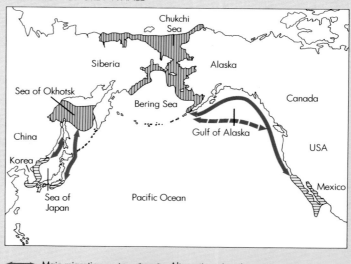

|||| Summer feeding grounds   ≡ Winter breeding grounds

◄——► Main migration route   ◄■■► Alternative migration route

An audience of penguins watch as an orca surfaces for air.

THE WORLD

G.L. Kooyman

OF THE WHALE

ANATOMY

R. EWAN FORDYCE

Cetaceans — whales, dolphins and porpoises — are often described collectively as 'whales'. They are remarkable among mammals in that they are fully aquatic and probably have been for 40 million years and their anatomy today reflects superb adaptation to life in the sea. But there are many ways to 'build' an animal suited to an aquatic lifestyle. As we look at cetacean anatomy it is interesting to ask 'Why are whales built like this, and not some other way?' Historical, functional and structural constraints all play a part in shaping anatomy.

BALEEN WHALE

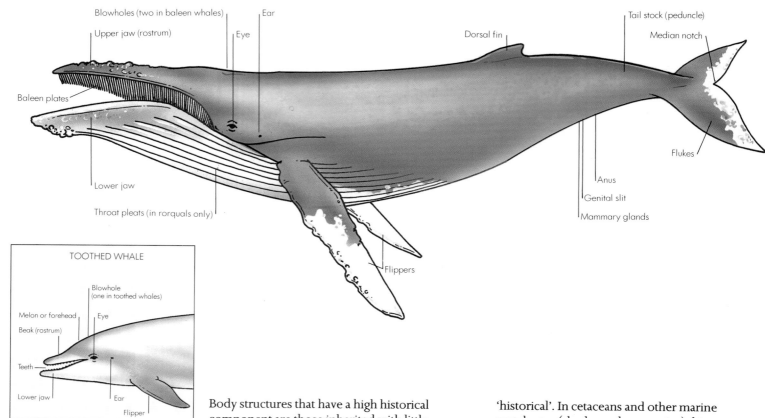

Blowholes (two in baleen whales)
Ear
Tail stock (peduncle)
Upper jaw (rostrum)
Eye
Median notch
Dorsal fin
Baleen plates
Flukes
Lower jaw
Anus
Throat pleats (in rorquals only)
Genital slit
Mammary glands
Flippers

TOOTHED WHALE
Blowhole (one in toothed whales)
Melon or forehead
Eye
Beak (rostrum)
Teeth
Lower jaw
Ear
Flipper

Body structures that have a high historical component are those inherited with little modification from distant ancestors. Thus, cetaceans have many features that occur in all mammals, for example, hair (albeit vestigial), a four-chambered heart, a single lower jawbone, three tiny bones inside the middle ear, mammary glands, and a placenta. These features need not be inherently present in a marine vertebrate, but they will always be present in a mammal. These historical structures are important in indicating ancestry, and thus relationships. In this case, they tell us that despite their misleading appearance, cetaceans are closely related to other mammals.

The streamlined profile, however, is not 'historical'. In cetaceans and other marine vertebrates (sharks, seals, penguins) this stream-lined torpedo-like profile has the function — as it does in fish — of allowing a smooth water flow across the moving body surface. This is an example of the effect of a functional constraint on morphology. Such features indicate the immediate working needs of day-to-day life. Other cetacean structures with a high functional component include the flattened forelimbs and prominent dorsal fin, which are probably important in controlling body orientation during swimming.

Finally, structural constraints have probably been important in limiting maximum and minimum sizes of cetaceans. As an animal increases in size the ratio of its surface area to volume decreases markedly. One reason why whales are so large is that a low surface area to volume ratio helps them to retain body heat in cold water. However, as a consequence of this structural constraint, their great mass requires proportionately huge amounts of food and thus the blue whale (*Balaenoptera musculus*) needs an enormous area of baleen (effectively, a large food-processing surface area) to support its mass.

The study of cetacean anatomy, then, can reveal relationships of animals (history) and the manner in which they live (function and structure).

PROFILE

Most living cetaceans have a streamlined, torpedo-shaped body that is propelled through the water by horizontal tail flukes that beat vertically. Paddle-shaped flippers, the equivalent of the human arm, help in steering. There are few impediments to efficient water flow; indeed, all living cetaceans lack significant body hair, an external ear lobe (pinna), a projecting nose, and externally projecting genitals or mammary glands. Body outlines do vary though, between species. Until the recent development of suitable underwater cameras, there had been little reliable information on the body profile of living large cetaceans. Even

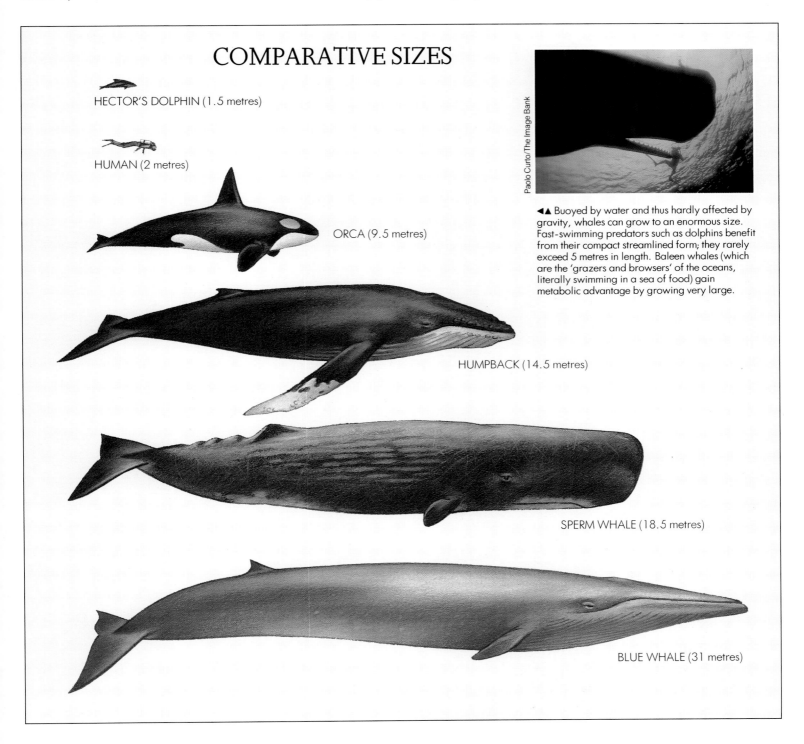

COMPARATIVE SIZES

HECTOR'S DOLPHIN (1.5 metres)

HUMAN (2 metres)

ORCA (9.5 metres)

HUMPBACK (14.5 metres)

SPERM WHALE (18.5 metres)

BLUE WHALE (31 metres)

Paolo Curto/The Image Bank

◄▲ Buoyed by water and thus hardly affected by gravity, whales can grow to an enormous size. Fast-swimming predators such as dolphins benefit from their compact streamlined form; they rarely exceed 5 metres in length. Baleen whales (which are the 'grazers and browsers' of the oceans, literally swimming in a sea of food) gain metabolic advantage by growing very large.

now, we do not fully understand the significance of differences in profile between species. For example, the slow-moving right whales (family Balaenidae) are fatter but otherwise do not differ radically in body profile from the typically much faster rorquals (Balaenopteridae).

HEAD

The structure of the head provides the best way of identifying families and species. Most cetaceans have a prominent upper jaw (rostrum), which sometimes forms a bird-like beak, in front of the eyes. The upper jaw is long in living baleen whales (suborder Mysticeti); it may be narrow and arched, or wide and flat, but it always carries baleen plates used for sieving food from the water (filter-feeding). Baleen whales are also distinguished by the flatness of the head above the eyes and the double blowhole. Toothed whales (suborder Odontoceti) generally have a narrow straight upper jaw, at least one pair of teeth in the lower jaw, a bulbous 'melon' (containing fat, muscles and nasal passage and sacs) above the eyes and upper jaw and a single blowhole high up on the elevated forehead.

Dolphins (family Delphinidae) seem to wear a permanent smile, but this is deceptive since the

head, like the rest of the body, carries significant blubber under the skin. Blubber, which occurs in all living cetaceans, prevents major muscles of the face reaching the surface. Thus whales and dolphins are capable of only a limited range of facial expressions. Some toothed whales can distort the external profile of the melon and in some the neck is slightly flexible.

All living baleen whales have widely separated lower jaws, in contrast to toothed whales, some of which have an extremely narrow lower jaw, in which two jawbones are fused together. In the slow-swimming plankton-skimming right whales the lower lips are arched up to cover the long baleen plates. In the rorquals the throat has conspicuous external grooves or pleats, which allow it to expand enormously when food is engulfed. Smaller double throat grooves in beaked whales (family Ziphiidae) are of uncertain function.

Cetacean eyes are rather small and expressionless. They lie on the sides of the head, just behind the gape of the mouth. There are no eyebrows or lashes. It is difficult to identify the former position of the external ear canal behind and below the eye in toothed whales since it is often hidden from external view.

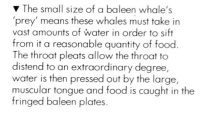

▼ The small size of a baleen whale's 'prey' means these whales must take in vast amounts of water in order to sift from it a reasonable quantity of food. The throat pleats allow the throat to distend to an extraordinary degree, water is then pressed out by the large, muscular tongue and food is caught in the fringed baleen plates.

Francois Gohier/Auscape International

Mike Osmond

◄ Humpback whales are noted for the size of their pectoral fins or flippers (their Latin name, *Megaptera*, means 'great wing'). The pectoral fins of all whales are highly mobile at the shoulder joint, while the rest of the fin, used as a stabiliser, is stiff and inflexible.

BODY AND FINS

All living cetaceans have well-developed forelimbs (flippers) placed behind the head and below the midline. The flippers vary widely in shape and size, although we do not know why. They are believed to be important in steering. In some cases, they are held rather rigidly out from the body, while in others, especially the long-flippered humpback whale (*Megaptera novaengliae*) the shoulder joint is remarkably mobile. All living cetaceans have a stiff foreflipper without the movable elbow joint seen in most mammals.

There is generally a prominent dorsal fin on the back at or behind mid-length though it is absent in a few species. The fin is supported not by skeleton, but by tough fibrous tissue inside it. Its size, shape and position vary.

Behind the anus the body tapers into the tail stock (peduncle), which has flattened sides, and the horizontal flukes. Sometimes the tail stock ends in a 'hump' before the flukes. They are stiff even long after death. Strongly interwoven tendons and fibrous bundles provide most of the stiffness.

THE SKULL

Most cetaceans have rather similar external features that differ in degree rather than in kind, but aspects of the internal skeleton vary greatly. In general, the postcranial skeleton (the vertebrae, ribs and flippers) varies less from group to group than does the skull. In all cetaceans, however, the skeleton is different from that of other living mammals.

The skulls and associated soft tissues of living toothed and baleen whales are so different from each other that it has been suggested that they represent two unrelated groups of mammals. However, the differences probably reflect their different feeding behaviours, and both types of skull can be derived adequately from the ancestral archaeocetes. In both groups, the skull has departed from the normal mammalian structure by being 'telescoped' (compressed from front to back so that certain parts overlap each other — just like the sections of a folded up telescope). But the details of the telescoping differ in the two living groups.

DORSAL FINS

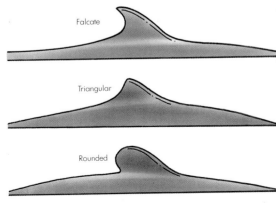

Falcate

Triangular

Rounded

▲ Dolphins include species with a fin that is falcate, triangular, bluntly rounded or absent. The functional significance of these different styles of fin is uncertain.

▼ Fluke profiles, viewed from above, vary considerably. Most are slightly convex at the back, but some are almost straight (sperm whale) and others are conspicuously curved (humpback) or even biconvex (narwhal). Most species have a notch in the centre of the trailing edge, but the notch is poorly developed in beaked whales.

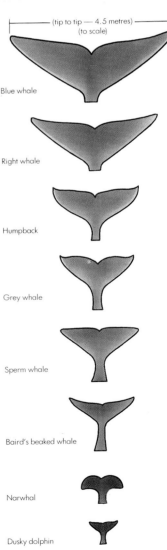

(tip to tip — 4.5 metres)
(to scale)

Blue whale

Right whale

Humpback

Grey whale

Sperm whale

Baird's beaked whale

Narwhal

Dusky dolphin

WHALE TEETH

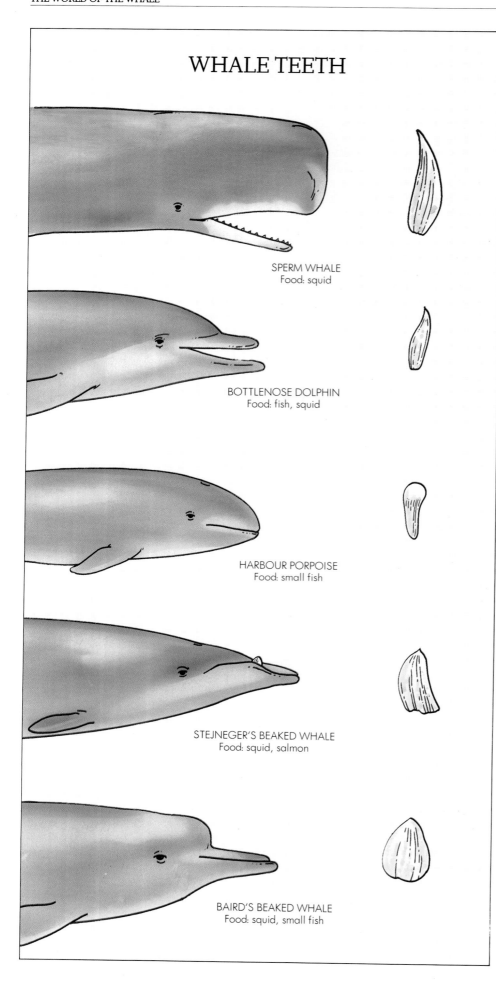

SPERM WHALE
Food: squid

BOTTLENOSE DOLPHIN
Food: fish, squid

HARBOUR PORPOISE
Food: small fish

STEJNEGER'S BEAKED WHALE
Food: squid, salmon

BAIRD'S BEAKED WHALE
Food: squid, small fish

TELESCOPING IN TOOTHED WHALES

In the skull of toothed whales, the main bones of the upper jaw have been thrust backwards and upwards over the eye sockets to extend across the front of the brain-case. In many cases they have become asymmetrical.

This type of telescoping of the upper jaw may be associated with the well-known ability of toothed whales to echolocate or use sonar. The expanded and backwards-shifted upper jaw bones hold a large volume of facial muscles, equivalent to those that in humans help move the lips and flare the nostrils. These facial muscles focus upwards and in towards the blowhole. Here they are attached to a series of sacs (diverticula) in the soft tissues of the nasal passages between the external blowhole and the bony nasal openings on the skull.

Other aspects of the skulls of these whales also seem to be adapted for producing or receiving such high-frequency sounds. For example, toothed whales have a reduced cheekbone that may help to insulate the sound-producing front from the sound-receiving back of the skull.

In each ear, the middle ear cavity is expanded into a complex sinus on the skull base. These sinuses may compensate for increased pressure on the ear cavities during diving, but they may also help to isolate the right and left ears from each other, making it easier for the animal to tell the direction of a sound source. The periotic, the earbone that carries the organs of hearing and balance, is not fixed to the skull in toothed whales, presumably so as to eliminate unwanted transmission of sound through the adjacent skull bones. The external ear canal is vestigial. Sound is probably transmitted from the water to the internally placed ear bones via a thin 'pan-bone' (shaped like a frying pan) in the lower jaw and a fatty channel from the pan-bone.

FEEDING ANATOMY OF TOOTHED WHALES

The upper and lower jaws are enormously varied in toothed whales, although both jaws are generally straight in side view.

All species have teeth and, generally, these differ from the teeth of other mammals. Many dolphins (family Delphinidae), for example, have dozens of simple conical teeth on both sides of each jaw — far more than the typical number for mammals. There is only one set of teeth in contrast to the juvenile and adult sets in most mammals. And, in most living toothed whales, the teeth are undifferentiated and the same shape (homodont) throughout the jaw, in contrast to the differentiated (heterodont) teeth of most mammals.

Some squid-eating species, however, have reduced numbers of teeth. Presumably simple conical teeth are effective in holding such prey, which must be eaten mostly whole, since the teeth are unsuitable for breaking up food in the mouth.

TELESCOPING IN BALEEN WHALES

Perhaps the most prominent feature of most baleen whale skulls, apart from their enormous size, is the large, bony, broad flat upper jaw. The main bones of the upper jaw carry a row of parallel horny, flexible flat plates of baleen (whalebone). The fringed inner edges of these plates filter food out of the water. In right whales, the baleen is long and the jaw is arched upwards. Rorquals, however, have rather short baleen and a flat upper jaw. The several bones of the upper jaw are rather loosely attached to each other, probably to help absorb the shock when the jaws close after gulping plankton-loaded water; the upper jaw is likewise attached loosely to the skull. The symmetrical upper jaw thrusts back under the eye region to extend the roof of the mouth backwards, perhaps increasing the food-processing area. Baleen whales lack the enlarged facial muscles and nasal sacs of toothed whales, and the brain-case is not expanded markedly upwards as in toothed whales.

But baleen whale skulls do have some unusual features of their own. The main jaw-closing muscles (temporal muscles) attach above the eye rather than behind it as in both archaeocetes and toothed whales. The lower jaws, like the upper jaws are toothless, and lack baleen. They typically bow outwards, and at the front they are not fused

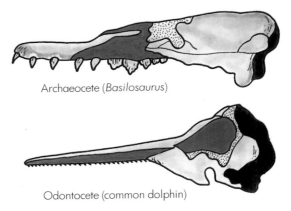

Archaeocete (*Basilosaurus*)

Odontocete (common dolphin)

together but are attached to each other by ligaments. This flexible joint presumably allows some independent movement of the jaws during feeding.

Baleen whales do not show the diversity of structure seen in toothed whales and species differ most obviously from one another in the proportions of the upper jaw. One of the most unusual features of these large animals, which are adapted so well for filter-feeding, is the presence of multiple simple teeth in the lower jaws of embryos — a reminder of the distant toothed ancestors of baleen whales.

◄ As cetaceans adapted to a marine existence, their skulls 'telescoped'. Some elements became shorter (the cranium became compressed to accommodate the echolocation 'melon'), some lengthened (the bones of the rostrum or 'beak' became more attenuated) and some changed position (the nasal bones gradually 'migrated' as the nostrils moved backward to the top of the head).

▼ Although the embryos of baleen whales have vestigial teeth in their upper jaws, these disappear and adults use the 'plates' of baleen to strain food from the water. Baleen is variable in length and shape and is found only in the upper jaw, which bows upward to accommodate baleen plates up to 4.3 metres long in right whales.

SKELETAL VIEW OF DUSKY DOLPHIN

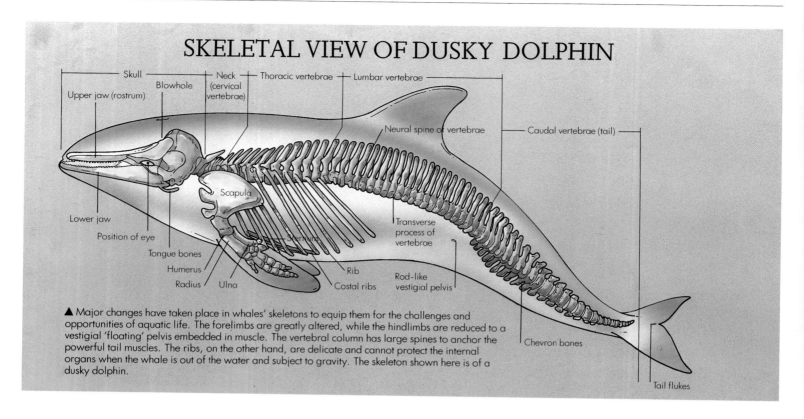

Skull — Upper jaw (rostrum) — Blowhole — Neck (cervical vertebrae) — Thoracic vertebrae — Lumbar vertebrae — Neural spine of vertebrae — Caudal vertebrae (tail) — Transverse process of vertebrae — Chevron bones — Tail flukes — Lower jaw — Position of eye — Tongue bones — Humerus — Radius — Ulna — Scapula — Sternum — Costal ribs — Rib — Rod-like vestigial pelvis

▲ Major changes have taken place in whales' skeletons to equip them for the challenges and opportunities of aquatic life. The forelimbs are greatly altered, while the hindlimbs are reduced to a vestigial 'floating' pelvis embedded in muscle. The vertebral column has large spines to anchor the powerful tail muscles. The ribs, on the other hand, are delicate and cannot protect the internal organs when the whale is out of the water and subject to gravity. The skeleton shown here is of a dusky dolphin.

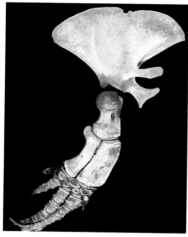

D.V. Weston

▲ Greatly compressed in length, the bones of the pectoral fin or flipper are nevertheless well developed, though movement is restricted to the shoulder joint. A reduction in the number of 'fingers' is common, with each finger usually having a greater number of individual bones.

THE REST OF THE SKELETON

The skeleton from the neck back differs radically from that of land mammals. Cervical vertebrae are foreshortened, and some or all of them fused, inhibiting the mobility of the neck. But cetaceans have been able to attain enormous sizes because they are buoyed by water and thus are not limited by the same constraints of body support as land vertebrates. Not surprisingly, then, cetacean ribs are often rather delicate in build, and not strongly attached to the spine or to the breastbone. This unfortunately means that the ribs of stranded large whales are not strong enough to support the weight of the body. There is great variation in form and number of vertebrae between species, but the significance of this is uncertain. There is only a remnant of the pelvic girdle that once supported hind limbs. The forelimb or flipper is always well

developed and, despite its hydrodynamic function, it retains the sequence of bones typical of many other vertebrates.

Phalanges, equivalent to individual bones of fingers, are generally increased (hyperphalangy) beyond the normal mammalian number, but the number of 'fingers' may be reduced to four. Such details are not apparent externally.

SOFT TISSUES

The soft tissues of cetaceans differ greatly from land mammals as do other parts of their anatomy. Sensory organs associated with the nervous system show many remarkable features. The olfactory (smelling) apparatus associated with the blowholes is greatly reduced in baleen whales and absent in toothed whales. In both baleen and

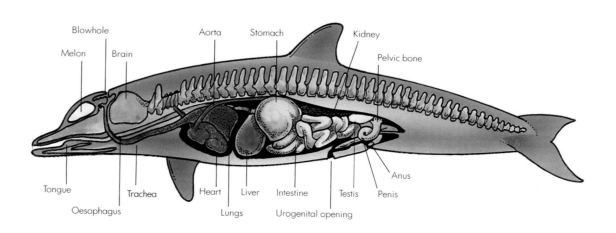

Blowhole — Melon — Brain — Aorta — Stomach — Kidney — Pelvic bone — Tongue — Trachea — Heart — Liver — Intestine — Testis — Penis — Anus — Oesophagus — Lungs — Urogenital opening

toothed whales the eyes are relatively small and the auditory organs are well developed. The ear canal from the side of the head is usually closed, and sound is probably transmitted to the ears through soft tissues. Some species appear to lack the eardrum, which is so critical for hearing in air.

Cetacean brains are large compared to body size, and the brains of large whales may be heavier than those of any other animals. Blood supply to the brain is not by the normal route of the carotid arteries, but instead by vessels associated with the spinal cord, the rete mirabile.

The lungs, which lie near the heart, are supplied by a short and often wide trachea. Cartilage rings support it and the bronchioles.

Cetacean stomachs, like those of some hoofed mammals, may be chambered. The similarity may be only superficial, however, since cetaceans do not chew their cud. The alimentary tract in fact varies widely between species. There are also other noteworthy features of the abdominal cavity. All species lack a gall bladder and appendix and the liver is not lobed. The kidneys are large and possess many separate lobes (renculi).

CONCLUSION

Less is known about the anatomy of cetaceans than for most mammal groups. These animals are difficult to study in the wild, which means that we still do not understand the function of many structures. And there are generally huge logistical problems encountered in dealing with dead animals, so that it is difficult to study fresh material. Nevertheless, several centuries of study have demonstrated the remarkable marine adaptations of much of cetacean anatomy, adaptations that overprint but never fully hide the unmistakable ancestry of these animals.

▲ Their environment — alien and dangerous to humans — and their sheer size have made whales difficult to study, and we still know very little, for example, about the function of the auditory organs or the mechanisms of these animals' astonishingly sophisticated ability to navigate by sound.

▲ Subtle physiological adaptations have enabled whales to take advantage of very cold but nutrient-rich polar waters.

G.L. Kooyman

ADAPTATION TO THE AQUATIC ENVIRONMENT

M.M. BRYDEN

W hales have evolved from mammalian ancestors that lived on land. For warm-blooded, air-breathing creatures, the aquatic environment in which they now live presents particular difficulties. Water is much denser and more viscous than air, making movement in it more difficult, as comparison between a sprinting swimmer and a runner readily testifies. Compared with air, water absorbs heat faster, transmits sound faster and with significantly less attenuation, and absorbs light more readily. Water also has a higher refractive index than air.

But although water — particularly very cold water — is an alien and in some ways hostile environment for mammals to live in, there are obvious advantages to be gained from exploiting it. Buoyancy in water counteracts the gravitational pull on the body, a major advantage to mammals that live in the sea. There are also vast exploitable resources in the oceans. A great many mammals feed on aquatic life and/or seek protection in water, including such seemingly unlikely candidates as certain cats, bats, pigs and primates, including of course humans. It should not be surprising that these advantages led to greater aquatic specialisation in certain mammals: the basic mammalian plan is easily adapted to the requirements of aquatic life (the partially aquatic polar bear, for example, is similar in appearance to other bears). Marked modifications of form and function became necessary only as mammals evolved to the point where they lived semi-permanently or permanently in water. And these modifications are greatest in the sea cows (order Sirenia) and whales (order Cetacea), the only mammals to have become totally aquatic.

▼ The similar body shapes of the shark (a fish), the extinct ichthyosaur (a reptile) and the dolphin (a mammal) are evolutionary responses to similar pressures, especially the need for streamlining to reduce friction in an aquatic environment.

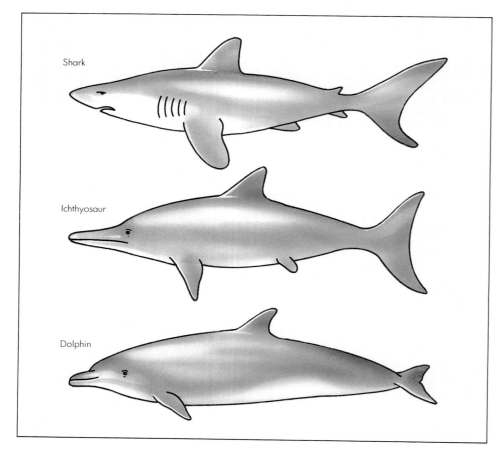

Shark

Ichthyosaur

Dolphin

EXTERNAL FORM, SIZE AND LOCOMOTION
The external form of cetaceans strongly reflects their watery environment. Because water is denser and more viscous than air, streamlining of the body was necessary, and the shape of whales became more like that of other marine vertebrates as evolution progressed. Superficial comparison of small whales, sharks and extinct fish-like reptiles (ichthyosaurs) reveals a remarkable similarity of form. This is an example of 'convergent evolution'

Whales and their kin are all comparatively large mammals. The large baleen whales are enormous — the blue whale (*Balaenoptera musculus*), which can grow to nearly 30 metres in length and a maximum weight of 170 tonnes, is by far the largest animal that has ever lived on earth.

Their large size conveys significant metabolic advantage to whales, many of which live in very cold seas. Like human beings, whales have a body temperature around 37°C, but sea temperature may be as low as –1.7°C. Heat loss from the skin surface in water is many times greater than in air of the same temperature, and the rate at which heat is lost depends on the area of the surface over which it is lost. Surface area declines relatively as body mass (or volume) increases, so that the surface area of a large mammal is relatively less than that of a small one. Thus the great size of whales, in polar

110

Heather Angel/Biofotos

seas particularly, has considerable adaptive value, because it slows heat loss.

As whales live permanently in water, their size is not limited by the effects of gravity as is that of land mammals. The whale's body is weightless in water and limbs are not required to support the body weight as in land mammals. The limbs are used only for control of movement and temperature regulation. In the dense aquatic medium, reduction in size of the forelimbs and loss of the hind limbs (replaced to some extent by development of the flukes) has had the dual advantage of making the limbs more efficient for steering and manoeuvring, and decreasing the surface area of the body.

Being viscous, water offers resistance to the application of a backward force by the animal, providing a forward thrust that drives the body forward. The propulsive force in whales is produced by the paddle-like tail flukes. The forelimbs (flippers) are also in the form of flat paddles, but are not used for propulsion; they act as balancing planes.

However, water also provides resistance against movement: a frictional resistance (drag) develops at the skin surface as the animal moves through the water. To minimise drag, the body has become smooth-surfaced and streamlined, with elimination of unnecessary protruding parts that would offer resistance to the water, such as

▲ The streamlining of the body does not reduce drag sufficiently to account for the extraordinary swimming speeds attained by some cetaceans. As it accelerates through the water, this bottlenose dolphin creates a laminar flow of water over its body to further reduce turbulence.

HOW A DOLPHIN SWIMS

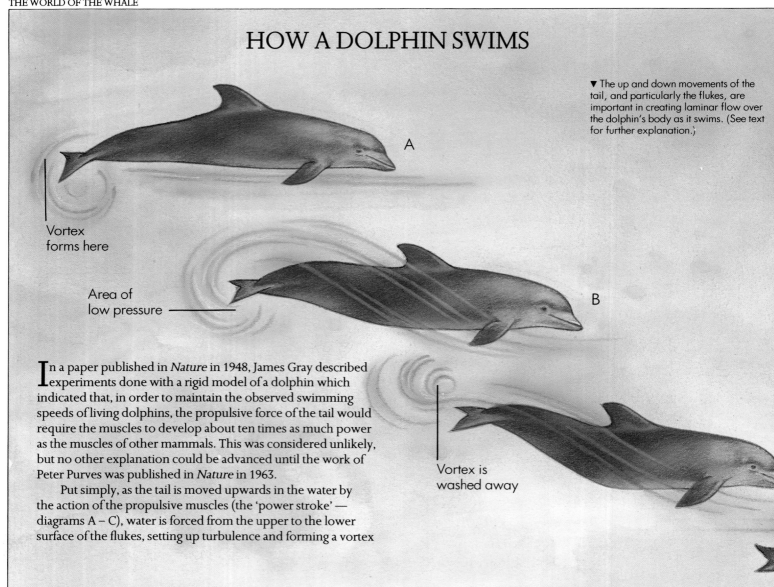

▼ The up and down movements of the tail, and particularly the flukes, are important in creating laminar flow over the dolphin's body as it swims. (See text for further explanation.)

Vortex forms here

Area of low pressure

A

B

Vortex is washed away

In a paper published in *Nature* in 1948, James Gray described experiments done with a rigid model of a dolphin which indicated that, in order to maintain the observed swimming speeds of living dolphins, the propulsive force of the tail would require the muscles to develop about ten times as much power as the muscles of other mammals. This was considered unlikely, but no other explanation could be advanced until the work of Peter Purves was published in *Nature* in 1963.

Put simply, as the tail is moved upwards in the water by the action of the propulsive muscles (the 'power stroke' — diagrams A – C), water is forced from the upper to the lower surface of the flukes, setting up turbulence and forming a vortex

▲ Just as the bulbous bow of large ships reduces drag, the bulbous forehead of some fast-swimming whales appears to contribute to their speed in the water.

external ear pinnae, protruding mammary glands or reproductive organs, and hair.

If one runs a hand over the surface of a whale, one is struck by the silky smoothness of the skin. As well, the skin surface bears no fold-lines or pores, and the body itself is very evenly contoured — there is no constriction at the neck, so that the head expands smoothly into the trunk, which then tapers toward the tail. All these features contribute to streamlining the body, but they do not explain fully the quite extraordinary speeds attainable by small whales. The rounded head, so marked in species such as the pilot whales (*Globicephala*), may play a part — we know that the bulbous bows of large ships reduce drag.

But the most important factor helping whales attain such high speed is the way the tail flukes act to create 'laminar flow' of water over the smooth body, greatly reducing drag. This enables a whale to achieve great speed with little exertion.

Dolphins also save energy during fast travel by leaping clear of the water, something that is seen

commonly at sea when dolphins are chasing prey.

The pliability of the skin may help at high speeds, too. Although the skin and blubber are firm, they are not rigid. When a dolphin changes speed or direction rapidly, folds appear on the skin surface at right angles to the direction of movement, indicating areas where turbulence is developing. The subtle alterations in shape at the skin surface probably eliminate the turbulence before it is fully formed.

There are two other means by which dolphins may reduce drag or even lubricate their passage through the water. The surface cells in the skin of the dolphin contain oily droplets and carbohydrates. Shedding of these surface cells may reduce drag. Cetaceans also have a large number of conjunctival glands that produce a copious mucous secretion, easily visible as a stringy material starting from the eye and passing back along the body toward the shoulders. This may have a similar function to the fine film of mucus secreted by fish as they swim.

at the trailing edge of the flukes (diagram A). An area of low pressure is created beneath the flukes as the upstroke continues, causing the blades of the flukes to bend down and drawing water backwards from the surface of the head and body. This causes the dolphin to move forwards and downwards against the hydroplaning action of the flippers (diagram B).

As a result of this forward and downward body movement, further upward movement of the flukes accelerates the passage of water obliquely over the body and down the back, and the vortex at the trailing edge of the flukes is washed away (diagram C).

The blades of the flukes relax before the downstroke of the tail begins (diagram D). As the tail is pulled downwards by the recovery muscles (the 'recovery stroke' — diagrams E and F),

the flukes begin to curl upwards and spill water sideways instead of accelerating it to the rear. The buoyancy of the head and thorax, enhanced by the large amount of oil and fat contained in them, causes the head to rise while the downstroke of the tail continues. The water flow over the rear of the body is similar to that during the propulsive stroke, but without positive acceleration.

The positive acceleration of water over the body during the power stroke allows laminar (non-turbulent) flow to occur at velocities well above those at which turbulent flow develops in the rigid body of Gray's dolphin model. A condition of laminar flow exists over the majority of the dolphin's body surface during swimming, thereby reducing greatly the power needed for high-speed swimming.

CONTROL OF BODY TEMPERATURE

Whales, as warm-blooded creatures, face particular difficulties in maintaining a steady body temperature (homeothermy) in an environment whose temperature is often considerably lower. Water has a much greater capacity to absorb heat (high specific heat), and it does so much more rapidly (high conductivity) than air. Heat exchange in water is consequently many times greater than in still air at the same temperature.

Whales are unable to conserve body heat by behavioural means in ways that some terrestrial mammals do, by curling up, building nests, huddling together, seeking shelter in protected places, or seeking out warm, sunny areas. For the whale, all the water available is at more or less the same temperature, and in the polar regions this is indeed cold.

To avoid excessive body heat loss, whales, like other aquatic mammals, have a heavy blanket of fat in the deepest layer of the skin, referred to as blubber, that acts as an insulator as well as an

important energy store. It varies greatly in thickness within and between individual whales and whale species, but it has been recorded up to 50 centimetres thick in one species, the bowhead whale (*Balaena mysticetus*).

Blubber has been shown to be an effective insulator, and it is clear from direct observation that whales in good physical condition do not suffer greatly from cold. However, the blubber is not a complete insulator, so that whales in very cold waters do lose more heat, and therefore require more energy from food, than those in warmer seas.

Although conservation of body heat is largely taken care of by the development of the blubber layer, there is a potential problem of overheating when a whale engages in bursts of activity. This is overcome by the presence of many quite large arteries running up through the blubber to the skin. If large volumes of blood are pumped through these vessels, the skin is warmed by all this blood and the heat is quickly dissipated to the

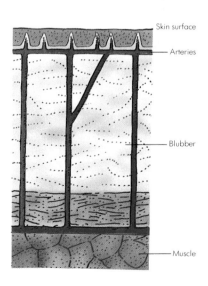

▲ Forming a layer up to 50 centimetres thick, the dense blubber that lies beneath a whale's skin insulates the body in cold waters. The arteries running through the blubber prevent overheating during intense activity.

David Rootes/Seaphot Ltd/Planet Earth Pictures

▲ A thick layer of insulating blubber and physiological adaptation of the blood vessels regulate heat loss. Many whales that live in high latitudes also grow to enormous size, thus reducing their surface area relative to their mass and making protection from cold waters even more efficient.

▼ Blood from the heart to an extremity flows through a central artery (shown in red) at 37°C and exchanges heat with surrounding veins to maintain a stable temperature gradient. Cool venous blood (shown in blue) flowing from fins or flukes is warmed gradually from 4°C to 37°C as it approaches body cavities.

surrounding water. The flow through the arteries is controlled by nerves. When the volume is decreased almost to zero, the blubber serves its normal function as an insulator.

But how is heat conserved in those parts of the body that lack blubber: the flippers, flukes and dorsal fin? These regions must receive some blood to supply their tissues with oxygen, but blood flowing through them at body temperature would

cause significant loss of body heat. An intriguing modification of the blood vessels minimises this loss by an elegant mechanism called 'countercurrent heat exchange'. The basic arrangement is present in many terrestrial mammals, including humans, where the deeply placed major arteries supplying the extremities are accompanied by two or more veins. Heat is transferred between artery and veins so that the blood is cooled as it approaches the extremity and warmed again as it leaves it. In the whale, the arrangement has been modified so that the arteries are completely enclosed in a plexus (bundle) of veins, increasing the efficiency of the counter-current heat exchange.

Venous return from the flippers, flukes and dorsal fin is controlled by a very simple mechanism. If the flow of blood to these extremities is increased, the arteries increase in

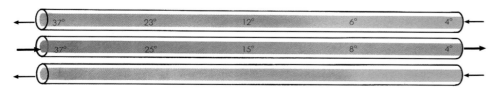

37°   23°   12°   6°   4°

37°   25°   15°   8°   4°

diameter to accommodate the extra flow. This in turn puts pressure on the surrounding venous plexus, restricting the blood flow in it (and hence preventing the cooling of the arterial blood) and forcing the blood to return to the body in surface veins. These are not accompanied by arteries, so heat is now lost from the relatively warm venous blood to the surrounding water.

This intriguing system can control the amount of heat lost from the surface of the extremities — heat is conserved when required by the countercurrent mechanism, or dissipated when this mechanism is closed off in conditions where surplus heat is produced, such as during physical exertion.

DIVING

All whales are skilled divers and take their food underwater in their natural environment, but being mammals they must surface at intervals to breathe. Until just a few years ago the only information about the diving capabilities of whales had been obtained either indirectly, by dissection of specimens or by examination of whales entangled in cables or other structures underwater, or directly but not experimentally, from observers attached to expeditions and whaling vessels.

Although such observations have been recorded for a very long time, it was not until the 1950s that detailed studies of the diving physiology of whales began, stimulated by the development of ways to capture and maintain small cetaceans. These were extended later by training dolphins to dive in the open ocean, follow commands and return reliably for further examination. Another method has involved the use of telemetry. A dolphin is captured at sea, fitted with a device to

Michael Bryden

▲ This cast of the whale's countercurrent heat exchange system is revealed by the scanning electron microscope as a web of veins surrounding a central artery, allowing for efficient warming and cooling of the blood.

record information about the dive and a signalling device to record the animal's whereabouts, and then released. Observers in a boat pick up signals transmitted by the equipment when the dolphin surfaces to breathe. The recording device is attached to the animal with a corrosive coupling designed to dissolve in seawater, and cause the equipment to fall off after a time. It can then be recovered and re-used.

Diving ability varies greatly among different whale species, but all are impressive divers. Sperm whales (*Physeter catodon*) and bottlenose whales (genus *Hyperoodon*) are the most accomplished, being able to stay down for up to 90 minutes and 120 minutes respectively. Rorquals (family Balaenopteridae) rarely dive for more than 40 minutes, while the bottlenose dolphin (*Tursiops truncatus*) dives for up to 15 minutes and the common dolphin (*Delphinus delphis*) for only 3 minutes.

It is often striking just how briefly a whale is at the water surface when it breathes. The nostrils, at the front of the head in most other animals, have in the course of whale evolution become a blowhole situated at the highest point of the head. Thus only a small part of the head region and back needs to break the surface during respiration, and the animal can exhale and inhale remarkably rapidly while swimming at speed.

DIVING AND 'THE BENDS'
Some whales, particularly the sperm whale, dive to quite phenomenal depths in excess of 2000 metres and possibly as deep as 3200 metres, and in doing

◄ The amount of time spent underwater varies greatly among different species but these spotted dolphins, like all cetaceans, require a remarkably brief time at the surface to take in oxygen, partly due to the convenient location of their blowholes.

▼ Before diving, whales must take in sufficient oxygen at the surface, to last the duration of the dive. The sperm whale when diving deeply (A) breathes more rapidly but less frequently than the fin whale diving for 10–15 minutes (B) or the common dolphin making short, frequent dives (C).

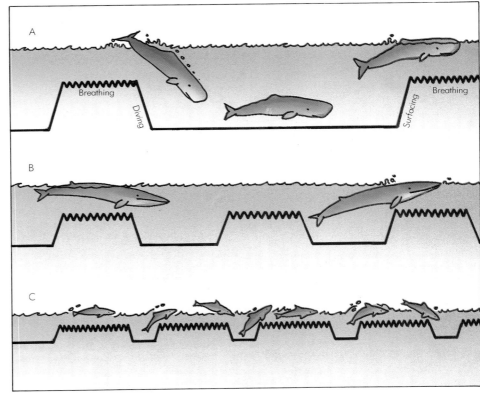

so are subjected to enormous pressure. How do they avoid getting 'the bends'?

For a long time it was believed that whales did not face such a problem because they do not breathe compressed gas as scuba and 'hard hat' divers do. These human divers have unlimited supplies of compressed air when submerged, and more and more of the nitrogen in this air dissolves in their blood as pressure increases with increasing depth. The bends, or caisson disease, occurs as a result of decreasing pressure during ascent after the dive, when the nitrogen comes out of solution in the diver's blood and other tissues more quickly than the lungs can get rid of it. It forms small bubbles in the blood vessels and tissues — exactly like the bubbles of carbon dioxide released in a bottle of soda water when the top is removed and the internal pressure is released.

The whale, on the other hand, is a breath-hold diver, taking down only the air contained in its lungs and respiratory passages, so there is relatively little nitrogen to dissolve in the blood and tissues and create what was thought to be the cause of the bends.

However, recently we have learned that a skindiver without compressed air who repeatedly descends to depth may also get the bends. A syndrome known as Taravana, observed in Polynesian divers of the Tuamotu archipelago, involves central nervous symptoms that appear to be the bends. And in experimental dives in the 1960s, a diver developed symptoms of the bends after making 60 dives to a depth of 20 metres and spending two minutes there each time, during a five-hour period. The symptoms disappeared rapidly when he was placed in a recompression chamber. How then does the whale escape the bends, as it makes frequent dives to feed at depths far greater than 20 metres, and remains submerged for considerably longer than two minutes? This question cannot yet be fully answered.

OTHER EFFECTS OF INCREASED PRESSURE

When a whale dives, the hydrostatic pressure, which increases at a rate of about one atmosphere for every 10 metre increase in depth of sea water, is transmitted to all parts of the body. Since a very large proportion of the whale's body consists of water, which is practically incompressible, most of its body is not deformed by the increased pressure. But the air in the lungs and respiratory passages is compressible and, with increasing pressure, the lungs collapse and much of the air is forced into the passages leading to the blowhole. The blood vessels supplying these passages are fewer and further from the surface than in the lungs, so that gas exchange from air to blood is reduced. In addition, when the lungs collapse their lining also becomes thicker, so that blood in the capillaries is further removed from the air.

There is another quite large air space surrounding the tiny structures of the middle ear. If the cavity did not collapse during a dive the way the respiratory spaces do, a pressure differential between it and the tissues and blood vessels lining its wall would develop. Only a small pressure difference is needed to make these vessels swell and rupture. The pain in the ears caused by such disequilibrium is appreciated by any diver.

The whale is protected against this by having extensive vascular sinuses in the lining of the middle ear space. Under pressure these swell with blood and reduce the volume of the cavity. This simple mechanism, which is quite automatic, keeps the middle ear always at the same pressure as the outside environment as the pressure changes with diving.

DIVING AND THE RESPIRATORY SYSTEM

A whale must obtain all the oxygen it needs for a dive during the brief period when it surfaces and breathes. Whales breathe less frequently than land mammals, but compensate by taking deeper breaths and extracting more oxygen from the air they breathe. They also exchange a greater percentage of lung air with each breath. The whale breathes in before diving, taking down at least partially inflated lungs, unlike the seal which breathes out before diving. But how can whales stay underwater for so long?

The first place we might look for an answer is in the respiratory system. The respiratory system of whales certainly has some unusual features, but they are adaptations to prevent water entering the airways: the nasal passages are complex and convoluted, and the larynx (the upper end of the respiratory tube) extends up into the nasal cavity rather than opening into the throat.

But do whales have an unusually high lung capacity? Proportionally the lungs of whales are not significantly larger than in land mammals, and more importantly lung *volume* in whales is small compared with land mammals. Even more

▼ Water is prevented from entering a whale's respiratory tract by a complex series of passages, sinuses, valves and plugs that can be opened or closed by the overlying muscle sphincters. Some water enters the outer vestibular sacs on either side of the blowhole but is prevented from entering the respiratory tube and is exhaled in the spray known as a 'spout' or 'blow' to whalers.

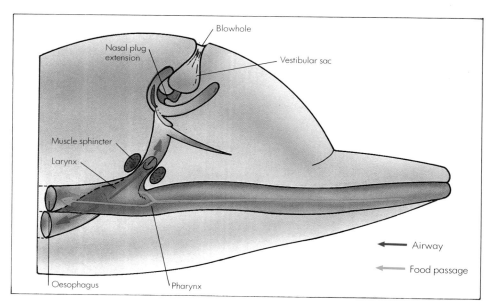

Blowhole

Nasal plug extension

Vestibular sac

Muscle sphincter

Larynx

Oesophagus

Pharynx

← Airway

← Food passage

Francois Gohier/Auscape International

surprising, the better diving whales have, relatively, the smallest lungs. Clearly, lung capacity does not explain how whales can store sufficient oxygen to hold their breath for minutes or even hours.

OXYGEN STORAGE AND BLOOD CIRCULATION

The way that whales have increased their capacity to store oxygen in the body is not by enlarging the lungs, but by modifying the circulatory system and the chemistry of the muscles.

In whales, blood makes up 10–15 per cent of the body weight, compared with about 7 per cent in humans. More important, the blood cells responsible for transporting oxygen, the red cells, are more abundant than in humans, and haemoglobin concentration in the blood of most whales is considerably higher than in land mammals. This increases the amount of oxygen the blood can carry.

Haemoglobin is also present in the muscles, where it is often called myoglobin. It has a greater affinity for oxygen than blood haemoglobin, so oxygen carried in the blood is readily given up to the muscles. Myoglobin is more abundant and

more concentrated in whales than in land mammals, giving the muscles a characteristic dark colour.

Even so, if we add up all the oxygen that could be stored in a dolphin, considering lung oxygen, blood oxygen, and muscle stores, and then divide this by the known resting oxygen consumption, we find that the oxygen stores are inadequate for the known durations of submersion. It is clear that other mechanisms must operate during diving or the animal would soon run out of oxygen.

The French physiologist Paul Bert described in 1870 a phenomenon of profound slowing of the heart beat, or bradycardia, when ducks were submerged. This has since been termed 'diving bradycardia', and is the most familiar cardiovascular response in diving animals, including whales. Observations of bottlenose dolphins have revealed that the heart rate fluctuates continually in concert with the respiration. While the dolphin is underwater between breaths its heart rate is fairly constant at 33–45 beats per minute, but when it takes a breath the rate rises sharply for a brief time to 80–90 beats per minute. The longer it has been submerged, the

▲ Whales use air more efficiently than other mammals, extracting a greater amount of oxygen and exchanging more air with each brief breath — up to 80 per cent of the lungs' contents compared with the 30 per cent exchanged by land mammals.

more the heart rate rises when it breathes.

In many aquatic animals diving bradycardia is accompanied by a redistribution of blood flow so that only essential organs are supplied with oxygenated blood. Blood flow to vital organs such as the brain and the heart wall is maintained during dives, whereas the arteries supplying other organs such as the stomach, intestines, kidneys and muscles may constrict to the point where blood flow is cut off almost completely. Large volumes of blood are stored in the veins (which are enlarged to form sinuses) in the abdominal and thoracic cavities.

Similar mechanisms may operate in the whale, although there is little experimental evidence of it, as such experiments are extremely difficult to perform. Certainly the veins in the body cavities of whales are large and distensible, indicating that redistribution of blood flow does occur during dives. Distension of the veins may have the added advantage of filling space in the body cavities as respiratory air is compressed during a dive.

Animals produce the energy they need for life and movement by breaking down glycogen. This is normally accomplished by the process of aerobic metabolism, which uses oxygen and produces carbon dioxide plus non-toxic waste products. The function of the respiratory system is to supply the oxygen to the blood and take away the unwanted carbon dioxide.

When insufficient oxygen is available for the complete breakdown of glycogen — for example, in a diving animal — the reaction is interrupted at an intermediate stage, producing toxic lactic acid. This is called anaerobic metabolism. In this case the animal incurs an 'oxygen debt', which can only be settled when it returns to the surface and breathes, replenishing its oxygen stores.

Increased tolerance to lactic acid and carbon dioxide is an adaptation to diving; terrestrial mammals tolerate only low levels of lactic acid, but seals, for example, accumulate large amounts of these chemicals in their blood during a dive.

It seems the whale takes down sufficient stored oxygen to permit most dives to be aerobic, and a principal feature of the more accomplished divers is an increase in the capability for storage and transport of oxygen.

However, during dives of very long duration, at least some tissues must be depleted of their oxygen stores and depend upon anaerobic metabolism. It has been suggested that during the later part of a deep dive, a whale has barely enough oxygen remaining in the body to maintain the heart, and that even the brain may be capable of some anaerobic metabolism.

THE WONDERFUL NETS

The blood system of whales is complex, and the full functional significance of all its features is not understood. Among the most intriguing structures are the 'retia mirabilia', ('wonderful nets') massive plexuses consisting of contorted spirals of tiny blood vessels that form great blocks of tissue on the inside wall of the chest near the backbone and elsewhere. How these retia function is not understood, though several functions have been postulated.

All of the blood flowing from the heart to the brain passes through a large rete mirabile in the upper part of the chest wall. It has been suggested that this arrangement has a pressure-damping function for the blood flowing to the brain. Another suggestion is that the retia mirabilia play some role in the whale's resistance to bends while making many repeated dives in the ocean, because the largest retia are found in the upper part of the body cavity and are well placed to trap bubbles of nitrogen that might be formed.

Other speculations on the functions of the retia suggest that they may help maintain steady blood flow or help equalise pressure differences, or that they act as temporary reservoirs of oxygenated blood (particularly for the brain), as space fillers or cushions, as thermoregulatory devices in countercurrent heat-conserving structures, or simply as stores used to help the redistribution of blood during diving.

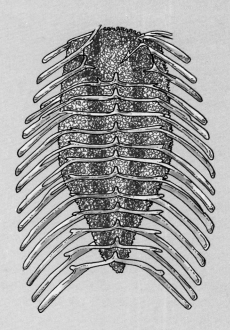

▲ One of the most intriguing features of whale anatomy is the existence of the large retia mirabilia ('wonderful nets'), massive structures composed of blood vessels beneath the backbone and ribs. Arteries feed into them to supply important organs such as the brain.

Flip Nicklin/Nicklin & Assoc.

BUOYANCY REGULATION

Most whales swim with a slight negative buoyancy. The animal's body becomes denser with increasing depth as the air in its lungs is compressed. This is of little consequence in many species because they do not dive to great depth, but it is extremely important in the very deep-diving species such as the bottlenose whales and the sperm whale.

The most striking characteristic of the sperm whale is its remarkable head, that huge, rather square structure usually depicted in diagrams or cartoons of the 'typical' whale. Those internal tissues of the head known collectively as the spermaceti organ are very rich in oil, which is different in composition from oils in the blubber and other parts of the body. A 30 tonne sperm whale may have as much as 2.5 tonnes of spermaceti in its head. Above 30°C this oil is a clear, straw-coloured liquid, but below that temperature it becomes cloudy, and eventually solidifies. The spermaceti organ is a huge component of the sperm whale's body; this fact, and the fact that it is present as a similar though less complex organ in other deep-diving whale species, suggests that it must serve an important

function. However, anatomists and physiologists have argued about its function for many years, and continue to do so.

A fascinating suggestion by noted biologist Malcolm Clarke is that it serves as a buoyancy regulator by cooling as the whale dives. He argues that as the whale descends in the ocean, it experiences colder and colder water. Cooling of the spermaceti oil changes its physical condition — it contracts and increases in density. Further, the density increase on cooling is enhanced by the increasing pressure as the whale goes down. As the spermaceti becomes denser, buoyancy decreases. Because so much spermaceti is present, a variation in temperature of only a few degrees would provide a sufficient change in density for a whale to regulate its buoyancy as it dives.

Others have questioned Clarke's hypothesis on a number of grounds, but it is an intriguing argument, and it is to be hoped it can be tested directly in the future.

By no means do we have all the answers about how whales as mammals cope with living in the sea. As we have seen, many fascinating aspects of their life are known to us, but far more remain to be elucidated.

▲ The oil contained in the spermaceti organ inside the sperm whale's massive head may act as a buoyancy regulator. As the oil becomes cooler and denser during the whale's prodigious dives, it may have the effect of reducing buoyancy, so making the hunting of giant squid at great depths easier.

THE WORLD OF THE SENSES

ROBERT MORRIS

Whales and dolphins evolved from a group of land mammals. We can assume that their ancestors had the same five senses as us — sight, touch, taste, smell and hearing — and that these senses were adapted, as they are in other land mammals, to receive messages through the medium of air rather than water.

As the early cetaceans moved into the sea it was vital for their survival that these aerially adapted senses became quickly re-adapted to life underwater. And if any sense could not be modified to function effectively underwater it was necessary to develop a new one to replace it.

▲ Here the spherical human eye is superimposed on the eliptical eye of a cetacean. The shape of the cetacean lens can be altered greatly so that the animal can focus both in water and in air.

Mike Osmond/Pacific Whale Foundation

▲ This humpback whale has eyes that are mobile and well adapted to life in the sea. The pupils are very large, at depth, enabling the eye to make maximum use of the low light intensity but are reduced to narrow slits, at the surface, where the light is very strong.

▶ The eyes of these spinner dolphins must be capable of adapting quickly to intense light at the surface and to hunting and navigating in the twilight world below. Some deep-diving whales may be able to detect the bioluminescent organs of their prey at great depths.

VISION

Being air-breathing mammals, cetaceans need to be able to see both underwater and in air. The eye of the cetacean was originally adapted only for sight in air, and important evolutionary developments occurred that allowed it to operate successfully in both media. One of the major problems is that light travels slower in water than in air and refracts, or bends, when it passes from air to water. Because of this, an eye adapted for focusing in air loses its focusing power in water. We humans have overcome the problem by wearing face masks when we dive, to keep our eyes in air when we are underwater. Whales have overcome the problem by means of a physiological change. During the course of their transi-

tion and evolution into marine animals they have developed strong muscles around the eye that can change the actual shape of the lens in the eye to suit either air vision or underwater vision.

There is another problem in using the eye both at the surface of the sea and at depth — light intensity. Underwater, particularly at depth, light levels are very low, while at the surface the light is very strong. Cetaceans have adapted to these extremes of lighting by developing an eye with a large pupil. This pupil can collect large amounts of light so that the animal can see even in very low light. In bright light, however, this pupil can be closed right down to a very narrow slit, so it can also be used for vision at the surface under the sort of lighting conditions for which our own eyes are designed.

When viewing objects, whales and dolphins often turn on their side and use a single eye which can readily be moved around to give a wide range of vision. This behaviour is often seen both underwater and at the surface. They can, however, also focus on objects quite close in front of their mouths using binocular vision.

It has been suggested that one effect of their living underwater might be that whales have a very limited colour vision. Red or yellow light is quickly absorbed by water and most underwater objects appear blue-green in colour. But in our own studies on wild dolphins we have found a strong preference for yellow and red objects, which would indicate that at least some dolphins do have the ability to discriminate between different colours.

The extent to which whales use their eyes at great depths in the ocean is not known. Below about 200 metres, light levels are very low, but many species of toothed whales regularly dive and feed well below these depths. Many of the deep-sea animals that they catch have light organs. These organs produce light of particular frequencies by a chemical process. Perhaps the deep-diving toothed whales have eyes specifically adapted to detect this 'chemical light' underwater.

Ken Balcomb/Earthviews

TOUCH

We normally associate the sense of touch with the use of our hands and fingers, and possibly our feet and toes. By touching or feeling a new object we get information on its three-dimensional shape, texture and consistency, and some idea of its internal structure.

Cetaceans no longer have 'hands' that they could use in this way, but the sense of touch is still very important to them. They have developed a highly specialised skin that is far more elaborate and contains a very complex system of organised, encapsulated nerve endings, which are more abundant in certain regions of greater sensitivity. The skin is soft and easily damaged, though it heals fast. In the wild, older animals often have a very battered appearance when viewed close-up as a result of the numerous scratches and wounds the delicate skin suffers during its life.

One important function of the skin is probably to help them swim more efficiently. Cetaceans need to achieve 'laminar flow' of water over the body if they are to swim efficiently at high speeds. If turbulence develops anywhere on the body surface the laminar flow is interrupted. Hence the animal's body shape needs to be adjusted constantly while it is swimming. Many species of whales and dolphins appear to be able to do this and it is thought that they manage it by using their highly sensitive skin as a pressure sensor. By monitoring the entire body surface for pressure or stretching points as it swims, the animal can continually keep its body in the correct shape for laminar flow to occur.

Particular areas of the skin may have specialised functions. For example, some cetaceans may be able to use the skin surface in the region of the jaw to detect sources of low frequency

Robert Morris

vibrations. And by sensing pressure build-up in this same region, they may be able to tell how fast they are swimming.

A major problem for air-breathing animals living in the sea is the proper co-ordination of their breathing so that only air is taken into the lungs and not a mixture of air and water — we have all coughed and spluttered after breathing in water while swimming. As they adapted to aquatic life, cetaceans developed a much more reliable system when the nostrils moved to the top of the head and powerful muscles developed to close them tightly when underwater. Unfortunately, if the opening for the lungs is on the top of the head, it is difficult to know exactly when it is clear of the water so that it can be used for breathing purposes. Snorkellers are familiar with this problem. We believe cetaceans solve the problem by using a specialised area of skin around the blowhole. Complex nerve endings are found in the skin from this region which sense pressure changes so that the animal can know exactly when the blowhole is in the air and can be opened. In calm weather wild dolphins have regularly been seen starting to blow

▲ The nerve-rich head and jaw region responds to pressure changes and may be able to sense speed as well as low-frequency vibrations that aid navigation and the detection of prey.

◄ Like all mammals, whales will drown if water enters their lungs. Highly sensitive nerve endings around the blowhole detect pressure changes as the water surface is broken. Powerful muscles close the blowhole when the whale dives and open it when it is clear of the water.

◄ The skin of whales is highly sensitive, not only to touch but possibly also to subtle changes in pressure, water pressure and density. These changes stimulate minute alterations in body shape and help maintain laminar flow, reducing turbulence as the whale moves through the water at speed.

▲ Dolphins use the sensitive skin on the lower jaw to investigate small objects in much the same way that humans use their fingertips, but they also make use of other senses that the vast majority of land mammals do not have.

air from their lungs just before surfacing and while their blowhole is still 5 or 10 centimetres below the surface. They then take a breath with the blowhole only just clear of the surface.

The behaviour of dolphins towards unusual objects in the water also provides clues about other means of touch sensing in cetaceans. A dolphin will often rest the tip of its lower jaw on an object it is investigating, or take the object into its mouth. Both of these behaviours may be associated with touch sensing but as we shall see later, they could be linked to a very different type of sensory system. Finally, there is a most unusual behaviour often observed in wild and captive male dolphins — the use of the extended penis apparently to 'investigate' an object. Whether the penis, which has abundant sensory nerve endings, is actually being used for touch investigation must remain as conjecture, but if this is what is indeed happening it does seem to be a somewhat hazardous operation!

TASTE AND SMELL

In land animals there is a clear distinction between taste and smell. Smelling (olfaction) is associated with detecting the source of chemical substances dispersed in the air at a distance from the source. Tasting (gustation) is concerned with detecting chemical substances dissolved in water that is brought into contact with the mouth. Both are examples of chemical sensing, which is believed to be the oldest sensory faculty in use by animals.

Underwater, the distinction between smell and taste is less obvious. The transfer of chemical information can only occur by solution in water. It is, however, still meaningful to separate the two as distinct senses. Smell in water is the chemical sense that provides information at a distance (presence of a predator or food), while taste gives mainly chemical information on objects near or in the mouth (generally food).

Water is an excellent solvent for many substances and acts as a good carrier for dissolved materials, which remain detectable for long periods. Many marine organisms rely on chemical sensing (chemoreception) as their major means of finding food or recognising a potential mating partner. Sharks, for example, have an extremely well developed olfactory system for distance 'smell' sensing of waterborne chemicals, and efficient gustatory receptors in their mouths for close-up 'taste' sensing.

We know that whales can see in air as well as in water. It seems reasonable, therefore, to ask whether they can also smell in both air and water. In fact, they do not seem to be very good at smelling in either.

Cetaceans appear to have largely lost the sense of airborne smell that exists in most mammals, as they have very limited olfactory receptors. They may have lost this sense with the repositioning of

Rosemary Chastney/Ocean Images/Planet Earth Pictures

the nostrils from the front to the top of the head when a number of important changes to the function and operation of organs associated with the nostrils must have occurred. The nostrils (blowhole) are usually closed except when the animal breathes at the surface and the breathing is so rapid that 'air smelling' must be of limited use. Baleen whales appear to have rather more olfactory receptors than the toothed whales and they may still be able to use these receptors to

'sniff the winds' in search of plankton-rich waters.

There is no indication of any system of waterborne smelling in cetaceans equivalent to the olfactory system in sharks. This would have required the development of a completely new sense of smell in the animals, but its absence must have put them at a great disadvantage compared with the sharks.

The sense of taste appears to be still present in at least some cetacean species. Dolphins can certainly detect a range of chemicals dissolved in water, distinguishing between what we would describe as sweet, sour, bitter and salty tastes. In addition, what appear to be taste buds are present on the tongues of several species of toothed whale. To date, no information is available on the taste sense in any of the baleen whales.

If some cetaceans do have a sense of taste they could use it in a number of ways. Taste might be used to investigate likely food items for signs of

▲ It is unlikely that humpback whales have anything but the most rudimentary ability to detect odours in the air, but they may be able to 'taste' small plankton concentrations in the water, which would make their search for food masses much more energy efficient.

Christian Petron/Planet Earth Pictures

▲ The function and importance of the outer ear is unknown: certainly its small size and inconspicuous opening, behind and below the eye, suggest it plays only a minor role in underwater hearing but it may be of use when the head is above water.

decomposition — we have regularly tried to feed wild dolphins on dead fish without success. Waste products of cetaceans (urine and faecal material) will only be dispersed slowly in the water and might be used to provide taste cues for other members of the species. They might, for example, contain sexual pheromones that would indicate readiness for mating, or they might provide trails for others in a herd during periods of migration. Taste might also be used to sense the presence of nearby food in the form of large shoals of plankton or blood from a wounded animal. Thus the gustatory detection of waterborne chemicals could provide a rich source of knowledge on the local environment and on social matters within a group. Unfortunately the extent to which cetaceans can use such a sense is largely unknown. It does, however, seem certain that it could not be used as a long-range sensory faculty to rival the olfactory sense of sharks.

HEARING

As with vision, important changes have been made in cetaceans' method of hearing as they adapted from hearing in air to hearing in water. Sound travels about five times as fast in water as in air owing to the much greater density of water. This density difference between the two also makes it very difficult for sound to pass between air and water. There is what is called an 'acoustic impedance mismatch' between the two media. Thus an air-filled ear is useless underwater.

An obvious physical characteristic of cetaceans is the absence of external ears. These have been sacrificed for the sake of a streamlined body shape for efficient swimming. Cetaceans do still have ears but they are barely noticeable, being marked only by a small hole just behind the eye. In the bottlenose dolphin (*Tursiops truncatus*) the ear hole is 5–6 centimetres behind the eye and is only 2–3 millimetres in diameter.

There is still considerable argument among scientists as to how cetaceans use their ears. The baleen whales have the external ears filled with a horny, wax plug, which is thought to transmit underwater sounds to the inner ear. Because the impedance of the wax plug matches that of sea water, baleen whales are probably deaf in air.

The toothed whales do not have earplugs and there is far more controversy about their hearing. Some scientists believe that the ear channel from the external ear hole to the inner ear is open and filled with sea water, and is fully operational underwater. However, there are reports that some dolphins can hear quite well in air, which, if correct, suggests that the ear channel is air-filled at least at the sea surface. Other scientists are convinced that hearing does not occur via the ear channel at all. They believe that in some dolphin species at least the ear channel is closed off and that during the course of evolution to a marine existence, the ear hole and ear channel have become redundant in the same way as our appendix has lost its function. Hearing in toothed whales, they suggest, occurs either by the bones of the skull transmitting sound to the inner ear — 'bone conduction', similar to the system of bone mikes used by many commercial divers — or by sound being conducted to the inner ear by deposits of fat that run up from the lower jaw — 'tissue conduction'. In some toothed whales an area of bone in the lower jaw, in the region of these fat deposits, has been found to be very thin and it has been suggested this might be an 'acoustic window' for sound reception.

THE ACOUSTIC SENSE AND ECHOLOCATION

So far we have dealt with senses familiar to us. Now we come to a sensory faculty with which we and most other land animals are very unfamiliar. Only a bat could properly appreciate the developments that have taken place in certain cetaceans relating to sound perception of the environment.

Perhaps the most serious problem for ancestral whales colonising the sea was that they were entering an environment where other animals had, over the course of many millions of years, already perfected sensory systems ideally suited to the marine environment. Sharks in particular had a very highly developed underwater 'smell' sense and a well-developed sense of sound detection with the result that they were undoubtedly the most successful predators. For the early whale, the shark must have been a major threat both as a predator and as a competitor for food. The baleen whales largely solved the problem by growing to enormous sizes and living on small plankton. For the toothed whales it was different. If they were to compete successfully with the sharks in the oceans of the world they had to develop a new sense faculty to match those of the sharks.

Many of the early whalers were baffled by the survival of the 'toothed' whales that actually had very few teeth but preyed successfully on the fast-moving squid. Most baffling was the great sperm whale (*Physeter catodon*), which hunted for squid in the depths of the ocean. The sperm whale had teeth only in its lower jaw and the males often had lower jaws so badly damaged from fights with other males as to be quite functionless. In spite of this, sperm whales that had obviously had such injuries for many years were regularly taken by the whalers in good condition and with full stomachs. They could think of only one explanation — the animals had supernatural powers.

The true explanation is that toothed whales had learned to 'see with their ears'. They developed this unique sensory system based on sound millions of years ago and the possession of such a faculty enabled them to catch food in the dark depths of the ocean and successfully compete with the shark in its own environment.

Sound communication in water is both effective and efficient. It is, therefore, not surprising that it has been used by the toothed whales as the basis for one of the most advanced sensory faculties in use on this planet — echolocation.

Echolocation involves an active process of emitting sounds in the form of short broad-spectrum burst-pulses (clicks) and gaining information on the surrounding environment (nearby objects, obstructions) by analysis of the returning echoes. Highly accurate echolocation, using a broad band of both low- and high-

▲ The apparently featureless ocean provides as much information to dolphins as the land does to us, but its initially alien nature and the presence of efficient, dangerous predators probably stimulated the evolution of new navigational senses.

Frans Lanting/Bruce Coleman Limited

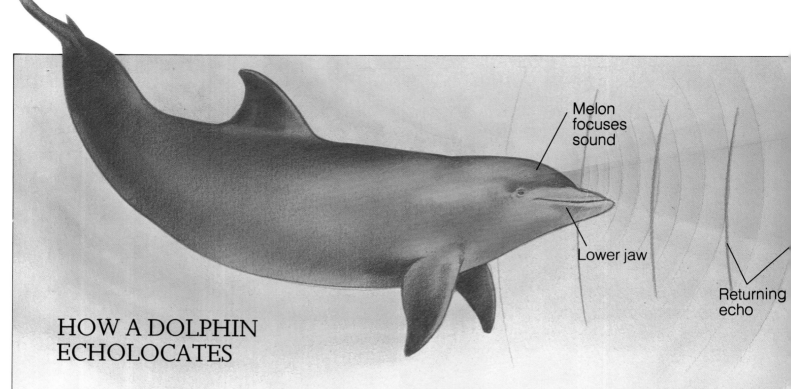

Melon
focuses
sound

Lower jaw

Returning
echo

HOW A DOLPHIN ECHOLOCATES

We believe that the likely sequence of events during a typical dolphin echolocation is as follows:

1. During normal swimming, with no specific target of interest, a general low-frequency echolocation signal of fairly pure tone is used. This acts like a ship's echo sounder, providing the animal with information on the topography of the area including water depth, changes in sea floor profile and position of any coastal features. The scan range will be determined by the time interval between the signals (clicks) and how much energy there is in the signal. For efficient echolocation one individual click must be sent out and the echoes (if any) received before the next click is emitted. Thus, we can estimate the range at which a dolphin is 'looking' by measuring the time between clicks. The maximum range is believed to be at least 800 metres. This type of echolocation will also tell the dolphin whether there are any large animals in the water nearby.

2. Once a new echo is received, the first requirement is to determine distance and direction, and to collect more detailed information on the target itself — for example, is it a predator such as a shark, or likely prey? The dolphin emits a series of clicks with a broad frequency band, the echoes of

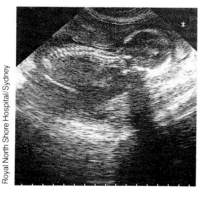

Royal North Shore Hospital/Sydney

▲ Only recently have humans taken their first steps into the sensory world of echolocation, with 'sound pictures' that are still very primitive by cetacean standards.

frequency sound emissions coupled with very sensitive directional hearing, has given toothed whales a sensory system unrivalled in the sea. Their prowess at navigating in turbid water and for locating and identifying objects well out of visual range has been marvelled at on many occasions.

When we look at an object with our eyes we are seeing reflected light. When toothed whales 'look' at an object with their echolocation system they are hearing reflected sounds from their echolocating clicks. Sound waves carry much more information than light. This is because sound has a more complex interaction with the environment. While light can give colour patterns by selective absorption of certain wavelengths, sound by a similar process can give a three-dimensional picture. A target object's material, internal structure and texture will all combine to produce a specific echo. It is only in recent years that we have properly appreciated what a powerful sensory technique this is and as a result ultrasonic exploration is increasingly replacing x-rays in medical examinations of internal human structures.

Although the various species of toothed whales have developed their own separate types of acoustic faculty, we believe they are all based on the same principle and have all involved major anatomical changes to the basic structure of the animal's head.

All the toothed whales examined so far have been found to contain large deposits of fat in their heads and lower jaws. Such deposits are unique in the animal kingdom and are remarkable for a number of reasons. First, they are large in relation to the size of the animal and represent an immense store of potential metabolic energy, yet they seem not to be used as a source of energy. Second, the chemical composition of these deposits is markedly different from that of the normal body fat and from that of the animal's normal dietary fat intake. Third, the shape and positioning of the deposits has apparently been so important that major changes in the shape and structure of the skull have been necessary in order to accommodate them.

These structures thus represent a major 'commitment' on the part of the animal, involving severe 'metabolic penalties' — they tie up large amounts of metabolic energy and valuable fat reserves, and they have required major anatomical

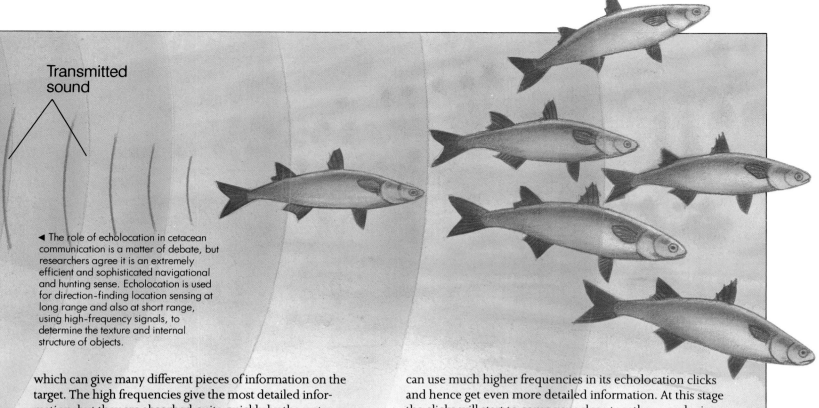

◄ The role of echolocation in cetacean communication is a matter of debate, but researchers agree it is an extremely efficient and sophisticated navigational and hunting sense. Echolocation is used for direction-finding location sensing at long range and also at short range, using high-frequency signals, to determine the texture and internal structure of objects.

which can give many different pieces of information on the target. The high frequencies give the most detailed information, but they are absorbed quite quickly by the water and so are useful only at closer ranges.

3. Once the bearing of the target is established, the dolphin focuses the signals on the target. This concentrates the power of the higher frequency components and gives a more detailed picture of the target. It can also scan the target by moving its head from side to side and so gain information on target size and movement.

4. As the range closes between dolphin and target, the dolphin can use much higher frequencies in its echolocation clicks and hence get even more detailed information. At this stage the clicks will start to come very close together, producing what sounds to us like a continuous 'creaking'.

5. Finally, at very close range, it may be necessary to determine texture or other fine structural information. In this case use of a short-range sonar system with very high frequencies would be necessary. It has been suggested that the habit of resting the tip of the jaw on objects or taking objects into the mouth may be associated with such a close-range acoustic sensory system rather than with the sense of touch.

modifications. To have evolved they must have a very important function that confers great advantages on the animal.

The largest fat deposits are in front of the brain-case. In the sperm whale these deposits (the spermaceti organ) are enormous, weighing many tonnes.

Most of the other toothed whales have a similar but smaller organ called the melon. The other large fat deposit, in the lower jaw, is strategically placed behind an area of the jaw where the bone is very thin. This deposit is similar in composition to the melon and extends up to the middle ear region. A widely accepted theory regarding their function is that they aid in echolocation. The process is believed to work like this:

1. Sound is produced internally by the animal.
2. The head fat organ focuses this sound into a directional beam.
3. Reflected echoes carrying information about targets are received at the 'acoustic window' area of the lower jaw.
4. This sound is transmitted by the fat organ in the lower jaw to the middle ear and subsequently to the brain for processing and interpretation.

Thus many scientists believe that the fat deposits in the head and lower jaw of toothed whales represent a completely novel physiological and biochemical development that provides the animals with the means to acquire their unique acoustic sensory system.

There are two other structural changes to the heads of the toothed whales that are thought to be linked to the development of the acoustic faculty. The first is the reduced number of functional teeth compared to their early ancestors. As the ancestral toothed whales perfected their sense of sound detection, food capture became much easier and teeth were no longer needed so much for this purpose. The second change is the immensely large brain. Echolocation is a highly sophisticated sense and requires much processing of information. We now know that a large part of the brain in toothed whales is involved purely in the storage, processing and interpretation of all the acoustic information that is continually coming in concerning their surroundings.

DO BALEEN WHALES ECHOLOCATE?

Toothed whales are the only group of whales to have properly developed sound for use as a sensory faculty. Baleen whales use low-frequency sounds for communication and produce complex 'songs'. But if baleen whales have an acoustic sense like the toothed whales, it must be, at best, primitive. There are some reports of certain species emitting fairly pure-frequency clicks and it has been suggested that these could have a sonar function for detecting targets or sensing water depth. Certainly such information would be useful. If, for example, they were able to obtain information on the topography of the sea floor during their long seasonal migrations across the oceans, this might enable them to recognise distinctive features (sea mounts, underwater mountain chains, deep trenches) and use these features as landmarks. This is one of the most common techniques used by humans in submarine navigation but, at present, we can only speculate on whether baleen whales can do this.

MAGNETIC SENSE

There is considerable evidence that many organisms, from bacteria upwards, have a sensory faculty that can receive directional information from the earth's magnetic field. Small crystals of the magnetic form of iron oxide (magnetite) have been found in certain species of mud bacteria, bees, butterflies, fish, birds, bats and reptiles. They have also been found in some cetacean species. In the higher organisms they are generally located either in the vicinity of the brain or near areas where there is a high concentration of nerve endings.

At present many other animals are being examined for the presence of magnetite crystals in their bodies, and this field of research is at a particularly exciting stage with many new and challenging ideas. In general terms, the magnetite crystals are thought to continually orientate themselves in line with the earth's natural magnetic force fields — just like mini-magnets. By sensing changes in the orientation of these crystals, the host animal is thought to be able to work out the direction in which it is travelling. Such a system would have obvious uses for long-distance navigation and could be used at most points on the earth's surface.

Cetaceans appear to be ahead of most other mammals in developing this unusual sensory faculty. Several species of toothed whales have been found to have magnetite crystals in their external brain tissues. In the marine environment, fixed points that can be used for navigational purposes are very scarce. Thus the development of a system of orientation based on the earth's magnetic field would be of great importance to all whales and dolphins — just as the invention of the compass was so important for human navigators.

Steven French

Normally the natural magnetic force fields run north to south at an even density. In places, however, the field is distorted by certain types of geological formations — for instance those rich in iron. Such distortions are called 'geomagnetic anomalies'. Areas of high or low geomagnetic anomalies are found all over the oceans, particularly in the vicinity of sea mounts, in areas where active continental drift is occurring and in some continental shelf areas. The result is a whole series of fixed, reliable 'landmarks' across the ocean if one has the sensory faculty available to recognise them. We believe that at least some of the cetaceans have that faculty by virtue of their magnetic sense.

Live strandings are believed to be the result of serious navigational mistakes on the part of the whale while attempting to use its magnetic sense for orientation. Possibly this is one sensory faculty in cetaceans that is still in its experimental stage.

▲ Geomagnetic anomalies occur where natural magnetic force fields are distorted by certain types of geological formations, particularly in the vicinity of sea mounts. Live strandings of whales are believed to occur in areas where geomagnetic anomalies are present. Serious navigational mistakes can be made while they are attempting to use their magnetic sense of orientation.

◄ Evidence is growing to support the theory that a sophisticated geomagnetic sensitivity enables whales and dolphins to navigate accurately across entire oceans.

REPRODUCTION AND DEVELOPMENT

M.M. BRYDEN

Most of what we know about reproduction and development in whales relates to species that, in the past, have been of commercial and economic value. Information was gained from observations of animals and their collected organs by investigators attached to whaling stations, ships and museums. More recently we have learned a lot about reproduction in certain species that have been killed accidentally in commercial ventures aimed at species other than whales. Notable in this regard is purse-seining of tuna, in which, to date, well over a million spotted and spinner dolphins (genus *Stenella*) have been caught and drowned in the nets. Gill-netting likewise has imposed heavy mortalities on some inshore species of small whales in various parts of the world.

EXTERNAL SEXUAL DIFFERENCES

During adaptation for a life in water, streamlining of the whale's body has involved modification of the external genitalia. It is difficult to distinguish between the sexes of most species of whales on superficial examination because the penis of the male is retained within a prepuce (except when it is erect), whose opening is a slit (the genital slit), similar in appearance to the genital slit or vulva of the female. The only conspicuous difference between the sexes is the distance between the anus and the genital slit, in the male it is approximately 10 per cent of the body length, but in the female the genital slit appears to be continuous with the anal opening. Even the mammary glands of the female are difficult to discern in whales. Each of the nipples, one on either side of the genital slit, is retained within a tiny mammary slit, which is often difficult to see. The nipple protrudes only during suckling, and the mammary gland itself lies beneath the blubber over an extensive area of the ventral body wall; there is no external sign of it except in heavily lactating females.

However, there are obvious sexual differences after maturity in some species, for example, the sperm whale (*Physeter catodon*) and the pilot whales (genus *Globicephala*), in which males are significantly larger than females. As well as being larger, the male orca (*Orcinus orca*) has a taller and more conspicuous dorsal fin than the female. But in no species is there any difference in colour pattern, or major difference in body form, between the sexes such as occurs in some other mammals.

▶ It is difficult to tell the sex of most whales without closely examining the ventral surface. Both males and females have a navel, genital slit and anus, but in females small mammary slits are usually visible on either side of the genital slit, which is much closer to the anus than in males.

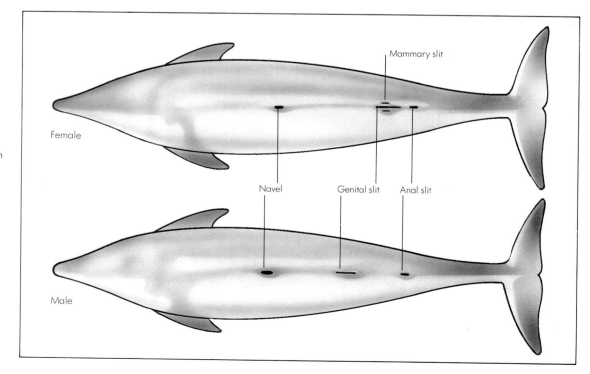

Female

Mammary slit

Navel   Genital slit   Anal slit

Male

M. Osmond

COURTSHIP AND MATING

Mating in whales has been observed very rarely in the oceans, therefore, little is known about it. What is known about courtship and mating has been gained from observations of captive dolphins and small whales.

Courtship display and mating in whales may not always be directed towards reproduction. It has been suggested that they may be used in the greeting and bonding of individuals or groups after a period of separation. Certainly a great deal of apparent sexual activity is common in captive groups, even juvenile animals being quite sexually precocious. Various behavioural signs considered to be associated with courtship, including chasing, nuzzling, rubbing, and even erection and intromission, have been seen sometimes in sexually immature males.

Whales have little sense of smell, the sense used extensively in sexual encounters in other mammalian species, and they probably use behavioural means to determine the sexual status of potential mates. In humpbacks (*Megaptera novaeangliae*) a range of activities has been described that probably indicate sexual activity, for example, rolling, slapping the water surface with the long flippers, fluke slapping, and breaching. Some of these may also be used as threats by males towards competitors, along with more aggressive and direct actions at close quarters such as lunging with the head or sideswiping with the flukes and tail stock.

We have almost no information concerning

Dean Lee

▲ 'Courtship' behaviour in many whales may be a displacement activity to ease tension — a kind of greeting ritual. Humpback whales may also determine sexual status with a variety of displays including flipper-slapping.

◀▼ Displays both above and below the surface become more dramatic as the humpbacks' mating intensifies, with competitive, sexually active males slapping flukes and rolling or butting heads in ritualised combat with other males. Females appear to ignore agonistic behaviour.

M. Osmond

Marty Snyderman

▲ The penis of most mammals has spongy tissue that fills with blood to produce erection. Whales have more fibrous tissue, the elasticity of which appears to assist in erection.

the duration and frequency of copulation in whales. However, in captive bottlenose dolphins (*Tursiops truncatus*) intromission lasts 2–10 seconds. The male swims up from beneath its partner and they mate with their bodies more or less at right angles to one another.

Male dolphins of several species in captivity will sometimes attempt to mate with other dolphins, male or female, of another species, genus or even family. Such cross-matings have sometimes resulted in offspring, even where the two parents were of different families. In the wild,

however, it is unlikely that such matings, if they occur at all, result in viable offspring.

PRENATAL AND EARLY POSTNATAL DEVELOPMENT

The general principles of prenatal development of whales are similar to those of other mammals.

Gestation lasts 10–12 months in most baleen whales; it probably lasts about 12 months or a fraction less in the migrating species such as humpbacks, which co-ordinate birth and mating with annual migrations.

THE MALE REPRODUCTIVE ORGANS

The penis is coiled or curved within the sheath (prepuce) except when erect; it is held in this position by a pair of strap-like retractor muscles. In most mammals the body of the penis is made up largely of three columns of spongy tissue and erection results when these fill with blood. Although the whale's penis contains the three columns, they are not very spongy but instead contain a relatively large amount of tough, fibrous tissue. It has been suggested that erection results simply from the elasticity of this fibrous tissue when the retractor muscles relax. Probably, however, the mechanism is more complex than that, as it has been shown to be in the bull, whose penis resembles that of the whale in many anatomical features.

The testes are elongated and lie not in an external scrotum as they do in most mammalian species, but within the abdominal cavity just behind the kidneys. This arrangement is

also found in the elephant and the hyrax. The testes increase dramatically in size at puberty — the testis of an immature dolphin is about half the size of a little finger and weighs about 20 grams, whereas in the adult it is as long as the forearm and considerably thicker, and weighs several kilograms.

Sperm are produced in the testis, then pass into the epididymis, which, as in all mammals, is a long, greatly con-voluted tube. The sperm mature as they pass along this tube to be stored near its end, the tail of the epididymis, which in some species forms several masses. From here the short ductus deferens conducts the sperm to the urethra.

Most of the fluid portion of mammalian semen is secreted by accessory sex glands of various kinds. The only accessory sex gland present in the whale is the prostate, quite small in immature whales but large in adults.

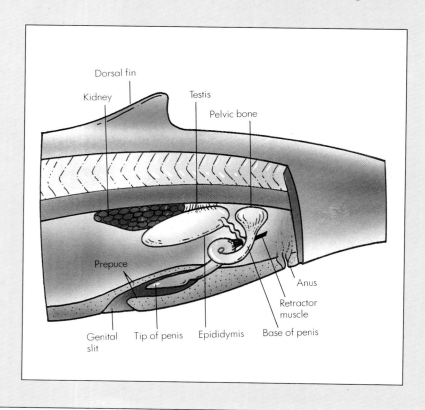

THE FEMALE REPRODUCTIVE ORGANS

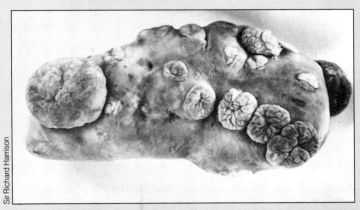

The anatomy of the female reproductive organs is similar to that in many other mammalian species. The two ovaries lie in the abdominal cavity behind the kidneys, as do the testes in the male.

The uterus consists of a body and two horns, which narrow at their ends to become the uterine tubes. The cervix, or neck of the uterus, opens into the vagina. On the vaginal walls are a series of folds projecting towards the vulva and resembling series of funnels. Their function is unknown, but they may prevent the entrance of water into the reproductive tract or possibly the loss of semen after copulation.

The ovaries of toothed whales are shaped like elongated eggs, with a relatively smooth surface. Those of baleen whales are highly irregular in shape, and studded with numerous rounded protuberances.

The mature ovary contains egg cells or oocytes surrounded by other cells to form follicles. Some of these follicles enlarge and develop a fluid-filled space. In baleen whales these enlarged follicles are responsible for some of the protuberances seen on the surface of the ovary.

As the breeding season approaches, one of the follicles enlarges further and around the time of copulation, eventually bursts (ovulation), releasing the oocyte, which is drawn into the end of the uterine tube.

The cells remaining in the collapsed follicle after ovulation multiply and form a large greyish yellow structure, the corpus luteum. If the oocyte is not fertilised, the corpus luteum

▲ The left ovary of a Pacific white-sided dolphin is marked with the remains of the follicles associated with ovulation and they provide a record of the animal's reproductive past; each excrescence, called a corpus albicans, represents one ovulation.

degenerates. If fertilisation does occur, the corpus luteum persists to the end of the pregnancy. In either case, the degenerated corpus luteum is white and is called the corpus albicans.

A peculiarity of whales is that their corpora albicantia remain for the rest of the animal's life, providing a record of past ovulations in the ovaries. This enables us to examine the reproductive history of individual whales; each corpus albicans represents one ovulation (though not necessarily a pregnancy).

It is often possible for the biologist to use this information to estimate how many pregnancies a whale has had, and this is an important part of the scientific basis for whale stock management.

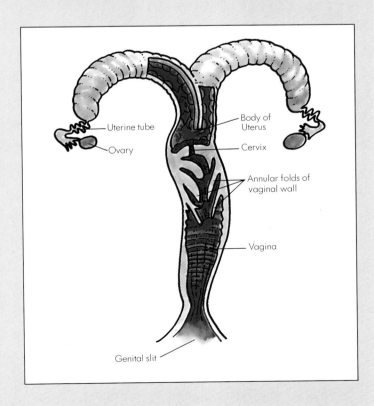

In toothed whales, gestation length varies more, from about 9 months in some species to 18 months in others.

The birth process of any mammal is stressful, but it must be particularly so in whales because the foetus is expelled from the uterus directly into the water, in which it can drown or lose body heat at an excessive rate. Observations of births in captivity have been made but only rarely have births in the wild been reported. In most if not all births the calf is born flukes first rather than head first, in contrast with land mammals, in which such a presentation (breech birth) can cause severe birth difficulties. The spindle-like shape of the foetal whale probably means that flukes-first presentation causes no more difficulty than head-first presentation — in seals, which are a similar shape, a relatively high proportion of births (up to 50 per cent) are also tail-first. Birth of the whale occurs rapidly, which is necessary because the young must surface for its first breath very soon after the umbilical cord breaks, otherwise it would die of anoxia. Some unknown mechanism must prevent the newborn whale from breathing in until its blowhole is above the water surface.

Multiple births may occur, but they are extremely rare. Twin, triplet and even quadruplet foetuses have been observed inside whales killed for commercial gain, but it is doubtful that they would have been born and reared successfully.

In seals, which like whales produce large and advanced (usually single) young, multiple births are extremely rare and even twins are rarely raised successfully.

The mother will actively protect her calf and will attempt to drive off intruders. There are many accounts of the propensity in whales, particularly dolphins, for other adults in the group to assist the mother. These animals, referred to as 'aunts', have been seen to help the mother guide the newborn calf to the surface to take its first breath, to protect it from other whales in the group, and to assist a sick or even dead calf by supporting it at the surface. It has been claimed that human beings have been saved in this way. However, in captivity at least, these 'aunts' have at times taken little interest in sick or stillborn calves, or have even mauled them. More than once, the mother or another dolphin has been seen to take a stillborn or weak newborn calf to the bottom of the pool and hold it there. Perhaps 'aunts' can tell whether their potential charges are dead or alive, and even estimate their chances of survival.

Such maternal care in whales is to be expected because the mother has, in genetic terms, made a very significant investment in the calf, and we would expect behaviour to evolve that will enhance its chances of survival. Probably the many stories of dolphins saving people in the sea are related to this behaviour (cases of mistaken

▲ Three stages in the birth of an Irrawaddy dolphin (*Orcaella brevirostris*) show the usual cetacean flukes-first or breech presentation. The newborn (often assisted by its mother or an 'aunt') swims to the surface for its first breath.

▶ Whales are assiduous mothers and will often support a calf at the surface, with an 'aunt' in constant attendance for protection.

Ken Balcomb/Earthviews

identity), rather than being the result of some special affinity that dolphins have for humans.

The calf is suckled underwater but close to the surface, so both mother and calf can breathe intermittently. The milk is actively ejected into the calf's mouth by muscle action, increasing the speed of transfer of milk from mother to calf — an obvious advantage underwater. A calf remains very close to its mother for at least the first few days or weeks after birth. Lactation lasts 4–11 months in rorquals (family Balaenopteridae), rather longer in the large than in the smaller ones. In most toothed whales it lasts considerably longer, about a year or more. There is evidence that older female pilot whales suckle young for up to 15 years.

REPRODUCTIVE CYCLES

Little is known about the relationship between the social structure of most free-ranging whale schools and reproduction. The major obstacle to examining this in the past has been that we have had no idea of the age or sex structure of schools, or of relationships among individuals that made up a school. However, something is now known of these things in a few species.

In sperm whales, for example, we now have a fairly good picture of social structure and migration. Older male sperm whales, the harem masters, migrate to high latitudes in search of food in the non-breeding season, but the 'nursery schools' containing the mature females and calves remain in temperate or tropical waters throughout the year. Because there is no marked seasonal migration of the breeding cows, the breeding pattern is not very clear. Mating occurs in winter,

WWF/Hal Whitehead/Bruce Coleman Limited

gestation takes about 15 months, and lactation lasts about two years. An adult female has a calf about every fourth year.

Recently, the collaborating Australian and Japanese biologists, Drs Helene Marsh and Toshio Kasuya, showed that the short-finned pilot whale (*Globicephala macrorhynchus*) has a most intriguing reproductive biology. Their research led to the conclusions that pregnancy rate decreases with age and reproduction ceases somewhere between the ages of 30 and 40 years. Lactation seems to be prolonged in the older females, lasting

▲ Top: This grey whale was born headfirst, unusual for cetaceans. Above: A miniature version of its parents, a baby sperm whale is 3.7–4.3 metres long at birth and will feed on its mother's rich, oily milk (ejected by muscle pressure into the calf's mouth) for at least a year.

DEVELOPMENT

SPECIES	LENGTH OF GESTATION (months)	BODY LENGTH AT BIRTH (m)	WEIGHT AT BIRTH (tonnes)	WEIGHT OF ADULT (tonnes)
Blue whale	11	7.5	2.2	150.00
Fin whale	11	6.5	1.8	70.00
Humpback whale	11	4.2	0.9	40.00
Long-finned pilot whale (male)	16	1.8	0.085	2.80
Harbour porpoise	9	0.7	0.009	0.070

▲ A section through the tooth of a short-finned pilot whale reveals cumulative growth layers, rather like the growth rings of a tree, which provide accurate information on age — in this case, 29.5 years.

Dr T. Kasuya

up to 15 years, and a close cow–calf association may last at least until the calf is sexually mature. Females less than 20 years old, by contrast, suckle their calves for much shorter periods, 2–6 years at most. Prolonged lactation does not mean that a calf feeds exclusively on the mother's milk throughout; on the contrary, all calves begin to take solid food when less than a year old.

Baleen whales have a regular breeding pattern. Most spend the summer months at feeding areas in high latitudes, and move to subtropical or tropical waters to breed in winter. Gestation takes about 11 months, lactation lasts less than 12 months, and an adult female produces a calf about every two years. However, it has been shown that some females at least have, on occasions, the capacity to produce a calf in successive years. Perhaps the incidence of having calves in successive years has increased in some species with the depletion in whale numbers by exploitation.

ESTIMATION OF AGE

Understanding of the biology of whales has been advanced significantly in recent years as a result of improvements made in the methods of estimating the ages of individual animals. This has permitted biologists to determine the ages at which animals mature sexually and at which they die, how fast they grow and how old they are when they first bear young. All these pieces of information are important if we are to build an accurate picture of the animals' life history, and absolutely vital for sound management of threatened populations.

For determining the reproductive potential of an animal it is particularly important to know the age at which it becomes sexually mature. The earlier it matures, the greater its potential number of offspring. Because sexual maturity is associated closely with physical size, a young whale that grows faster will become sexually mature at a younger age. One reason for faster growth and earlier maturity might be the increased availability

of food, which could result from reduction in the numbers of whales. This, coupled with increased frequency of pregnancy as discussed earlier, would accelerate the rate of increase in the population. There is good evidence that a reduction in age at first breeding observed in southern fin whales (*Balaenoptera physalus*) and sei whales (*B. borealis*) is the result of overexploitation of large baleen whales in antarctic waters. Mean age of sexual maturity of female fin whales declined from ten years to six years between 1930 and 1950. The same may be true of southern humpback whales, in which age of first breeding may have dropped as well, because one population has been shown to have been increasing at an extraordinarily rapid rate in recent years.

A method of age estimation developed in seals — counting growth layers in the teeth — has been applied successfully to toothed whales and has proved to be of considerable value. The details of the method vary among species, but the principle is similar. Layers can be seen in a thin lengthwise section of a tooth. Patterns of these layers, referred to as growth-layer groups, occur in cyclic fashion, somewhat like the growth rings in trees. There are some problems with the method, and the actual rates of deposition of layers are known for only one or two species, so it is not always possible to put an absolute figure on age. However, the layered structure of teeth is essentially similar among species, varying only in detail, and sufficient is known at present for the method to be very useful and widely applied.

In baleen whales, which lack teeth, a different method has been developed. When the peculiar horny plug that lies in the ear canal of these whales is cut lengthwise, it too shows a layered pattern. Layers of shed skin cells alternate with layers of ear wax, so that sections of the plug have alternating light (horny) and dark (waxy) layers. Again, these occur in cyclic fashion, but as in the case of the teeth there has been controversy about the rate of accumulation of the layers.

GROWTH

The rate of growth of the foetus, as in all mammals, is greatest in the later part of pregnancy. Quite astonishing figures are recorded in the large whales — in the last two months of pregnancy the foetal blue whale (*Balaenoptera musculus*), for example, increases its weight by 2 tonnes, the daily weight increase being about 100 kilograms at the end of pregnancy. This growth is greater than in any other whale, at least ten times that of any mammal other than a whale, and 500 to 1000 times that of the human foetus. Whales differ from land mammals in that species' differences in birth size are achieved mainly by altering the rate of foetal growth rather than the gestation period.

Now that we are able to estimate the age of individual whales, we can also determine the rate of growth after birth. A characteristic of marine mammals is that they grow very quickly in early postnatal life. Like the seals, whales produce milk very rich in fat and, to a lesser extent, protein, therefore, growth of the calf is rapid, so much so that although it is possible to estimate the age of the calf reasonably well by its size for its first year or so, after that it is very unreliable. A two-year-old animal may be as big as, or bigger than, a five-year-old. During the suckling period of about seven months, the blue whale calf increases in weight by approximately 17 tonnes, at a rate of 80 kilograms per day. A blue whale calf that is 8 metres long at birth may be twice that length or more when it is two years old.

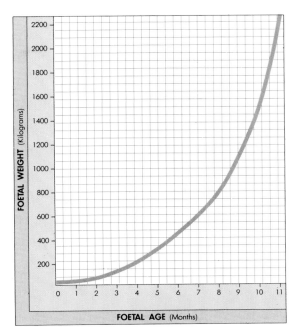

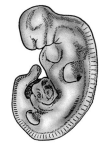

◄▲ The extraordinary growth of the blue whale is achieved mainly during its last two months in the uterus. While a human foetus increases in weight by 2 kilograms during the last two months of pregnancy, a blue whale foetus adds 2 tonnes to its weight in the same time.

▼ A blue whale, 8 metres long at birth, may be twice that length by two years of age, increasing weight by 80 kilograms a day on the fat- and protein-rich milk actively ejected from its mother's mammary slits.

Francois Gohier/Auscape International

SOCIAL BEHAVIOUR

PETER CORKERON

The social systems of all animals are the result of evolutionary developments, but the question of why animals form groups is a difficult one for biologists to answer. Because natural selection operates on the individual, not on groups, it must be in the long-term interests of the individual animal to remain in a group — in other words, the overall costs to the individual of remaining in a group must be outweighed by the benefits of group living.

Assessing the relative costs and benefits of group living is complicated by the fact that animal social systems are also adaptations to ecological conditions; and that the evolution of social behaviour is influenced by how closely (or distantly) individuals are related.

The ecological factors that appear to affect the social behaviour of whales include rates and types of predation, the quality and spacing of food patches (and the ease with which they can be located), and the constraints placed on mammals in an aquatic environment.

Don Croll

How do these factors affect cetaceans? On a fairly simplistic level, habitat can influence sociality: river dolphins, for example, live in shallow, structurally complex habitats that offer escape routes or hiding places from predators, with low apparent rates of predation, and with prey more or less evenly dispersed.

These dolphins are found in small groups or are often solitary. Inshore dolphins, which live in bays or along ocean beaches, are found in slightly larger groups from about six to twenty animals. Their habitat is slightly more open, prey patches are somewhat larger and more clumped, and predation pressure is greater. Pelagic (open ocean) dolphins are found in extremely large groups — up to thousands of animals — in very open habitats where huge prey patches are distributed in clumps, separated by vast expanses of ocean, and predation pressures are assumed to be more substantial.

The way the relatedness of individuals affects their social behaviour is somewhat harder to assess. It is assumed that individual animals attempt to maximise the proportion of their genes transmitted into the following generations; referred to as maximising their 'inclusive fitness'. The most obvious way to achieve this is by producing sons or daughters. However, if an animal assists in the survival of its nieces and nephews, aunts, uncles, sisters, brothers or cousins, then the helping animal's genetic complement carried by its relative is carried on.

Another way that an animal can maximise its inclusive fitness is through 'altruistic' acts. The helping behaviours observed in many animal societies certainly do not appear to fit the concept of competition: mathematical modelling has demonstrated that it can sometimes be in an animal's best interests to assist a group mate, if all animals in a group adopt this attitude and none 'cheat'.

▼ Pelagic or open-ocean dolphins hunt large patches of prey scattered over huge areas. Gatherings of a thousand or more animals can herd prey more efficiently, leading to the formation of highly co-ordinated groups that appear to emphasise their co-ordination with a 'choreography' of leaps and sudden changes of direction.

Altruism doesn't necessarily imply a conscious intent to carry out an act of kindness: instead, the term refers to the evolutionary development of a 'suite' of behaviours involving the assistance of a group mate, with the assumption that group mates will reciprocate such behaviour — in what is known as 'reciprocal altruism' — should the need arise.

Examples of altruistic behaviour among cetaceans are common, and while there are many examples of altruistic acts among terrestrial mammals, the fact that cetaceans live in an aquatic environment appears to provide an impetus for altruistic acts. An injured whale or dolphin incapable of swimming to the surface to breathe

may rely on its group mates to support it; whether cetaceans learn that assistance to group members is one of their social rules, or assist an injured animal instinctively is not at issue here. The need (induced by living in an aquatic environment) to develop such behaviour is what is important, and appears to be sufficient for acts of reciprocal altruism to form an integral part of cetaceans' social behaviour.

To add to the complexity, the long-term interests of males and females differ. Males need to compete for access to breeding females, and need to 'convince' females that they are the female's best choice of a mate. Females have to maximise their energy input, as the energy costs of reproduction

▼ More is known about the social behaviour of humpbacks than of any other baleen whale. The protection of females and their calves appears to be the prime purpose of the social group.

Mike Osmond/Pacific Whale Foundation

(and especially of lactation) are great. To put all this simply, males invest in obtaining the greatest number of mating opportunities, while females invest in ensuring that their young survive and get a good start to life. Nepotism, as the assistance of kin is called, is also common among cetaceans. (Again, the term does not have the political connotations it attracts in human society).

The basic unit of cetacean society appears to be the bond between mother and calf (rather than, for instance, the bond between a mated male and female). This translates under suitable conditions into female-bonded or matrilineal groups.

Pilot whales, for example, seem to display this form of social system, and there is good evidence that females of this species undergo menopause, a rare phenomenon in the animal kingdom. There is also evidence that the 'grandmothers' of a group are the repositories of learned information — for example, where to find the best food patches in different seasons — and may act as group leaders in much the same way that tribal elders do in human society. The existence of menopause also suggests that as the females of some species age, they invest more in the rearing of an individual

calf, while young females invest in producing many calves.

Regrettably, cetacean social behaviour is far from completely understood. However, over the past fifteen years or so, the number of studies of cetaceans in their natural habitat has increased greatly. A good start has been made in the study of social behaviour, and some excellent studies of free-ranging cetaceans have thrown light on how the behaviour of whales fits into what we know of the social behaviour of mammals in general. While free-ranging animals have provided most of the information on cetacean social structures, the observation of captive cetaceans is still necessary to improve our knowledge of their social organisation — the different interactions between members of dyads. This has obviously been impossible for the great whales, as they are far too large to be kept in oceanaria. Any attempt to discuss what is known of every species' social behaviour would provide little more than a great number of snippets of information, so it is necessary to take some broadly representative samples of different cetacean social systems, and examine them in detail.

▲ The study of social behaviour involves recording the interactions between individual animals. At its most basic level, any social network is a series of interactions between pairs of animals, called dyads. Thus, the social network of six animals involves the interaction of 6 + 5 + 4 + 3 + 2 + 1 dyads. This network can change, and each interaction of each dyad depends both on the previous interactions of that dyad and on the overall social network. Studying these networks is a basic part of the research into all forms of social behaviour. Compare the problems associated with studying a terrestrial mammal with those of a group of inshore dolphins — probably the easiest cetaceans to study.

THE BOTTLENOSE DOLPHIN

Bottlenose dolphins (*Tursiops truncatus*) are found throughout the world in both coastal and offshore waters. As they were among the first cetaceans to be kept in captivity, and have proved remarkably adaptable to their life in oceanaria, a large body of data on their dyadic interactions has been collected. Dominance hierarchies are obvious from captive studies, with the largest adult male being the dominant animal; female dominance patterns appear to be less rigid. Agonistic or aggressive behaviour patterns observed include dolphins chasing each other, ramming, biting, slapping a subordinate with their flukes, and jaw clapping, where a dolphin shuts its

Bernd Würsig

▲ The leaping of the bottlenose dolphin has probably been witnessed by more people than any other aspect of cetacean behaviour. With its long history in captivity and its inshore habitat in the wild, it is certainly the best studied of all cetaceans.

jaws firmly, causing a sharp report in the water. Adult males display aggressive behaviour toward calves as well as adults. In these instances, the calf's mother will fight back or try to escape the male's aggression.

Other social behaviour includes dolphins rubbing against each other; leaping simultaneously; a female presenting her belly to a male (presumably a mating invitation) and copulation. For one group of captive animals under observation, these behaviours peaked in mid-afternoon.

Because they are found close inshore, bottlenose dolphins are the best-studied cetaceans in the wild. Groups have been studied in the waters off the United States, South Africa, Argentina, England, France and Australia. This spread of studies has allowed differences in habitat and variation in social structure within one species to be studied, and has thus thrown some light on the influence different ecological conditions have on social behaviour. Social groups being ecological adaptations, different ecological regimes should, in theory, result in different social structures and allow hypotheses regarding the relative importance of different ecological factors on sociality to be tested.

Bottlenose dolphins are found as solitary individuals or in groups ranging in size from two

to more than a thousand animals. Populations studied in detail have revealed a fairly fluid social structure, and groups seem to change composition with remarkable regularity. However, there are some underlying patterns. Small 'subgroups', usually of two to six dolphins, tend to remain quite stable, and it is the mixing of these subgroups that creates larger groups. Some subgroups — especially groups of juvenile and adult males — tend to avoid each other. It seems, too, that there is patterning in the way larger groups associate. While the dolphins within one area may associate in this manner, they do so within communities that are rigidly demarcated. One study looked at dolphins in a restricted Florida bay. The bay contained a community of about 100 dolphins, all living within a range of about 85 square kilometres, which showed no signs of interacting with dolphins in waters outside their range. On a larger scale, a study in a Queensland (Australia) bay looked at a community of more than 250 animals inhabiting a much larger range, with individual animals' ranges reaching 250 square kilometres. These bay dolphins were never seen to associate with the many other bottlenose dolphins found in coastal waters just outside the bay.

It has been argued that the dominance hierarchies of captive dolphins are responses to the stress of captivity, and that no such hierarchies exist in free living populations. However, dominance hierarchies have been shown to exist in wild dolphin society. In the waters off the coast of Queensland (and, indeed, in many other places around the world), bottlenose dolphins feed behind trawling (shrimp) boats. These boats discard non-commercial fish that are caught incidentally in the nets, and this by-catch is eaten by the dolphins. In Moreton Bay, dolphins that obtained a large percentage of their food requirements in this manner displayed definite dominance patterns. The most dominant individuals — generally adult males — had first choice of the by-catch and were very selective in what they ate. Other, lower ranked animals (generally females and juveniles) took the scraps and ate fish species that more dominant animals were never observed eating.

This situation demonstrates the bottlenose dolphin's remarkable range of feeding methods. In open waters, dolphins herd large schools of fish while in rocky reef areas they feed individually. In one shallow, marshy habitat, they have been seen driving fish ashore, then almost stranding themselves to catch the struggling fish. There are accounts of bottlenose dolphins herding fish co-operatively with humans to the benefit of both groups: a diversity of feeding techniques that suggests bottlenose dolphin groups act as teaching institutions, with young animals learning from their elders.

This remarkable ability to develop feeding

Ben Cropp

techniques to fit the circumstances presents problems in deciding the role of food availability in determining group size. Assessing the role of predation on dolphin group size presents other problems: many of the animals observed feeding behind trawlers in Moreton Bay show scars from encounters with large sharks, which also follow the trawlers. However, these wounds heal quickly, and being bitten by a shark does not seem to discourage dolphins from feeding behind trawlers. Dolphins studied in Florida waters tended to move into shallower (and presumably safer) waters at times when sharks known to feed on dolphins were in the area. Despite the folklore that

bottlenose dolphins attack and kill sharks, and that sharks and dolphins are never found together, the evidence for dolphins killing sharks has yet to be presented — and they have been seen with sharks nearby, when both species are hunting schools of fish.

Bottlenose dolphin communities are female-bonded, or matrilineal, but their mating system is uncertain and the role that male competition for mates plays in their society remains a mystery. To explore these areas, the sex of free-ranging animals needs to be determined, yet identifying the sex of bottlenose dolphins is extremely difficult, as males and females look much the same.

▲ Like a cat toying with a mouse, the bottlenose dolphin will sometimes play with its prey, grasping it gently before releasing it, then darting forward to seize the hapless fish or squid again.

THE ORCA

Orcas or killer whales (*Orcinus orca*) are found in all the oceans of the world, in both inshore and offshore waters. One population in the waters of British Columbia, Canada and Washington, in the United States, has been studied since the 1970s. The animals are identified by their distinctive dorsal fin patterns and by the size, shape and position of the light 'saddle patch' behind the dorsal fin. There are three separate communities in this population: a resident northern community, a resident southern community and a transient

▲ Studies of orcas on the northern Pacific coast of Canada and the United States have shown populations to be relatively stable, with groups of up to fifty animals maintaining their cohesiveness with constant acoustic communication. Each pod has its own 'dialect' of clicks, whistles and pulsed calls.

▶ Orcas are among the more obviously sexually dimorphic whales. Males grow to 9.75 metres in length and have a distinctive dorsal fin that is sharply triangular and may stand almost 2 metres high. Females are lighter in weight, shorter (a maximum length of 6.5 metres) and have a smaller, less robust dorsal fin.

community, which comprises whales seen only occasionally within the areas where the two resident communities are found.

These whales live in relatively stable groups, called 'pods', which appear to be made up of animals related to each other. The pods range in size from one to fifty animals and there are about thirty pods, numbering about 260 individuals. One pod will regularly combine with others, but not all pods associate with all other pods; only with those pods that are part of the same 'community'. Pods of different communities never join together. Solitary animals of either sex are rare; some small pods contain no males, for example, or more than half a particular pod's members may consist of adult males, though adult males make up only 23 per cent of the overall population. (Ascertaining the sex of individual orcas is relatively straightforward. Males are at least a third larger than females, and dorsal fins are up to twice the size of females.)

All the resident pods have a range of at least 500 kilometres along the coast, while the transients occupy at least 630 kilometres of coast and extend an unknown distance offshore.

Orcas are extremely vocal animals, and produce three different types of sound:

Jen and Des Bartlett/Bruce Coleman Ltd

▲ Orcas, the most predatory of the dolphins, gather at seal pupping grounds and swim close to shore, intentionally stranding themselves during the hunt or harrying the seals until they panic and attempt to escape through the surf — where they are seized by waiting pod members.

▶ There are records of orcas attacking larger baleen whales, harrying them until they are too weak to escape, wounding or drowning them. This blue whale was attacked by a pod of orcas off Baja California and eventually died of its wounds, whereupon it was partially eaten.

echolocation clicks, whistles and pulsed calls. Pulsed calls are characteristic of orcas, and can be divided further into discrete calls and variable calls. Discrete pulsed calls are the most common form of sound produced by active resident orcas: analysis of the discrete pulsed calls of the British Columbia and Washington State pods has revealed that every pod has its own 'dialect'. Each pod has a limited repertoire of calls that remain stable over several years and the dialects of pods within a single community are similar, while the repertoires of pods from different communities share very few calls.

Orcas' vocalisations have also been recorded in antarctic waters: the sounds produced by antarctic orcas, while recognisable as orca sounds, are different from those recorded off the west coast of North America, providing further evidence for the existence of dialects. Incidental observations of orcas in other areas have shown intriguing, apparently learned, aspects of their hunting behaviour. They move close inshore

around sub-antarctic islands during the pupping seasons of the seals that inhabit the islands. In the coastal waters off Argentina, where they arrive for the seal pupping season, they have been seen to strand themselves intentionally in their hunts for seals. In fact, intentional stranding is the most successful hunting technique adopted by this group of orcas. If they attempt to catch seals in the surf, where the seals are in difficulty — not really swimming and not ashore — the whales also put themselves at some risk by entering an alien environment. It also appears that young whales are taught how to strand themselves to catch seals from observing older animals. Orcas also demonstrate an impressive degree of social co-ordination when attacking other cetaceans. There are some records and reports of controlled/co-ordinated attacks on great whales, and accounts from different parts of the world over many years show striking similarities. The whales are seen to be 'herded' by the orcas and stopped from sounding. Members of the orca pod may throw

themselves over the whale's head, apparently in an attempt to cover their quarry's blowhole and thus prevent it breathing. Further evidence that orcas understand other cetaceans' breathing behaviour comes from observations in the waters off British Columbia, where a minke whale was drowned by being forced to remain underwater until it died.

When feeding on smaller cetaceans, orcas herd animals into tightly packed groups, then individual whales dart through the mass of milling animals, killing as they go.

One unusual and fascinating account of orcas' hunting co-operation involves them working with the whalers of old. At Twofold Bay in southern New South Wales, Australia, a shore-based whaling station sometimes worked with the assistance of a group of orcas. The orcas would herd migrating whales into the bay and keep them on the surface to allow an easier kill by the whalers, or would alert the whalers to the presence of migrating humpbacks outside Twofold Bay. The whalers would usually leave the dead whale tethered for a couple

Bob Vile / Hubbs - Sea World Research Institute / Harcourt Brace Jovanovich

surfaces facing each other, while the male's penis is extruded; swimming in this position with the penis retracted; one whale gently butting its head against the genital region of the other; whales slowly and gently rubbing their bodies together; one whale draping itself over the other, which lies motionless in the water; two whales swimming towards each other, gently touching heads; and one whale gently nibbling the tongue of another. An extruded penis is apparently a sign of pre-copulatory behaviour.

Antagonistic, or aggressive, behaviour includes one whale lunging at another, a whale shaking its body or flukes at another (which may or may not be followed by a lunge), a whale deliberately bobbing its head at another and, most serious, whales biting each other.

While studies of captive animals have recorded many examples of the behaviour patterns outlined above, comparisons with free-ranging animals have yet to be made. What little we know of the grouping patterns of orcas in places other than British Columbia and Washington, for example, suggests that these animals may live in small groups that may not be stable. The reported joining of the pods at Twofold Bay suggests that pods can coalesce to form a permanent, larger pod — something quite at odds with the suggestion that pods are necessarily stable social units. The presence of single whales in the waters off British Columbia and Washington suggests rather that pods *cannot* be completely stable — these animals must at some stage have belonged to a pod. How many animals, and what conditions, are needed to ensure stability? What effect does the distribution and abundance of prey have on pod size? The mating system of orcas also remains a mystery. If males of a species are much larger than females, this generally indicates some sort of polygyny — one male mating with several females. We simply do not know if this is the case among orcas: there are even suggestions that males remain in the group in which they were born for their entire lives. If so, this raises a fairly obvious question: who mates with the females of a pod? Perhaps transient males do, or perhaps mating takes place when pods unite with other pods in communal mating and breeding areas. In the majority of polygynous mammals, juvenile males leave the group in which they were born and migrate elsewhere; if this happens with orcas, it would explain the small percentage of adult males in the population of British Columbia and Washington. Observations of orcas' hunting behaviour suggests that males play a major role in subduing large, dangerous prey. The low percentage of adult males in the North American studies may simply be due to the higher mortality of males carrying out these hazardous 'duties'. Yet to confuse the issue further, these orcas are supposed to feed mainly on fish.

▲ Explanations for orcas' fluke-slapping vary from ritualised aggression between adult males or attempts to defend calves against aggression to signals that alert the group to intruders or predators.

Dean Lee

of days to let their assistants feed on the lips and tongue. Interestingly, these orcas lived in what were described as three 'mobs' or 'families' that, over the years, combined to form one group; a social pattern quite similar to that described for orcas off the west coast of North America.

Orcas also associate with human activities today. Herring seining in the waters off Norway and Iceland attracts hundreds of orcas to feed around the fishing boats as they work. This poses some interesting questions. How does the social organisation of orcas allow for the development of such large aggregations? In such situations, do the divisions between pods and communities remain and, if so, how are they maintained?

The social behaviour of orcas has not been studied in great detail, but some work has been undertaken with captive animals. Patterns of interaction within dyads can be separated into locomotive patterns, play, apparent courtship, pre-copulatory and agonistic behaviour. Locomotive patterns include whales chasing each other, as well as co-ordinated swimming patterns such as side-by-side swimming. Play includes activities such as whales brushing against each other while swimming at high speed. Apparent courtship involves whales lying still, with their ventral

▶ As part of their co-ordinated swimming patterns, orcas often 'spy-hop', thrusting their heads and upper bodies above the surface to inspect their surroundings. Studies of free-living orcas suggest that 'spy-hopping', usually associated with complex and highly efficient hunting techniques, is learned by young orcas from observation of adults.

▲ Spinning, leaping and breaching abilities, common to many species, reach their apogee in spinner dolphins. Although normally gregarious, lone spinner dolphins are also observed leaping and spinning.

SPINNER DOLPHINS

Spinner dolphins (*Stenalla longirostris*) are found in tropical, subtropical and occasionally warm temperate waters all around the world. They are found both around islands and in the open ocean, and live in groups numbering from about twenty to more than a thousand individuals. The population sizes and stock separation of spinner dolphins that inhabit the waters of the eastern tropical Pacific ocean have been studied in some depth. Unfortunately for the dolphins, most of this information comes from animals killed in tuna fishing operations. Millions of these dolphins and their close relatives, the spotted dolphins, have been killed 'incidentally' due to their association with tuna. While some information on their social behaviour has been gleaned by observations from tuna vessels, other studies have provided more widely based data on their social behaviour.

From studies of Hawaiian animals, it is apparent that spinner dolphins make use of different habitats during the course of a day. In daylight hours they rest close inshore in bays, while at night they move offshore to deeper waters, where they feed on fish at great depths. As they move into these different habitats, their group sizes change: during the day's rest they swim slowly in groups of twenty or so, while at night they congregate in groups that may number several hundred. These feeding groups, which appear to help co-ordinate the search for food patches, comb large areas of ocean.

The transition from rest to active travelling and feeding is quite marked. As evening draws near, the aerial activity of spinners (indeed, they were named in honour of their impressive acrobatic displays) increases, and is followed by a period of zig-zag swimming, apparently to ensure every member of the group is acting in a cohesive fashion. Then the group will move offshore, where it joins other groups. Spinner dolphins appear to have a fairly loose social structure, with group composition changing on a daily basis. However, some small groups (generally pairs) seem to remain constant.

This social structure and pattern of behaviour appears to demonstrate how ecological factors can bear directly on social behaviour. Spinners move to inshore areas to rest, apparently because they need to find protection. Because they feed on midwater fish, which occur in large, dispersed clumps, they need to form groups large enough to search vast areas efficiently. These combined factors operate to produce the observed social behaviour. In the oceanic waters of the Pacific, spinner dolphins are seen in large schools with spotted dolphins. As spinner dolphins feed at night and rest during the day, while spotted dolphins rest at night and feed during the day, it has been suggested that these combined schools work to the advantage of both species. While one part of the overall group is resting, the other is alert so at all times some dolphins are keeping an eye out for predators.

Analysis of dead spinner dolphins suggests

► Spinner dolphins earned their common name from their exuberant acrobatic displays, but during the day they rest close to the shore, conserving their energy for the evening's fishing.

Marc Webber/Earthviews

that groups are segregated according to sex and age; however, little is known about the way the sexes interact in the wild. One study of captive spinner dolphins has produced interesting results.

This study looked at specific social behaviour: genital-to-genital contact; beak-to-genital propulsion (where one dolphin places the tip of its rostrum, or 'beak', in the genital slit of another, and pushes gently); other genital contact (which included one animal inserting its fin into the genital slit of another, or rubbing or stroking the other's genital area); non-genital contact (where dolphins caressed each other with the rostrum, flukes, head, flanks or pectoral fins); ventral presentations (where one dolphin tilted its belly towards another) and chases. The study found that genital-to-genital contact and ventral presentations were most common when the males' testosterone levels were high, and beak-to-genital propulsion appeared to be associated with ovulation. Other behaviour, and the amount of time dolphins spent

swimming with members of the opposite sex, did not correlate with changes in levels of sex hormones. Although these studies have shown us little more than some very basic behavioural characteristics, they represent a significant advance in our knowledge of a species whose open-ocean habitat has presented great difficulties in obtaining information on more complex issues.

THE SPERM WHALE

Sperm whales (*Physeter catadon*) are found in deep water throughout the world's oceans. Unlike the other species described here, most of the information on the social behaviour of sperm whales comes from the study of whales taken by the whaling industry. As they are inhabitants of the open oceans — generally in deep waters off the continental shelves — they are not easy to study, but recent behavioural studies conducted from small sailing vessels have proved it *is* possible to study them, alive and in the wild. Records from the

▲ Spotted dolphins have developed a mutually satisfactory social arrangement with spinner dolphins — while one group rests, the other group is alert and feeding.

Carl Spencer/Earthviews

▲ Despite centuries of being hunted, the sperm whale remains the most mysterious of the great whales. Recent studies have revealed that 'nursery schools' form the basic unit of sperm whale society, and during the breeding season come under the control of large bulls ('harem masters') for brief periods.

Ben Cropp

▲ As elusive as the great hunter that pursues it through the depths of the ocean, the giant squid grows almost as large as the sperm whale. This 12-metre specimen was recovered from the stomach of a sperm whale harpooned off Albany, Western Australia.

time when sperm whales were hunted from open boats also provide some insight into their social behaviour.

Sperm whales are the most sexually dimorphic of the cetaceans: when physically mature a bull sperm whale can be half as long again as a mature female, and may weigh up to three times as much. This great difference is associated with the different patterns of migration of male and female sperm whales. It is important to realise that there is something of an evolutionary chicken-and-the-egg question here: are male sperm whales larger because they migrate to polar waters where there is more food, or do they migrate to polar waters because they are larger? To answer this question, we need to return to the concept of males seeking to maximise their number of mating opportunities.

From whaling data and from recent behavioural studies, it seems clear that the basic social unit of the sperm whale is what is referred to as the 'nursery school'. Adult females, calves and juveniles, found in warmer waters, form groups of two to 50 individuals that seem to be fairly stable. Since female sperm whales appear to engage in communal nursing (in other words, mothers share the responsibility of providing milk for calves), it is likely that these are matrilineal, female-bonded groups. But why should these groups exist? Nursery schools may provide protection for juveniles and calves, which are preyed upon by orcas and large sharks. There are reports of nursery schools of sperm whales keeping sharks and orcas at bay, and it would appear that a group response can successfully deter predators. These nursery schools also provide a valuable, concentrated resource of reproductively active females during the breeding season. The largest bulls, called 'harem masters', battle for right of access to a nursery school, and the nursery school then becomes that male's harem. Recent behavioural observations of males in their mating grounds

indicate that two large males may form a 'coalition' and work together to exclude other males from female groups. Coalitions move between female groups, searching for sexually receptive females, so it appears that males hold their harems for very short periods — probably a few days at most.

Accounts of battles between harem masters, mostly from old whaling boats' logs, tell of mammoth contests between these magnificent adversaries. Many accounts suggest that the whales attack each other with their jaws. While a battle between harem masters must be an amazing spectacle, it is unlikely that bulls would regularly do themselves serious injuries; most battles between animals tend to be ritualised affairs, with serious damage to either opponent a very rare occurrence. It seems male sperm whales have evolved great size (up to 19 metres) to intimidate their rivals — a case of 'honest advertisement' that enhances a larger animal's chances of mating.

For large male sperm whales, feeding on almost equally large prey such as giant squid — which seem to be in great numbers in polar waters — would be more energy efficient than feeding on many smaller fish and squid; so large male sperm whales migrate to polar waters to feed because they are large, and they are large because their social system has assisted them to grow large.

The social behaviour of immature bulls raises other interesting questions. These animals migrate to higher latitudes than nursery schools and form 'bachelor schools'. The smallest males (who would only recently have left their nursery schools) form groups of up to fifty animals. As they mature, their school size decreases to between three and fifteen animals, and the largest males — the harem masters — are either solitary or found in pairs. We do not know why males live in progressively smaller groups as they age; or whether the smaller squid hunted by the younger males are schooling species. If they are, do the young whales hunt co-operatively? Until the way sperm whales catch their prey is resolved (the fact that sperm whales can have mutilated jaws, yet still seem quite capable of feeding has, incidentally, led to the suggestion that these whales stun their prey with biosonar) the role that the distribution and abundance of their prey plays in their social structure remains an open question. The need to defend prey patches could also play an important role in determining the size of schools of whales. The smaller whales — especially the calves and juveniles — are probably under threat from predators. It seems unlikely that large bulls (which are reliably reported to have sunk wooden whaling ships) could not outswim, outdive or outfight sharks or orcas. Bulls also show a definite seasonal pattern of testicular activity, so aggression between bulls is probably seasonal and aggression between members of bachelor schools as they mature may lead to these groups breaking up.

Al Giddings/Ocean Images, Inc. /Planet Earth Pictures

THE HUMPBACK WHALE

Most studies of cetacean social behaviour have been conducted on the toothed whales. Over the past ten years or so, however, work on two species of baleen whales — the humpback and right whales — have shed light on the social behaviour of these great whales. Humpback whales (*Megaptera novaeangliae*) migrate from high-latitude summer feeding grounds to low latitudes in the winter to mate and calve.

Humpbacks have been studied intensively at their wintering grounds in the waters off Hawaii and the West Indies. In Hawaiian waters, humpbacks are found as individuals or in groups ranging in size from two to around twenty animals; off Silver Bank in the West Indies, groups range from two to about a dozen whales. In both groups, male humpbacks compete for access to females using songs and fighting. Humpback whale songs were first recorded almost thirty years ago, though intensive study of the relationship between singing

and behaviour is a more recent development. Humpback songs are long and elaborate with cyclic patterns that seem too melodic and complex to be described simply as vocalisations. The songs are heard infrequently on the feeding grounds and during migration; they seem to be virtually restricted to the mating season. Their content changes each year, and alters slightly during each breeding season and the songs of each population are quite distinct.

Establishing the sex of humpback whales in the open ocean is difficult, but to date every singing whale — with one possible exception — has been a male. Usually, songs are sung by solitary whales that cease singing when they join other whales. Overall, it appears that humpbacks' songs function in a similar way to the singing of songbirds — as a form of courtship display.

When (presumably male) whales congregate around a female, they engage in an activity that is

▲ One explanation for the humpback's breaching is that it is simply adding an exclamation mark at the conclusion of some other behaviour. Another explanation is that it is an effective means of long-distance communication — a highly visible method of announcing its presence to other whales.

▲ Herman Melville described the humpback as the most 'gamesome' of whales. However, much of the humpback's apparently sociable behaviour, including the head lunging shown here, has more to do with dominance and aggression than with cetacean high spirits.

far more common among these animals; they fight for the prime position near the female, presumably to increase their chances of mating. Fighting between humpback males involves adversaries lunging at each other, sometimes with their throat pleats extended (to appear as a larger, more formidable competitor) and hitting each other with their flukes. Less dramatic forms of aggressive behaviour include lifting the head from the water while swimming, fluke slapping, slapping the pectoral flippers and releasing a stream of bubbles underwater (presumably in an attempt to disorient an opponent). These contests can leave rivals with raw and bleeding patches on their backs and fins. Unfortunately, no-one has so far observed copulation between humpback whales, so we do not know what it is that leads to a successful mating attempt.

Another aspect of humpback whale behaviour that has attracted much attention is breaching, when a whale leaps clear of the water. Various interpretations have been attached to this behaviour, including aggression, inspecting the environment, long-distance communication, or simply an 'exclamation mark' at the end of some other behaviour. Which, if any, of these possibilities is correct is still not known. Another intriguing example of humpback behaviour is fin waving, where the large pectoral fin (from which this species got its name *Megaptera*, or 'great wing') is waved in the air while the rest of the animal leaps clear above the surface. Explanations of fin-waving vary from aggressive displays to simply 'waving goodbye'.

At their summer feeding grounds, humpbacks behave in a totally different fashion. They are found in groups of from one to about ten animals, which show no stability over time. Only mothers with calves form stable groupings. The size of feeding groups seems to depend on the size of the prey patch on which they are feeding. These groups seem to co-ordinate their activities, presumably to enhance their feeding success. Short-term 'companionships' are also observed when non-feeding whales travel together for a while, usually less than a day.

▶ Boisterous group behaviour has been observed in humpbacks during feeding, when males are fighting over access to a female or, occasionally, when large numbers of whales congregate for their ocean-spanning annual migrations.

What does this tell us about the social system of the humpback whale? Their mating system seems to involve a sort of harem, dispersed in both time and space, so that only a few males have the opportunity to mate successfully with ovulating females. We can do no more than speculate about the purpose of their elaborate songs, or their fighting. Neither do we know why songs change over time, or why different populations sing different songs. The importance of predation on grouping patterns is also unknown: there are accounts of orcas unsuccessfully attacking pairs of adult whales with calves, and records of large sharks following humpbacks with calves, but the success of such attempts at predation is unknown.

The co-operation between whalers and orcas at Twofold Bay demonstrated that orcas can successfully attack humpbacks, though human assistance appears to have benefited the orcas. An interesting account of a pack of orcas harassing several feeding humpbacks, taking small pieces from several whales, suggests that they may 'test' whales, attempting to find one that is most vulnerable, perhaps due to old age or injury.

In conclusion, these few examples of cetacean social behaviour give some idea of the little we do know, and show how much there is still to learn. The social behaviour of pelagic dolphins, beaked whales and most of the baleen whales remains a mystery and many of the factors that affect the social behaviour of the better studied cetaceans need further research. The use of techniques such as the identification of individual whales and dolphins using natural marks; radio and satellite telemetry both to track animals and to provide physiological data; DNA 'fingerprinting' to reveal the relationships between individual animals and to provide some information on mating systems; the recording and analysis of sound patterns and simple observation will add to our understanding of these magnificent but enigmatic mammals.

INTELLIGENCE

M.M. BRYDEN and PETER CORKERON

The frequent stories about whales, dolphins and porpoises in newspapers and magazines almost always refer to the 'high intelligence' of these animals. It has become widely accepted that dolphins are highly intelligent. But is there evidence to support this?

The study of human intelligence is difficult, and there are many illustrations of just how complex it is to measure. But the mental processes of animals other than human beings are even more difficult to investigate, and as a result any discussion of relative intelligence among animals is highly subjective. We tend to form opinions about whether a dog is more intelligent than a sheep, a horse more so than a pig, and so on. Individuals' opinions vary, often depending on the amount of time they have spent observing or interacting with a particular species.

▼ Despite the popular belief that all cetaceans are highly intelligent creatures, there is no clear supporting evidence. One problem with assessing their behaviour is that we have only a human perspective — experimental results may thus owe more to our techniques of measurement than to objective criteria of intelligence.

Australian Picture Library

The 'cleverness' of a trained dolphin is impressive and it is tempting to equate this cleverness with a high degree of intelligence, particularly given the faculties these animals possess, such as sonar and the production of complex sounds.

A few biologists have assumed dolphins to be very intelligent, but this assumption has been based solely on the fact that they have large brains. In the seventeenth century, biologist John Ray was sufficiently impressed by the large size of the dolphin brain to state that 'this largeness of brain, and correspondence of it to that of man, argue this creature to be of more than ordinary wit, and capacity'. In the 1960s John Lilly achieved considerable notoriety when he wrote about the large, complex cetacean brain and his belief that these animals possess a high level of 'non-human intelligence'. However, such assumptions are pure speculation, as is Lilly's belief that dolphins have a complex language that they use to exchange significant amounts of information. No research has lent direct support to his belief.

BRAIN SIZE AND STRUCTURE

The size of the cetacean brain is quite large and it is tempting to speculate that this may have something to do with higher mental processes.

Attempts have been made to measure the relative extent of brain development among animals, and the term 'encephalisation' has been used to refer to an index of the degree of brain development. Studies of the dolphin brain show that it is less developed than the human brain, but more so than other highly encephalised mammals such as the chimpanzee (*Pan troglodytes*).

The feature of the human brain that sets it apart from most other mammals is the advanced development of the region known as the cerebral cortex. It is very large and extensively folded. This is the region of the brain where conscious control of body functions occurs, and where complex functions such as correlation, association and learning are centred. A feature of the cetacean brain, similar to the human brain, is the large size of the cerebral hemispheres. They are also folded in a complex way, although the cortex is significantly thinner than in the human brain as well as in some other mammalian brains. Apart from this, the brain of a cetacean bears little resemblance to a human brain; the pattern of folding is much more like that found in the brains of hoofed animals, such as cattle, sheep and deer.

The structure of the dolphin brain is known in some detail through the careful work of many respected biologists. However, little is known about its functional organisation, in particular, that of the cortex in whales and dolphins. Modern anatomists have often used terms such as 'primitive' and 'undifferentiated' to describe the microscopic architecture of the cetacean cortex. Certainly it is different from that seen in other mammals.

Brain size in cetaceans may not mean the same thing as it does in land mammals such as the apes and human beings. An explanation of why the dolphin brain is so large, and whether its brain is functionally primitive or not, is not available. One intriguing possible explanation of the large brain size in dolphins has been advanced by the Nobel laureate Francis Crick (who made major contributions toward the discovery of the double helix molecule of DNA). Crick has related brain size in mammals to their metabolic rate, and to whether or not they experience 'dream sleep' or REM (rapid eye movement) sleep. He observed that those mammals in which dream sleep is absent or reduced (which includes both dolphins and whales) have large brains, and proposes that their brains may be large because they require a much larger storage area for the unwanted associations (what he calls 'parasitic modes') that in other mammals can be eliminated during

dreams. Like so many other theories of brain function in whales and dolphins, this is only a hypothesis, but it does provide an alternative explanation for the large size and structural complexity of the whale brain.

HOW INTELLIGENT ARE WHALES?

In an excellent book entitled *Whales,* Nigel Bonner has expanded the debate centred around brain size and intelligence. He argues that it is futile to attempt to apply human concepts of intelligence to an animal that inhabits a medium so different from ours.

What is intelligence? In general terms it is the faculty of understanding, and often involves the mutual conveyance of information. It may involve a choice of several actions, the choice requiring foresight and judgments about possible consequences. Of course this cannot be achieved in the absence of processes of thinking; do animals other than humans experience any thoughts and subjective feelings at all? Konrad Lorenz is one of the few who have discussed animal thought processes and feelings. He emphasised that it is extremely difficult, perhaps impossible, to learn anything at all about the subjective experiences of another species. But behavioural scientists are examining once again the possibility that animals have conscious awareness. In a recent book *Animal Thinking,* Professor Donald Griffin discusses what it might be like to be an animal; what dolphins, monkeys, crows, bees and ants might think about or whether they think at all.

The whale obtains most of its information about its surroundings from touch-sensitive organs on or in its skin, and from the sounds in its environment. Toothed whales supplement this information by adding their own clicks to provide reverberating echoes in a mechanism called echolocation, or sonar.

People who have spent much time with dolphins and whales have been impressed by their

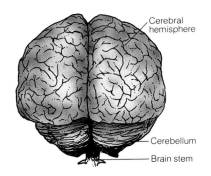
Cerebral hemisphere — Cerebellum — Brain stem

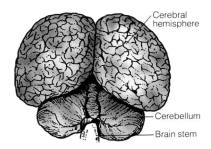
Cerebral hemisphere — Cerebellum — Brain stem

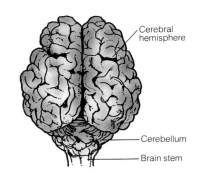
Cerebral hemisphere — Cerebellum — Brain stem

▲ The brains of a human (top), bottlenose dolphin (centre) and cow (bottom) seen from above show some basic similarities, though they are of different sizes relative to body weight. The folding of the dolphin cerebral cortex resembles that of the cow but differs from the folding of the human cortex.

BRAIN AND BODY WEIGHTS

ANIMAL	BRAIN WEIGHT (grams)	BODY WEIGHT (tonnes)	BRAIN WEIGHT AS A PERCENTAGE OF BODY WEIGHT
Human (*Homo*)	1500	0.07	2.1
Asiatic elephant (*Elephas*)	7500	5.00	0.15
Bottlenose dolphin (*Tursiops*)	1600	0.17	0.94
Common dolphin (*Delphinus*)	840	0.11	0.76
Pilot whale (*Globicephala*)	2670	3.50	0.076
Orca (*Orcinus*)	5620	6.00	0.094
Cow (*Bos*)	500	0.6	0.08
Sperm whale (*Physeter*)	7820	37.00	0.021
Fin whale (*Balaenoptera*)	6930	90.00	0.008

Alan Levenson/Courtesy Kewalo Basin Marine Mammal Laboratory

▲ Responding to the artificial gesture 'language' developed by researchers at the University of Hawaii, a bottlenose dolphin named Akeakamai obeys the instruction 'get a hoop and carry it to the pipe' by picking up a plastic hoop with her rostrum and swimming with it to a floating pipe.

Alan Levenson/Courtesy Kewalo Basin Marine Mammal Laboratory

▲ Dolphin trainer Jane Taylor communicates instructions to Akeakamai with stylised gestures for (from top) 'pipe', 'hoop' and 'fetch'. She wears reflective goggles that eliminate the possibility of providing eye-gaze cues to the dolphin, and restricts arm movements to the 'vocabulary' of the sign system.

gentleness towards people, and many have equated this with some kind of special understanding between humans and animals. This gentleness certainly makes dolphins among the most appealing of animals, but it is folly to regard it as proof that they perceive some special relationship between themselves and humans. The ability of trained whales and dolphins to execute complicated routines should not be equated with intelligence. A skilled trainer can teach a wide variety of animals, including parrots and pigeons, and even some invertebrates, to perform quite complex routines. Such performances tell us more about the skill, patience and intelligence of the trainer than of the animals they train.

There is no doubt that whales, and dolphins, in particular, can mimic the action of others. They are able to observe other animals, even other species, and mimic their behaviour in a short space of time.

HOW CAN WE STUDY INTELLIGENCE IN WHALES?

Despite the difficulties, it would be contrary to our natural inquisitiveness simply to consign the study of intelligence in whales to the 'too hard basket'. With the skills and knowledge available, however, the best we can do is examine possibilities.

Research on the evolution of intelligence has increased in recent years. The group of animals most interesting to behavioural scientists in this field is the primates (especially the monkeys and apes), because much research is centred around human evolution. It has been shown that group-living animals whose food is either difficult to capture or hard to find show the greatest potential for the development of intelligence. Thus, we find the more intelligent land mammals among the primates and the dog family. Ecologically, the toothed whales show similarities to both these groups, whereas the baleen whales are closer to the large grazing herbivores such as cattle and giraffes — animals not renowned for their great intellects.

Attempts have been made to assess dolphin intelligence both by experiments on captive dolphins and by observing dolphins in the wild.

EXPERIMENTS ON CAPTIVE TOOTHED WHALES

The early work on captive dolphins had serious flaws in both design and execution, and so is of little value, but more recent work, notably by Dr Louis Herman and his colleagues at the University of Hawaii, has made some headway.

Bottlenose dolphins process information about their world through their auditory (hearing) centres. As sound is a major part of the undersea world, this is to be expected. Dolphins in captivity performed quite badly in tests of their visual memory until a connection was introduced between visual information and an auditory code, further indicating the importance of auditory processing to these animals.

Louis Herman's group has taught artificial languages to two bottlenose dolphins, one of them a language based on gestures, the other a sound-based language. Unlike the language studies conducted with apes by other research groups, these studies tested the dolphins for sentence comprehension, rather than language production. A variety of objects (such as balls, pipes, frisbees and hoops) were placed in the dolphins' pool, and they were taught to associate a sound or gesture with each object. They were then taught a variety of verbs (for example, 'touch' and 'fetch') and were given simple command sentences (for example, 'touch the ball with your tail'). From these studies, it has been shown that dolphins can be taught to understand semantics and syntax, the rules underlying language. They also understand qualifiers such as up and down; over, under and through; and left and right.

Other results from these studies indicate that bottlenose dolphins can devise generalised response rules, that is, they understand a set of rules underlying the behaviour that they may carry out. Trainers working with false killer whales (*Pseudorca crassidens*) have reported that these animals, too, seem to comprehend the rule sets underlying their training.

Other studies of captive dolphins can shed light on the way that dolphins perceive their environment, although they may not be specifically designed to do so. A captive bottlenose

Alan Levenson/Courtesy Kewalo Basin Marine Mammal Laboratory dolphin was taught to attack sharks. It would attack sandbar sharks (*Carcharhinus plumbeus*), lemon sharks (*Negaprion brevirostris*) and nurse sharks (*Ginglymostoma cirratum*), none of which is known to attack dolphins. However, the dolphin refused to attack a bull shark (*C. leucas*), a known predator of dolphins. This indicates that bottlenose dolphins are capable of classifying species of shark according to the threat that they present.

One factor often overlooked in discussions of odontocete intelligence is the differences among the toothed whales themselves. Little is known about most aspects of the natural history of many of the toothed whales. The best known are the dolphins (family Delphinidae) and the sperm whales. 'Dolphin intelligence' is probably the most commonly considered form of cetacean intelligence, but there are great differences between the various dolphin species in their behaviour and ecology, which may mean that there are great differences in their intelligence. To investigate this, one study asked dolphin trainers to rate the apparent intelligence of other dolphin species relative to bottlenose dolphins. Even though these ratings were subjective estimates of some poorly defined concept, they were in general agreement — some species were considered more intelligent than bottlenose dolphins and others were considered less so.

FIELD RESEARCH

As the larger toothed whales and the great whales are too large to be maintained in captivity, any information on their intelligence must come from the study of free-ranging animals. Similar studies have added to our knowledge of the intelligence of the smaller toothed whales as well.

There are several examples of toothed whales displaying what appears to be an understanding of cause and effect. Orcas (*Orcinus orca*), for example, display an understanding of cause and effect in catching prey. Small groups have been observed co-operating to create waves sufficient to tip seals off ice floes in antarctic waters. The intentional stranding of orcas in Argentina to catch seals, a behaviour that these whales teach their young (see chapter on social behaviour), provides an interesting example of social communication playing an important role in the development of behaviour.

Bottlenose dolphins also strand themselves intentionally to catch prey. In marshy areas of the southeastern states of the USA, bottlenose dolphins drive fish on to mud banks. The dolphins drive the fish then rush at them, setting up a small wave that washes the fish ashore. The dolphins then semi-strand themselves to eat the stranded fish.

It appears that bottlenose dolphins can undo some knots that fishermen tie in the ends of

trawlers' nets. Even if the dolphins are pulling with no set pattern at the net's drawstring, this at least demonstrates that they understand how the net is held together.

When being hunted by whaling boats equipped with depth-sounding gear that could locate them, sperm whales (*Physeter catodon*) would swim to the deep scattering layer. This layer of mid-water fish provided an acoustic hiding place, making the whales invisible to the whaler's sensing equipment. In earlier times, when sperm whales were hunted by sailing ships, it is reported that they would frequently swim into the wind. This behaviour may have been due to the whales' learning that their pursuers could not sail to windward.

What do these examples tell us of the intelligence levels of toothed whales relative to other animals? The examples of orcas and bottlenose dolphins using topography to trap prey can be equated with the use of tools by other animals to catch prey. While such behaviour is often thought of as a characteristic of the 'higher' primates, some other animals, particularly birds, also use tools. It has been shown that some seabirds employ the use of tools according to environmental conditions in a highly sophisticated manner.

Alternatively, some dolphin species have been observed behaving in a remarkably unintelligent

▲ Learning to jump through a blazing hoop is more a tribute to the trust that develops between a dolphin and its trainer than an example of intellectual ability.

◀ 'Intelligence' includes the ability to manipulate the behaviour of others to one's own advantage. Orcas teach their young to harry seals and sea lions on land or on ice floes until their prey panics — the seals attempt to escape by diving into the water and are seized by the waiting orcas.

fashion, similar to other herd animals. For example, 40 to 60 spinner dolphins were trapped by a net made of a floating cork line, from which 6 mm lines were hung every 2 metres, for nearly 4 hours, in an area 6 by 10 metres. However, when caught regularly in tuna purse-seines, spinner dolphins learn to avoid the net, and to wait near the area where they will be released.

The study of how individual monkeys and apes use the social rules regulating their inter-actions to their own advantage is a developing subject of behavioural research. The discovery that some animals 'cheat' by bending the rules to their own advantage demonstrates that some apes

Deborah Glockner-Ferrari/Center for Whale Studies

▲ How bottlenose dolphins interact socially is not known, but some researchers suspect they may use sonar to communicate — 'seeing' with sound echoes each other's body flexion and muscle tension or the disposition of air in body cavities.

▶ False killer whale society is highly regulated according to age, size and sex — older, larger males appear to dominate most social interaction and to co-ordinate group hunting activities. Nothing is known, however, about the rules that keep group order and that provide protection against predators.

Robert Pitman/Earthviews

and monkeys understand the rules on which their society is based.

Research has shown that bottlenose dolphins and false killer whales are capable of developing generalised sets of rules, but we do not know whether they apply such rules to their social systems. As they have the capacity to develop these rules, the possibility seems likely.

We still do not understand how dolphins communicate with each other. Field studies of social behaviour in land mammals includes extensive research on the role of social communication, but this has been impossible to study in dolphins, because field studies of dolphin behaviour have only developed recently; it is difficult to view dolphin social interactions, as they occur underwater; and most importantly, we have no idea of the role of dolphin sonar in their social communication.

The traditional picture of dolphin communication assumes that sonar is used only for investigating the environment, while other sounds are used in social interaction. There is no evidence that this is so, but it is difficult to conceive how an active remote sensing system, such as sonar, might be used for communicating. Whatever role sonar plays, it is sure to vary greatly among the different types of dolphins, and even more so among the toothed whales as a whole. There is evidence that comprehending sonar signals has to be learned by bottlenose dolphins, although whether this is so for all dolphin species is unknown.

This raises again the issue of whether dolphins have a language. We have seen that bottlenose dolphins are capable of following and interpreting sets of instructions. However, there is no evidence that these dolphins use anything resembling language in the wild. This could be due to the lack of suitable research on free-living animals, and our lack of understanding of dolphin communication generally. Dorothy Cheney and Robert Seyfarth have demonstrated that free-living vervet monkeys (*Cercopithecus aethiops*) use a 'primitive language' to warn of predators, and that they learn to classify the animals around them. Such classification has also been observed in bottlenose dolphins, as discussed, but research on the whistle sounds made by dolphins has produced no evidence that these dolphins use particular sounds to represent particular types of animal. Such research is confounded by the role of sonar in social communication, but indicates that dolphins do *not* have a whistle language.

Another difficulty with assessing dolphin intelligence is the assumption by many observers that, if an animal is shown to demonstrate a reasonable level of intelligence in one field, it will also show that intelligence level in all areas. Research by Cheney and Seyfarth on vervet monkeys has shown that, while monkeys are good primatologists (they understand the way *their* society is organised), they are hopeless naturalists (they do not recognise subtle signs indicating the presence of predators). Like the monkeys, dolphins may be good acoustic signal processors and mimics, but less adept at understanding the nuances of their social situation.

The song of the humpback whale (*Megaptera novaeangliae*) is cited as an example of baleen whale behaviour that may indicate intelligence. However, the only significant difference between the songs of humpback whales and those of birds is the extraordinary length of humpback songs. Bird songs, like those of the humpback, also change over space and time. Because of its repetitive nature, humpback whale songs appear to lack the information content that a language usually possesses. Neither can it be said that the ability of humpbacks to recall the previous mating season's song, and to navigate across large ocean basins, is a sign of any great intelligence. Such behaviour in birds has been shown to be genetically controlled, rather than learned.

The emergence of 'cognitive ethology' as a valid form of scientific endeavour will hopefully help us to see cetaceans in perspective.

▼ Although humpback whale songs have been cited as evidence of intelligence, their rigid structure and the fact that the sequence is unvarying within an entire population suggest that they are simple communications.

Claire Leimbach

WHALES

AND PEOPLE

WHALES IN ART AND LITERATURE

RUTH THOMPSON

The earliest-known portrayal of whales, dolphins and porpoises in art dates from about 1500 BC when the early Greek and Roman artists — inspired by the dolphin's intelligence and kindness to humans — began to adopt dolphin motifs in sculpture, drawing, painting, on mosaic floors and on coins. This artistic tradition based on the idea of the dolphin as a source of creation, survives to the present day, with sculptures, paintings and murals, such as the evocative scene of whales, dolphins and sea lions in the wild painted by Lou Silva in 1979.

▲ This dekadrachm coin from Syracuse (480–400 BC) shows the head of Arethusa, crowned with an olive wreath and surrounded by four dolphins. In Greek mythology, the nymph Arethusa was changed into a spring on the island of Ortygia in Sicily, to escape the amorous advances of the river god Alpheus. The dolphin motif appeared frequently on coins — dolphins held a special significance for travellers, similar to the St Christopher medallion today.
Michael Holford/British Museum (Natural History)

▶ A contemporary artist's depiction of a whale can be seen in this mural painted by Lou Silva in 1979 on a wall of the building that houses Berkeley University Press.

Lou Silva/Photo courtesy of Berkeley University Press

The authors and poets of the Mediterranean regarded whales and dolphins as sacred creatures. Many believed that they were reincarnations of the human soul and represented the vital power of the sea. To some, like the Greek philosopher Aristotle (384–322 BC), they were objects of great curiosity and scientific observation. He observed that whales and dolphins were mammals, and recorded the fact in *History of Animals*.

> The dolphin, the whale and all the cetaceans — that is, all that are provided with a blow-hole instead of gills — are viviparous . . . All animals that are . . . viviparous have breasts, as for instance all animals that have hair, such as man and the horse and the cetaceans.

Aristotle, like other writers of his time, embellished his factual descriptions with stories told to him first-hand. In these stories dolphins appeared as gentle creatures with an almost human-like intelligence. In one story a school of dolphins entered a harbour and stopped there until a fisherman, who had caught and wounded a dolphin off the coast of Karia, let his captive free. Only then did the school depart.

Like Aristotle, the Roman soldier–traveller

Pliny the Elder (AD 23–79) collected stories for his *Naturalis Historia* but, unlike Aristotle, these were often second- or third-hand accounts, which led to inaccuracies in his writing. In *Naturalis Historia*, he wrote one of the most famous stories about dolphin and human relationships. It involved a boy who would go to the 'poole Lucrinus' at noon, with bread to attract the dolphin he called 'Simo'. The dolphin would emerge, take the bread, and gently offer the boy his back to ride on to Puteoli where the boy attended school. When the boy became sick and died, the dolphin mourned him deeply. Some time later, the dolphin, overcome with grief, was found dead on the shore.

The Dolphin Rider at Iassos is a similar tale of love between a boy and a dolphin. It is a powerful evocation of love and death, in which the beginning of the world, the sea's creative and destructive elements and the ambiguities of human sexual relations are vividly depicted. The story may have had its basis in fact: it was written at a time when whales and dolphins were the familiar companions of fishermen, who considered it a bad omen to kill one, and when boys (and possibly girls) rode gentle dolphins in almost every bay and inlet of the ancient Mediterranean Sea.

AELIAN:
THE DOLPHIN
OF IASSOS

A dolphin's love for a beautiful boy at Iassos: a famous story:
here it is

Iassos' gymnasium is near the sea
after running and wrestling all afternoon
the boys went down there and washed
a custom from way back when
one day a dolphin fell in love
with the loveliest boy of the time
at first when he paddled near the beach
the boy ran away in fear
but soon by staying close by and being kind
the dolphin taught the boy to love

they were inseparable
they played games
   swam side by side
      raced
         sometimes the boy would get up on top
            and ride the dolphin like a horse
he was so proud his lover carried him around on his back

so were the townspeople
visitors were amazed

the dolphin used to take his sweetheart out to sea
   far as he liked
      then turn around
         back to the beach
            say goodbye and return to the sea
               the boy went home

when school was out
there'd be the dolphin waiting
   which made the boy so happy

everyone loved to look at him
he was so handsome
   men and women
      even (and that was the best part) the dumb animals
for he was the loveliest flower of boy ever was

but envy destroyed their love
one day the boy played too hard
tired he threw himself down belly first
   on the dolphin's back
      whose back spike happened to be pointing straight up
it stuck him in the navel
veins split blood spilled
   the boy died
the dolphin felt him riding heavier than usual
(the dead boy couldn't lighten himself by breathing)
saw the sea turning purple from blood
knowing what had happened
   he chose to throw himself on their beach by the gymnasium
      like a ship rushing through the waves
         carrying the boy's body with him

they both lay there in the sand
   one dead
   the other gasping out life's breath
Iassos built them both a tomb
   to requite their great love
they also set up a stele
      which shows a boy riding a dolphin
         and put out silver and bronze coins
            stamped with the story of their love death

on the beach
they honor Eros the god who lead boy and dolphin here

In the 'dolphin rider' stories the dolphin and the boy are clearly distinguishable as separate creatures. Other stories take the ancient view of creation flowing from the womb of a dolphin; *delphys,* the Greek word for dolphin, is related to *Delphis,* which means womb. In Greek mythology, the story of Apollo the Sun God and his defeat of Delphyne, the dolphin/womb monster, illustrates this aspect of the Mediterranean creation story. Apollo's triumph over Delphyne leads him to build a temple at Delphi (Dolphin Town) and take on the title of

Delphinius, or 'dolphin-god'. Apollo then becomes a giant dolphin, commandeers a boat of Cretan merchants, and at Delphi reveals himself as a god. Thus Apollo emerges victorious from the sea of creation (embodied by the dolphin) to command the universe.

Stories about friendship between dolphins and children are not limited to ancient Greek and Roman writings. In 1945, a thirteen-year-old American schoolgirl, Sally Stone, made friends with a dolphin at Long Island South and between 1960 and 1966 a dolphin played among the boats

◄ The dolphin fresco, a decorative panel on the wall of the Queen's Room at the Palace of Knossos, Crete, was painted by an unknown artist probably in the late Minoan II period, c1450–1400 BC. It is one of the earliest known portrayals of dolphins in art, probably dating from the last phase of the New Palace. Around the door are rosettes, a decoration typical of the Minoan period. The dolphins compare favourably with medieval drawings of dolphins which often depicted them with scales or gills.

Michael Holford

and swimmers at Elie in Fifeshire, Scotland, and at Seahouses in Northumberland, England. From New Zealand comes an account remarkably reminiscent of Pliny the Younger's story of the dolphin in Africa. In 1956 the New Zealand parliament passed legislation to protect a dolphin at Opononi Beach, Hokianga Bay. The bottle-nose dolphin 'Opo', allowed the children to pet her, play ball with her and clamber on her back. Opo proved such a popular attraction that tourists began to flock to the town, but it was not long before Opo died.

Dolphin legends and motifs featured in a variety of art forms in pre-Biblical times. Cretan artists of the Minoan civilisation, which flourished from the end of the fourth century to 1400 BC, used realistic motifs, based on floral and marine forms including dolphins, in their decorative painting. The murals and frescoes that adorned Cretan palaces like Knossos and Phaestos depicted dolphins as realistic, lively creatures, unlike the paintings of later medieval artists that often portrayed whales and dolphins with scales and gills.

▼ The *Dionysus Cup* (540 BC), by Exekias, illustrates the Greek legend of Dionysus, god of wine and frenzy. Dionysus is sailing between the Greek islands of Ikaria and Naxos. He learns of the crew's plot to sell him into slavery and plans his revenge — their oars become snakes, vines sprout from the loins of the god and flutes begin to play. The terrified sailors dive overboard where they are rescued by the Greek god of the sea, Poseidon, who turns the sailors into dolphins. In gratitude for their lives, they draw his sea chariot and obey his commands.

In Greek and Roman art, dolphins appeared on mosaics (for example, the dolphin mosaic from 'The House of Tridents' in Delos) and in sculptures, many of which were inspired by the tales of friendship between boys and dolphins. The Greek genius for sculpture is most evident in the minting of their coinage, although the best examples of this art were not produced at Athens, but at Syracuse. Dolphins were a favourite motif for ancient coins as they were thought to provide safety for travellers. About 650–500 BC, potters from Athens, like Exekias, began to use a process

of depicting black figures on a red ground. Mythological scenes, like that shown on the Dionysus Cup, were introduced about this time.

BIBLICAL STORIES

Greek and Roman mythology underwent a rapid metamorphosis in the age of Christianity. Previously dolphins had served pagan gods like Apollo and Poseidon, but now they became agents of the one deity. Dolphins saved St Martian, St Basil the Younger and Callistratus from martyrdom, and when the dead body of the martyred St Lucian of

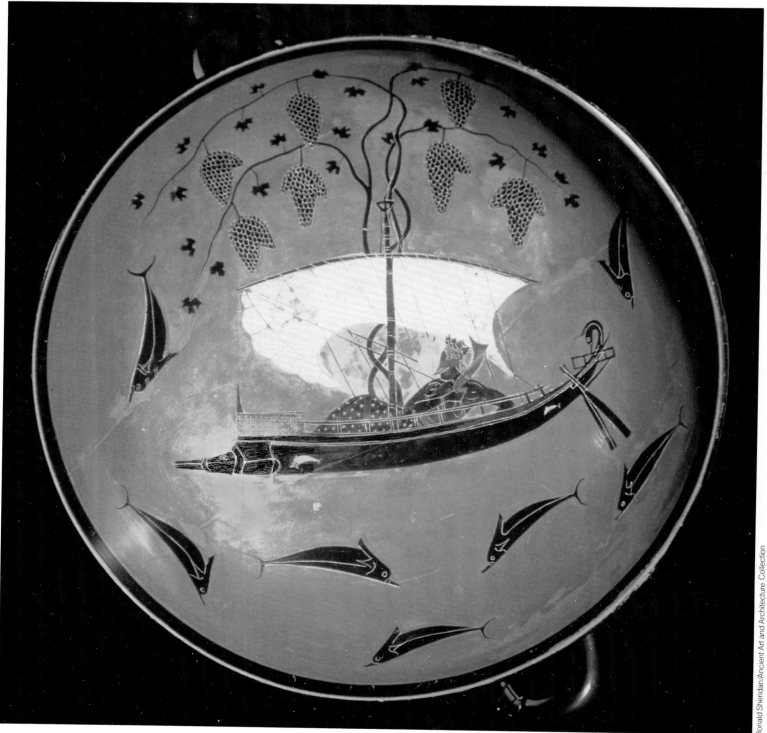

Antioch was thrown into the sea for predators large and small, a dolphin bore his body to Drepanum for a proper burial.

The affinity between man and dolphin is less apparent in stories about whales. The sheer size of the animal instills a sense of life on a huge scale. Its enormous size suggests a terrifying monster ready to prey on man. This is apparent in many of the references that appear in the Bible. Job, for example, describes Leviathan:

▲ This depiction of Jonah and the whale, is from a woodcut, 1493. A naked Jonah is emerging from the whale's mouth, beseeching deliverance. The city of Nineveh is in the background but it is the huge whale, with its scaly skin, that dominates the scene. Medieval artists frequently portrayed dolphins and whales with scales.

Ronald Sheridan/Ancient Art and Architecture Collection

Canst thou draw out leviathan with an hook? . . .
I will not conceal his parts, nor his power,
*   nor his comely proportion . . .*
Who can open the doors of his face?
*   his teeth are terrible round about.*
His scales are his pride, shut up together as with a close seal.
One is so near to another, that no air can come between them.
They are joined one to another, they stick together,
*   that they cannot be sundered.*
By his neesings a light doth shine, and his eyes are like
*   the eyelids of the morning.*
Out of his mouth go burning lamps, and sparks of fire leap out.
Out of his nostrils goeth smoke, as out of a seething pot or caldron.
His breath kindleth coals, and a flame goeth out of his mouth.
In his neck remaineth strength, and sorrow is turned to joy
*   before him.*
The flakes of his flesh are joined together: they are firm in
*   themselves; they cannot be moved.*
His heart is as firm as a stone; yea, as hard as a piece
*   of the nether millstone.*
When he raiseth up himself, the mighty are afraid:
by reason of breakings they purify themselves.
The sword of him that layeth at him cannot hold: the spear,
*   the dart, nor the habergeon.*
He esteemeth iron as straw, and brass as rotten wood.
The arrow cannot make him flee: slingstones are turned with him
*   into stubble. Darts are counted as stubble:*
*   he laugheth at the shaking of a spear . . .*
He maketh the deep to boil like a pot:
*   he maketh the sea like a pot of ointment.*
He maketh a path to shine after him; one would think the deep
*   to be hoary.*
Upon earth there is not his like, who is made without fear.
He beholdeth all high things:
*   he is king over all the children of pride.*

From the Book of Job, Ch 41, verses 1-34

The most well-known whale story in the Bible is the story of Jonah. When Jonah disobeyed God's call for him to go to Nineveh to preach against the city's wickedness, a violent storm erupted, which prompted the sailors aboard Jonah's ship to throw him into the sea. A whale swallowed Jonah and he spent three days and nights in its belly. Finally, the whale spat Jonah on

to land and he proceeded quickly to Nineveh as God had told him to do. The sinful Ninevites repented and God spared the city. Jonah, however, who had wanted to see the city ruined, felt angry at this turn of events. He prayed to be allowed to die if his enemies lived, but God responded:

Thou hast had pity on the gourd, for the which thou has not laboured, neither madest it grow; which came up in a night, and perished in a night. And should not I spare Nineveh, that great city, wherein are more than sixscore thousand persons that cannot discern between their right hand and their left hand; and *also* much cattle?

(Job 4,10-11)

In the story of Jonah the image of the whale is an instrument of divine will that vividly conveys God's object lesson in true mercy.

MYTHS AND LEGENDS

In Japanese folklore and mythology, the whale is depicted as the hare in Aesop's fable of the hare and the tortoise. The monster whale boasts that he is the greatest animal in the sea and challenges the slow sea slug to a race. They agree to begin the race in three days. The sea slug asks each of his sea slug friends to travel to a different beach and wait for the whale. The day of the race arrives. The whale surges forward leaving the sea slug to follow slowly in his wake. At the appointed beach the whale calls out 'Sea slug, sea slug where are you?' The waiting

sea slug calls back 'What, whale? Have you only just arrived? The sea slug suggests a second race to another beach. When the whale arrives he calls out 'Sea slug, sea slug where are you?' The waiting sea slug responds 'What, whale? Have you only just arrived?' The race continues with the same result until finally the whale admits defeat.

One of the few stories that depicts whales in a similar way to the dolphin myths of Greece is a tale from Polynesia about Putu (or Tinirau in a similar Maori legend), queen of the island of Nuku Hiva in the Marquesas. Putu rides on the back of the

great sperm whale Tokama (or Tutunui in the Maori tale), while her twin daughters travel astride Tokama's twin sons. The evil Kae arrives from Upolu, 2400 kilometres away, intent on kidnapping and marrying the twin princesses but he is held captive by the islanders. He begs to return to Upolu. Putu's daughters suggest that Tokama take Kae home, rather than risk a ship and crew. As Tokama bears Kae into the harbour of Upolu, the villagers attack the sperm whale viciously with spears and axes. Finally, Kae drives a spear into her skull and she dies, the first whale to

do so by human hand. Tokama's sons return to Nuku Hiva to bear witness to the treachery. Although Putu realises that whales will no longer want to serve humans she asks a final favour of Tokama's sons: to seek revenge for Tokama's death. Putu's twin daughters ride on the backs of Tokama's sons to Upolu, and capture Kae. The priest of Nuku Hiva curses Kae and sacrifices him to the gods. Putu commands the sons of Tokama to take to the open water, away from humans, and the villagers of Nuku Hiva bade the twin sons a sad farewell.

▲ This Japanese print by Ichiyusai Kuniyoshi, c1851, shows a stranded whale. The triptych is entitled *Diagyo kujita no nigiwai* ('Big fishing: crowding round the whale').

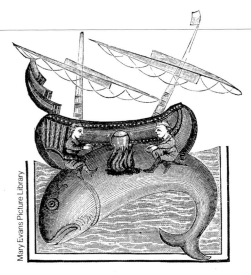

▶ This etching by Richard Furnival entitled *Bestiaire d'Amour* shows medieval navigators mistaking a whale for an island. A number of such stories circulated in medieval times and usually the denouement came when the heat of the fire penetrated the skin of the whale causing it to dive. Only then would the sailors realise the true nature of their 'island'.

Mary Evans Picture Library

In this Polynesian story, the innocence of the animals, the sexual connotation of women on the bull whales, the treachery of man towards these mammals and the notion of whales and humans living in harmony reflect the elements of the Greek dolphin myths.

THE MEDIEVAL AGE

The medieval age heralded a significant shift in the mythology surrounding whales. For the first time they began to appear as animals that were not always what they seemed, for example, the story of St Brendan, the Benedictine monk who left his native Ireland in 565 AD to find the Promised Land

MOBY DICK

by HERMAN MELVILLE

OBY DICK is a classic work written in the nineteenth century. It is the story of Captain Ahab's revenge against the white whale that had brutally mutilated him, causing his severed leg to be replaced by a gleaming ivory jaw. The book is based on the author's personal experiences of whaling aboard the sperm-whaler *Acushnet,* which set sail for the Atlantic in 1841. Ten years later New York-born Melville published *Moby Dick.* It was poorly received by the critics, and it was not until Melville's death in 1891 that interest in the book was renewed. It soon became the focus of considerable scholarly and literary criticsm.

The story of *Moby Dick* opens with the now-famous words 'Call me Ishmael', a Biblical reference (one of many that abound in the book) to Abraham's son by a slave woman. Ishmael becomes the unwanted wanderer when Abraham's wife Sarah produces a son and drives out Ishmael and his mother to prevent them from claiming the inheritance.

In *Moby Dick,* the young man Ishmael is attracted by 'a portentous and mysterious monster', the whale, and by a desire to see 'the wild and distant seas where he rolled his island bulk'. He decides to join the whaler *Pequod,* which on a cold Christmas Day 'blindly plunged like fate into the lone Atlantic'. On board the *Pequod* are Captain Boomer and three officers: Starbuck, the God-fearing, prudent Quaker; Stubb; and Flask. The three harpooners on board are all pagans: Queequeg, a tattooed Maori; Tashtego, a Gay Head Indian; and Daggoo, an African. The rest of the crew consists of what Ishmael calls 'isolatoes', loners and misfits like himself. They learn later that, as part of his plan for revenge, Ahab has secreted in his cabin an additional crew of pagans headed by Fedallah.

The novel reaches its climax when the white whale is finally sighted. Starbuck, the Christian among pagans, tries to dissuade Ahab from his quest for vengeance but Ahab refuses. When the glow of St Elmo's fire lights up the mast in a typhoon, a sign that death is near, Ahab ignores the omen. The chase begins. Armed with a specially-fashioned harpoon, edged with his own razors, Ahab battles with Moby Dick for three days. Moby Dick, his

huge body writhing from embedded harpoons, rams the lowered boats of the *Pequod* with his head. The foaming sea is a confused mass of half-drowned sailors, tangled lines and sinking boats. On the third day the whale sounds, rises from the sea and smashes into the bow of the *Pequod* itself. Ahab, inflamed with vengeance, harpoons an iron into Moby Dick but as the monster threshes to his death, Ahab becomes entangled in a line and is sucked into the sea and dies. Only Ishmael survives.

Moby Dick contains a plethora of allusions and symbols, conveyed superbly in eloquent language, ominous portents and brooding reflections. Critics have considered their significance at great length. One concludes that *Moby Dick* reflects the Nordic consciousness of the endless struggle against the elements. Others have argued that the whale is a symbol of vested privilege, which impedes the spirit of man; or that Ahab is doomed because he is guilty of the Christian sin of pride; or, according to Freudian psychoanalysis, Ahab is the id, Moby Dick the ego, and the upright Starbuck the super-ego, and, when Ahab dies by the line attached to Moby Dick, it is a symbol of the umbilical cord, or of Melville's submission to parental conscience.

Yet Melville did not set out to write an allegorical novel as some might suggest. He described his work in a letter to his English publisher as 'a romance of adventure based on certain wild legends of the Southern Sperm Whale Fisheries, and illustrated by the author's personal experiences of two years or more, as a harpooner'. There is nothing to suggest that Melville had a symbolical plan in mind rather, as Robert McNally sums it up in *So Remorseless a Havoc,* 'he worked with his meanings and symbols as they revealed themselves in the course of the writing. Criticism assumes deductive art; Melville wrote *Moby Dick* inductively'.

The writers D. H. Lawrence and E. M. Forster perhaps have come the closest to understanding what *Moby Dick* is about. D. H. Lawrence wrote an essay about Melville in his *Studies in Classic American Literature.* He notes that 'of course [Moby Dick] is a symbol' but poses the question 'Of What?' Lawrence doubts that even Melville knew exactly, but goes on 'That's the of the Saints. St Brendan put ashore to say Mass on what he thought was an island but in reality was a whale. God transforms the whale into a 'real' island, named St Brendan's Island. Such was the credibility and superstition of people at the time that explorers searched for the Atlantic 'island' as late as the mid-eighteenth century.

Folktales about whales began to disappear around the fifteenth century, with the rise of commercial whaling. People began to perceive whales in terms of their income-producing capacity rather than as powerful creatures of the sea. Yet, it is remarkable that given the huge whaling industry that had developed by the nineteenth century, more writing about whales did not appear in contemporary novels by authors such as Alexander Dumas and W. H. G. Kingston. One of the few novelists who did write about whales was London-born Frank Bullen. *The Cruise of the Cachalot* is an account of a voyage in which Bullen vividly recalls the customs and dangers of hunting sperm whales. In the 17 years before his death, Bullen wrote 36 books, mostly based on his experiences as a young man on a whaling vessel.

Perhaps the greatest, and certainly the most well-known novel about whales, is Herman Melville's *Moby Dick*.

▲ This eighteenth-century Chinese porcelain dish for the European export market shows a whale hunt amid the ice floes of the Arctic.

best of it. He is warm-blooded, he is loveable. He is lonely Leviathan, not a Hobbes sort. Or is he?' On Melville, Lawrence writes that he was

> a deep, great artist, even if he was rather a sententious man. He was a real American in that he always felt his audience in front of him. But when he ceases to be American, when he forgets all audience, and gives us his sheer apprehension of the world, then he is wonderful, his book commands a stillness in the soul, an awe. (Lawrence 1924,146)

It was this 'awe in the soul' that led Lawrence to conclude that Moby Dick is the 'deepest blood-being of the white race, he is our deepest blood-nature'.

> And he is hunted, hunted, hunted by the maniacal fanaticism of our white mental consciousness. We want to hunt him down . . . And in this maniacal conscious hunt of ourselves we get dark races and pale to help us, red, yellow, and black, east and west, Quaker and fire-worshipper, we get them all to help us in this ghastly maniacal hunt which is our doom and our suicide.

In *Aspects of a Novel*, E. M. Forster argues that both Melville and Lawrence are what he calls 'prophetic novelists'. Their novels reach back to universal themes, which strike deep and often disturbing chords and give us 'the sensation of a song or of sound'. Thus for Forster 'the essential in *Moby Dick*, its prophetic song, flows athwart the action and the surface morality like an undercurrent'.

The mystery of *Moby Dick* lies in its transcendant glory, the majesty of the sea at once hated and loved and, above all, in the mystery that lay within Moby Dick. As Melville movingly writes:

> For that strange spectacle observable in all Sperm Whales dying — the turning sunwards of the head, and so expiring — that strange spectacle, beheld of such a placid evening, somehow to Ahab conveyed a wondrousness unknown before. He turns and turns him to it — how slowly, but how steadfastly, his homage-rendering and invoking brow, with his last dying motions. He too worships fire; most faithful, broad, baronial vassal of the sun!

▲ Rowland Hilder captured the terrible beauty of Melville's story in his illustrations, for many of the most moving scenes in *Moby Dick* are set on the sunlit ocean. Here the *Pequod* sails to where Daggoo is about to harpoon a sperm whale.

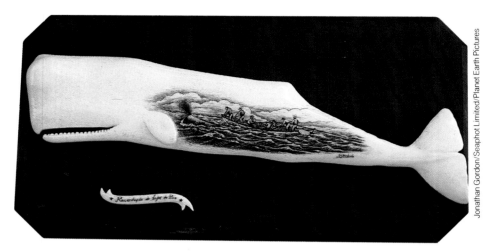

▲ Using a jack knife or a box of 'dentistical-looking implements', sailors created objects of startling beauty from sperm whale teeth and bones. This scene of open-boat whaling in the Azores would have been familiar to Herman Melville.

Jonathan Gordon/Seaphot Limited/Planet Earth Pictures

SCRIMSHAW

SIR RICHARD HARRISON FRS

In *Moby Dick* (1851), Herman Melville described the 'lively sketches of whales and whaling-scenes, graven by the fishermen themselves on sperm whale teeth, or ladies' busks wrought out of the right whale-bone, and other skrimshander articles, as the whalemen call the numerous little ingenious contrivances they elaborately carve out of the rough material in their hours of ocean leisure.'

Leisure is hardly the right word for the monotonous idleness and inactivity faced by the crews of whale ships. Whaling ships' crews were much larger than those of merchant ships of similar size; all four or five whale catchers needed to be manned and the mother ship had to be worked when the chase was on and the catchers were away. So there were many idle hands when the ship was cruising to the whaling grounds, when it was becalmed or halted by foggy weather. Days, weeks, even months could go by with nothing to do . . . and some trips could last four years!

Whalers turned to their own craft skills to occupy their minds and their fingers. Melville continued: 'Some of them have little boxes of dentistical-looking implements, specially intended for the skrimshandering business. But, in general, they toil with their jack-knives alone; and, with that almost omnipotent tool of the sailor, they will turn you out anything you please . . .'

It might have been a Mr Scrimshaw who gave his name to the art; it would have been a fine name for a scrimping second mate, for it was he who usually doled out the raw material on board ship. Or the term might have been one of derision by the 'real' sailors, who navigated whale ships far into the southern ocean — and often sailed them safely home — for the idle 'scrimshankers' who did nothing until a whale was sighted.

The products were decorative, sometimes artistic, and often practical, and were made from whale teeth and bones

distributed by the second mate as occupational therapy. Wood, shells and metal — even stones — were also worked, carved and etched. Designs tended to be nautical, patriotic or jingoistic; many represented the chase and the kill or the hazards and dangers of whaling. Also common were sea monsters, mermaids, seals, seahorses, whales, dolphins and porpoises.

Some were complicated traceries depicting lace, or intricate geometrical figures; another group was sentimental, affectionate, poetic or, occasionally, mildly erotic.

Although some designs clearly had a particular person in mind and sent loving thoughts embellished with hearts and pretty flowers to a sweetheart, there was occasionally a slight doubt about her devotion . . . 'This my love I do intend, for you to wear and not to lend'. Few were initialled or signed by their makers; perhaps they were never too sure about their sweethearts' faithfulness . . . or of their own chances of a safe return home. Some sperm whale teeth bore a demure Victorian lady on one side and a grass-skirted maiden on the other, perhaps expressing the hope that wives and girlfriends might never meet. I have a tooth etched with a scene of a whaling disaster with the inscription 'The Great Whaler Claims All'.

The technique was fairly simple, but in a sailing ship with no lathes or electrical machinery, a lot of elbow grease was needed. The tooth or piece of bone had to be cleaned, prepared and polished to perfection. It was then engraved, using a jack-knife, a sail needle or a carefully filed nail, fitted into a handle. The etchings were often freehand drawings, but could be made by pasting pictures from naval annuals and popular magazines on the tooth or bone, then cutting through the paper to obtain an outline. The engraved lines were filled with lamp black and other colouring materials, and burnished with wood ashes or a substitute polish.

Other objects classified as scrimshaw were made from a

Hull Fisheries Museum

▲ Scrimshaw for personal use or for gifts to wives and sweethearts were the result of patient work and skills born of whaling voyages that could last for four years. Sometimes articles were made for sale back in port.

whale's hard lower jawbone, for example, a corrugated wheel set in a decorated handle, called a jagger, used for crimping the edges of pastries or pies.

The most skilled workers (or the most patient) made whale jawbones into splendidly ornamented snuffboxes for men and workboxes for women. Carved and decorated slats were made into front 'busks' for ladies' corsets, and were often inscribed with dedications to the future wearer. Napkin-rings, bodkins, thimbles, knitting needles, buttons, brooches, walking-sticks, sword-sticks, handles for riding crops and toothbrushes were other popular products. Skilled men also made 'swifts', adjustable frameworks on which silk or yarn could be wound; some were so well made they were still in daily use many years after their maker had died.

Some scrimshaw dates from the late eighteenth century, but most was made between about 1830 and 1860. Since then, craftsmen, in many countries, sometimes connected with the whaling industry, or in the back rooms of shops where sperm whale teeth are available, have carried on the tradition. It is virtually impossible to ascribe any particular scrimshaw item to a known 'artist' or date of manufacture, and sometimes only an expert can tell if the object is made from tooth or bone.

Most old scrimshaw now resides in museums, but should you find any in attics, be careful. Recent scrimshaw is covered by the Convention on International Trade in Endangered Species of Wild Fauna and Flora (CITES) and cannot, since 1976, be imported or sold on the open market in the countries that are party to the Convention, unless the item can be proved to have been obtained or made before the Convention came into force . . . and that can be *very* difficult. This is not some meddlesome piece of bureaucracy designed to restrict the taking of rare and protected animals whose parts or products are valuable, it has probably done more than any other legislation to save endangered species.

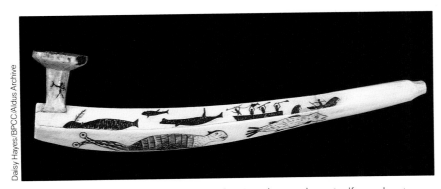

Daisy Hayes/BPCC/Aldus Archive

▲ Although the origin of the word 'scrimshaw' is unknown, the art itself was almost certainly learned from the Inuit or Eskimo whale hunters who first encountered, and traded with, European whalers in Greenland during the sixteenth and seventeenth centuries. This ivory pipe has a scrimshaw decoration of Eskimo whaling scenes.

▲▶ French artist Jean-Luc Bozzoli sees a synthesis of human aspirations, the mathematics of the universe and the grace of dolphins. He describes his art: 'Have you ever gone inside a flower or imagined yourself in crystal-like oceanic waters? Moving through the splendours of the planet, Nature's geometry connects us with universal patterns . . . I step into this dance . . . and build gateways to dreamtime . . . to a place where my heart becomes magic.'

Jean- Luc Bozzoli/Ocean Bozzoli Productions

HISTORY OF WHALING

SIR RICHARD HARRISON

Whales have been hunted since before the beginning of history. Our Stone Age ancestors, and their Bronze Age successors on Orkney, off Scotland, used whale bones as rafters for their dwellings. Neolithic people on the coast of Denmark were mostly shellfish eaters, but whale bones have been found in their immense kitchen middens. The occasional stranding of a large whale would have provided primitive peoples with an unexpected food source and many other welcome products.

Pliny the Elder (24 –79 AD), a famous collector of rumours and tall stories, reported accounts of dolphins that were 'enamoured of little boys'. Pliny witnessed the attack launched by Emperor Claudius and his Praetorian guards on an orca in the bay at Ostia, but the encounter was more of a sporting event than the start of commercial whaling. For many hundreds of years after this incident there is no written record of whaling activities.

▼ Relatively poor soil encouraged the Stone Age inhabitants of northern Europe to turn to the sea for food. This Neolithic rock carving from Skegerveien, Norway, demonstrates the importance of the occasional stranded whale as a source of protein.

University Museum of National Antiquities, Oslo, Norway

The Inuit (Eskimo) people of Greenland and arctic Asia and America hunted marine mammals once they learned how to make a harpoon that could be recovered if it missed its target. Single and double cockpit kayaks were used to hunt seals and narwhals, using harpoons fitted with floats and drogues. Hunting of bowhead whales was more hazardous and required a team effort with a larger, skin-covered whaleboat, the umiak, manned by a crew enlisted or bribed by an acknowledged leader: temporary wife exchange between the leader and a crew member often helped cement the hunting relationship.

Primitive whaling elsewhere involved men in rowing boats herding small whales, then driving them ashore. Long-finned pilot whales in particular were slaughtered in shallow waters or after being hauled ashore. This technique may have been practised in Japan, for example, as early as the tenth century; it was also used in Orkney and Shetland but has long been abandoned. In the Faroes, pilot whales have been driven ashore and killed over many centuries; there are records dating from 1584 showing that catches ranged from about 300 to 1700 each year.

The catching of large whales as a regular industry demands considerable skill, organisation and equipment. It is thought to have been first practised by the Basques of northern Spain, who were catching northern right whales in the Bay of Biscay as early as the twelfth century. Whales prefer deep water, and there is a tongue of very deep water that extends close to the shores of the Basque country at the western end of the Pyrenees. Fishermen used to set out in boats from the shore to attack the whales, but later took to larger ships and by the sixteenth century had ventured into the western North Atlantic as far as Newfoundland.

Watchtowers gave early warning of whales and men were ready to launch boats immediately. Many towns on the Basque coast have a whale in their coats of arms: royal personages of the thirteenth century gave grants to coastal villages to encourage whaling. In return the king could claim a slice of meat extending from head to tail, or even the whole of the first whale caught — though he often gave most of his 'perk' back to the people as a public relations gesture.

Around 1250, a Norwegian work called *Kongespeil*, an account of the whales off Iceland, gave the first description of the differences between local species. This work is of particular interest in that it ascribed good and bad attributes to the various whale species. Some were thought to be ferocious monsters that hunted and sank ships. These were evil whales, and longed to consume human flesh: 'never mention them by name when you are at sea, or . . . years later, when you sail again a whale will get you'. There were good whales too; fin whales 'will protect you but do not throw stones at them, or they will become evil'. These beliefs persisted late into the nineteenth century, and perhaps illustrate our deepest feelings about the 'moral' qualities of animals.

Nothing of real importance comes down to us about whaling during the Middle Ages. The learned scholars repeated what the ancients had claimed; indeed, it was close to blasphemy to question Aristotle and Pliny, and almost anything that seemed new was entirely anecdotal. In illustrations, whales were given chimneys for nostrils, tusks and beards and bushy eyebrows, and were shown devouring ships and their crews. The whales in Basque fishermen's home waters became scarcer as they were exploited. The population may never have been large, but by the middle of the seventeenth century Basque sailors had begun to hunt whales in Newfoundland waters. Their long voyages in pursuit of the whale were noted by others (who also had considerable maritime experience) interested in harvesting rewards from the sea. In 1578 a Bristol adventurer found French, British, Portuguese and Spanish ships visiting Newfoundland to fish for cod; but the Spanish were also after whales.

The discovery of the Davis Straits in 1585 by English Captain John Davis in the barque

▲ The Inuit or Eskimo people of arctic lands made use of almost every part of a stranded or harpooned whale: meat, blubber for lamp oil, sinews, skin and bone for kayak building, and air-filled intestines for harpoon floats.

◄ Knowledge of whales languished for a thousand years after Aristotle and Pliny. This woodcut by Conrad Gesner, from *Historia Animalium*, first published in 1551–58, shows a hazy appreciation of the size and power, if not the anatomy and behaviour, of a whale.

Shelburne Museum, courtesy American Heritage/BPCC/Aldus Archives

▲ *Capture of a Sperm Whale,* an early nineteenth-century American painting, is alive with the drama and the immediate peril of open-boat whaling. An injured and enraged sperm whale or cachalot could easily smash a small whaling boat to matchwood with a blow from its flukes.

Mary Evans Picture Library

▲ This eighteenth-century Dutch tryworks fouled the air with smoke and the stench of blubber being rendered into oil, but shore-based tryworks offered far greater efficiency and safety than the same operations carried out at sea.

Sunshine, and the rediscovery of Bear Island and Spitzbergen (an archipelago 930 kilometres north of Tromso in Norway, and also known as Svalbard, which means Cold Coast) in 1596 by the Dutch explorer William Barents, at once attracted the Basque whalers. They were soon followed by Dutch and English sailors with the scent of whale oil in their nostrils. The Muscovy Company of English adventurers, who had earlier been encouraged by Queen Elizabeth I to trade with Russia, sent out the first whaling enterprise from England in 1610 to Spitzbergen.

It was a profitable voyage. In the following year six veteran Basque harpooners were engaged to go with the two larger company ships to act as instructors on whaling. That same year other interested parties joined the hunt; French, Dutch, Danish, Norwegian, German and Portuguese whalers, and, of course, the Basques, who seemed prepared to help others (especially the Dutch) for a fee. Rivalry for the spoils intensified. The English claimed sovereign rights and prepared to fight. Well-armed Muscovy Company ships tried to drive away interlopers, even those from the English ports of Hull and Yarmouth. Quarrels over whaling rights resulted in divisions of the coast, and the English wasted much time trying to exert their alleged authority. It was the Dutch who gained supremacy by bringing in more ships and more men.

The cities of Amsterdam, Flushing, Middleburg and others in the Low Countries contributed to the establishment of a veritable whaling town on Spitzbergen (called Smeerenburg, or 'Blubber Town') by sending out a shipload of building materials in 1622. This coped with the housing problems of all employed in the whale business, namely 'men busy at the oil cookeries, besides shopkeepers, vintners, tobacconists, bakers and all kinds of artisans', and the shore crews. On one occasion one such Dutch 'barn' (or 'tent', as it was called in those days) provided winter protection to a crew of the Muscovy Company that had been separated from its ship.

At the height of activity at Spitzbergen the Dutch claimed to have 300 ships in the region and to have employed 18 000 men. The attraction for some kinds of men to go whaling was inevitable at the time; there was, potentially, a fortune to be made from whaling. The work was hard, but only for short periods when catches were made and cutting-up took place. This could be done on shore at 'Blubber Town' or at some other shore station, until it was realised that middlemen could also be cut out by the simple method of taking the raw blubber back home and boiling it down at home base.

The catching of northern right whales increased with such international activity, so attention moved to the Greenland right whale or bowhead. This little-known whale, by swimming in coastal waters, became vulnerable to hunting. Both species were reduced by Spitzbergen whalers to a tiny remnant of their original populations, and seemed in danger of extinction.

New catching endeavours were established in the waters off Greenland and in the Davis Straits. The Dutch appeared in 1719 and the English in 1725; the Dutch were dominant for much of the eighteenth century, but suffered from the predatory activities of French and English privateers. English whalers were encouraged by a government bounty which was also paid to the colonists, and helped stimulate the development of American whaling.

Political events — namely the American War of Independence (1775–83), then the French Revolution, with the outbreak of a virtual world war from 1793 — were now having effects across the world. The seas became increasingly the possessions of the dominant warring nations. France and Britain forced the Dutch out of the whaling business, and by 1798 Dutch whaling interests in the north Atlantic had been destroyed.

Meanwhile, a new interest in whaling had been generated in Nantucket and Long Island from as early as 1644, when colonists became aware of the value of drift whales cast ashore. In 1690, American whaling had its humble beginnings in shore-based boats. By 1700 matters were well organised, with watchtowers erected along the shore from which lookouts could spot the numerous right whales in the vicinity. This practice continued until about 1712, when 'an accident of the weather' caused Mr C. Hussey to be blown far from land and to encounter a school of sperm whales. He killed one, towed it back to port and so established a business that at once brought wealth. There were more sperm whales out there in the ocean, but to the 'southward', and larger ships and crews were needed to hunt them.

Trading jealousy and general disputation about whaling rights between the neighbouring settlements were made worse by the imposition of taxes and regulations from England, but by 1715, six Nantucket sloops were busy whaling, away at

sea for about six weeks and returning with a valuable catch. Right whales began to grow scarce near the shore; another reason for venturing farther out into the 'deep'. Whalers also turned their attention to humpback whales, slow swimmers that passed close to the eastern coast of North America during their annual migrations.

By the 1730s many more Nantucket whalers were in operation, helped by the bounty from England. Vessels became larger and voyages much longer, to the Equator and even beyond. Many ports on the east coast of America had become well known for their early whaling activities. Besides Nantucket, Bedford (later New Bedford) was a leading centre, along with Martha's Vineyard, Cape Cod, Sag Harbor, Salem, New Haven and Providence. Many of these ports still retain evidence of their whaling past in churchyards and local museums.

A technological advance in the 1760s was the installation of tryworks — brick ovens in which blubber was rendered into oil — on the decks of the whaling ship. This was clearly a fire hazard, but few of the wooden ships seem to have been lost and it meant long voyages could be made southward into the deep. It also opened up whaling into warmer climates, since tryworks on board removed the need for the cooling of a dead whale which occurred quite naturally in cold northern waters.

The American whaling industry declined during the early part of the nineteenth century, but offshore and distant pelagic hunting increased and the sperm whale began to be exploited, mainly to meet the increasing demand for lamp oil and

▼ Its dying breaths tinged with blood, a victim of the nineteenth-century South Seas whale fishery is shadowed by a whaleboat. In the background, the tryworks on an early version of the factory ship converts another whale into oil and corset stays.

Ann Ronan Picture Library

▶ *A Whale Brought Alongside a Ship,* published around 1813, illustrates the centuries-old technique of flensing or cutting up a whale that has been lashed to the whaleship, but conveys nothing of the dangers of working in a heavy sea, or of the filth and discomfort of a whaler's working life.

Coo-ee Historical Picture Library

AFTER THE HARPOON HAD STRUCK

In the old whaling days a dead whale was towed back by a catcher to the whaleship and secured alongside at head and tail, with a line through a flipper to haul it up high in the water. A ship's boat or two then took up position beside the whale and the harpooners and other crew members started to 'flense' the corpse. They fitted metal spurs to their seaboots to grip the whale surface and, armed with long-handled, keenly sharpened 'spades', cut the blubber into long strips. At the start of each strip a hole was cut for a rope, which was fastened in with a toggle and then led through a heavy tackle fixed to the mast. Men pulled on the ropes to peel away strips of blubber from the body. These 'blanket' pieces were cut up into smaller chunks in a process called 'making off'. The skin was stripped from the outside and the unwanted fibrous 'kreng' from the inside was removed, and after more chopping the small pieces of blubber were sent down below deck to be put into casks under the supervisory eye of the 'skee-man'. Much continual stowing and restowing of empty and full casks made activity in the hold hard work, and if it was not done properly a cask might explode as the 'kreng' decomposed and gave off gases.

When the head was reached, the whalebone was hacked out from each side and hauled on the deck. What was left of the carcase was abandoned to the sea as 'kreng', to be recycled by sharks and any other animals capable of taking a bite.

Later techniques differed somewhat according to the species taken and the use of a new modification — a cutting-in stage rigged over the side of the whaleship with a handrail to give support to those plying the cutting-in spades. In whaleships equipped with try-works fitted up on deck, the blanket pieces of blubber were further reduced on a mincing-horse with wicked mincing knives and the pieces were forked into the try-pots for rendering into oil. Much care was taken to ensure that the fires lit below the pots did not set the wooden ship alight, but occasionally such a disaster did occur. Alternative solutions to this fire problem were properly equipped modern factory ships and efficient shore stations.

The floating factory ships were popular for a while. They could take aboard the entire whale and process it completely, either at sea or at a good anchorage. They could arrive laden with supplies at the start of a season and return with a load of oil and other basic whale products. But quarters were cramped, welfare and cleanliness were difficult to maintain and shelter from weather was essential for high efficiency.

Shore stations had obvious advantages — space; plenty of fresh water for making steam to work winches and saws, and for cleansing down; protection from storms; facilities that allowed the processing of a whale carcase to be undertaken at leisure with methodical precision. There was room for the flensing plan on to which the corpse was winched from the sea and secured by a chain. There was also room for boilers, cookers, meat stores, bone lofts, storage tanks, glue pots, workshops, staff houses and recreation huts. All of this made it easier to obtain as much as possible from the whale in the way of marketable products.

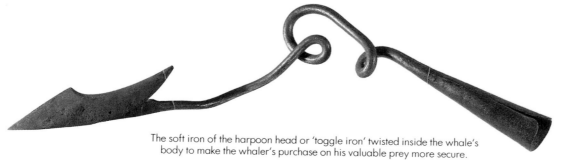

The soft iron of the harpoon head or 'toggle iron' twisted inside the whale's body to make the whaler's purchase on his valuable prey more secure.

The Whaling Museum, New Bedford, Mass.

candles. The southern right whale was also hunted throughout the southern hemisphere; European whalers continued to go north for northern right whales and American whalers from west coast ports penetrated the Pacific Arctic for right whales in 1848. Soon, right whales became so scarce that many of these and other fishing areas were abandoned.

In 1857 there were 429 whalers registered at New Bedford; the American Civil War of 1861–65 restricted American whalers, but a more lethal blow was delivered by the discovery of petroleum in Pennsylvania in 1859. Petroleum replaced whale oil as an illuminant almost immediately, but was slower to replace it as a lubricant.

Modern whaling is often said to have begun in 1864, when the Norwegian whaler Svend Foyn invented a type of harpoon gun that was fired from the bow of a small catcher. It was not just the gun that marked the era of modern whaling since a harpoon gun mounted on a swivel had been in use since 1731 in a boat that carried sails and oars. The gun's recoil was considerable, because of the heavy harpoon, so the boat's sails had to be lowered, its mast unstepped and the final approach to the whale made under oars.

The real advances were the mounting of the gun in the bow of a small (later to be oil-fired) steam catcher, the improved design of the catcher

so that the gunner could move quickly into position by running along a gangway, and the use of explosive harpoon heads. Catchers became higher powered, faster and more manoeuvrable, had a crow's nest for observation, and later were to be guided to whales by planes and helicopters. The lines from the harpoon became longer and stronger, were wound on special engine-driven winches and run over a block hung on special springs, or accumulators, so the struggles of the whale would not break the line. Machinery was installed for inflating the dead whale with air so

◄ The cry of 'Thar she blows!', though now a cliché, was a real enough concern to the wind- and spray-lashed lookout, swaying wildly in his barrel crow's nest. First sight of a whale meant extra income for a vigilant lookout.

▼ Norwegian whaler Svend Foyn spelled the doom of entire species of whales with his development of the grenade harpoon and the bow-mounted cannon. Although the harpooned whale's agony was no less, the harpoon's greater penetrating power dramatically increased the efficiency of whaling in little more than a decade.

Colin Monteath/Hedgehog House New Zealand

Colin Monteath/Hedgehog House, New Zealand

▲ ▶ The 'slum of the Southern Ocean' was the name whalemen gave to the shore stations of South Georgia, a barren sub-Antarctic island east of Cape Horn. Now abandoned, Grytviken was the focus of an appalling slaughter of whale populations for more than half a century.

that the carcass would float: one disadvantage of hunting humpbacks, for example, is that they sink to the sea bottom very quickly after death and only surface again when decomposition is well advanced.

The mother ships became floating oil cookeries by 1903, and by 1924 were fitted with a chute at the stern. The entire whale could be hauled on board and processed in a more orderly and complete manner than when it had been secured alongside and stripped until what remained had to be cast away unused. During the last thirty years of the nineteenth century the main activity had been in the north Atlantic, conducted at first from land stations in northern Norway; catches peaked in 1885.

Then, in 1904, a land station on the sub-antarctic island of South Georgia allowed increasing exploitation of the southern whale population. At this time factory ships were also moored in harbours as near the whaling grounds as was convenient. In the late 1920s factory ships became so large and well fitted that they could operate on the high seas without need of moorings or land stations.

Pelagic whaling reached a peak in 1930–31 with more than thirty factory ships, each 'mother' to eight or more powerful oil-fired catchers, equipped with a gun firing a harpoon which carried a fuse and 400 grams of explosive (the 'granat') at its head. This was specially shaped to avoid a ricochet, but more than one charge often had to be delivered into the dying whale.

Pelagic whaling has never entirely superseded shore-based methods, but it was the main factor responsible for the decline of southern whales until stocks were almost commercially exhausted. It was said in 1912 that, 'Foyn's harpoon gun still pursues its march of death through the oceans . . . with so limited a power of reproduction the stocks of whales will inevitably be reduced'. It was the speed of the catchers and the improved techniques of dealing with the whale after it had been struck that really did the damage: a radio beacon could be planted on the corpse, allowing the catcher to move on to the next kill so the dead whale could be collected later.

Navigational aids had also improved, weather forecasting was more accurate and new technology did much to make whaling both safer and more profitable. Whale products helped the economy of countries such as Norway and Japan, which rely on the sea for much of their protein. Countries short of oil in the eighteenth and nineteenth centuries, like Britain and those of western Europe, also encouraged whaling.

By 1911, the British Museum (Natural History), had called for scientific research into the immense and unrestricted slaughter of Antarctic whales, especially of humpback whales. Protective measures on an international scale were demanded from the Colonial Office; committees sat and reports were published after World War I. In 1924, the *Discovery* began research on whales in the southern oceans and over many years made important contributions to our knowledge of large cetaceans. Whaling crews generally knew far more about what they were doing and what a whale was than their predecessors had a century earlier, but despite all the research, an expert was to write 'As all the world knows, the immense expenditure of time, effort and money was futile, for the information that should have guided the whaling industry was constantly disregarded, the populations of whales were severely reduced and the whaling industry, once profitable in material and money, was ruined'.

In 1929 a Bureau of International Whaling Statistics was established in Norway in an attempt to record details of catches. By 1930–31 there were 41 factory ships with more than 200 catchers, and the total catch was about 38 000 whales. In 1931 the League of Nations drew up a Convention for the Regulation of Whaling, to come into force in 1935. Sadly, nothing happened because not all countries adhered to the regulations. Over-exploitation

caused a marked reduction in catches in 1932 but from 1934 onward, excluding the years of World War II, catches exceeded 30 000 whales a year. At this time Norway was the largest pelagic whaling nation, with the United Kingdom second.

International conferences in 1937–38 and in 1944 and 1945 (the International Council for the Exploration of the Sea), had at last begun to look to the future. For the first time the need to protect young, immature whales was announced, right and grey whales were recognised as being first in need of security, humpback whales were at last considered to be at risk of total extinction, and it was resolved that the activities of factory ships should be limited, a sanctuary should be established in the South Pacific, catching seasons should be shortened and an inspector should be appointed.

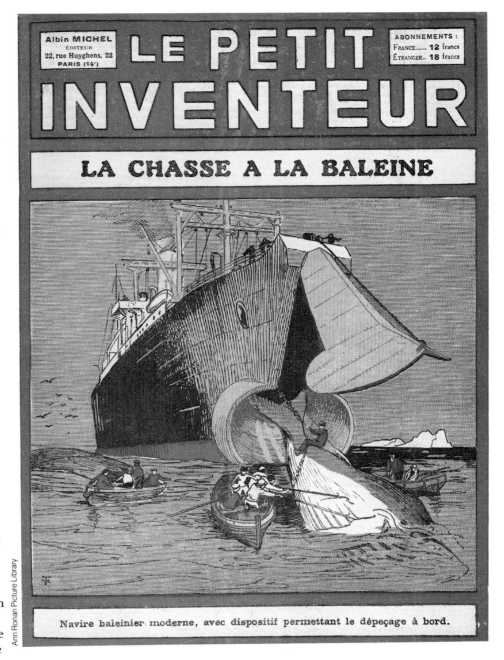

Ann Ronan Picture Library

LE PETIT INVENTEUR

Albin MICHEL
ÉDITEUR
22, rue Huyghens, 22
PARIS (14')

ABONNEMENTS :
FRANCE...... **12** francs
ÉTRANGER.. **18** francs

LA CHASSE A LA BALEINE

Navire baleinier moderne, avec dispositif permettant le dépeçage à bord.

▲ Disturbingly similar to the snout of a bowhead whale, the hinged prow of this Norwegian-owned factory ship took the conversion of whales into margarine and soap to a new height of efficiency, and was suitably feted in the technology-mad 1920s.

▲ Raw material which contributed to a whaling captain's fortune was the layer of insulating blubber, which was rendered into oil for lighting and lubrication.

▶ Shore-based whaling stations made the processing of whales more efficient. Protection from bad weather meant wastage was minimised and more of the carcase could be utilised.

WHALE PRODUCTS

Whale meat was consumed by Eskimos, American Indians, Japanese and natives of the Pacific Islands long before European whaling started. Meat was the main reason for hunting whales, particularly in mountainous countries such as Japan and Norway where a source of protein needed to be found outside territorial boundaries. But even for these earliest whalers the carcase, once stripped, would also have provided hide and bones useful as protective and supporting materials.

Early American colonists needed time to develop their land for agriculture, so they turned to the ocean to supplement their economy. New World whalers started by harvesting the whale crop close to land and then moved further out into the deeps for more. Whales were no longer being killed primarily for food. The northern right whale *(Eubalaena glacialis),* the first species to be hunted, and the bowhead whale *(Balaena mysticetus)* also provided blubber. This could be rendered into oil and the even

more valuable whalebone, which gave stiffening to garments, whips and umbrellas and had a sizeable influence on fashions. For more than a century whale products were used extensively by people of fashion and class — in their dress, to enhance their figures and posture, and in their homes, to provide lighting in the form of whale oil lamps and whale candles.

The captains of the whaleboats made sizeable profits from their long and hazardous voyages, although the real whalers — the crew — did not do so well. One large right whale could provide nearly 2 tonnes of whalebone and 25 tonnes of oil. On a good market the yield would cover all costs and give, in today's money, a profit of many hundreds of thousands of dollars. Only one whale was needed to pay for the venture. It is not surprising, then, that the overexploited right whale soon became rare, and whalers turned their attention to other species.

The really big business in whale products started with the

▲▶ Whalebone processed from baleen plates established fortunes and fashions for much of the nineteenth century. Trimmed of its fibrous 'hair', the whalebone was softened, trimmed and shaped to make corset stays, umbrella ribs and shoehorns.

hunting of sperm whales *(Physeter catodon)* in the early nineteenth century. The most important product was sperm whale oil, used in the manufacture of margarine and soap. A by-product in soap preparation was glycerine, an essential war material when turned into the explosive nitroglycerine. The oil was also used as a drying oil in the making of paints, and in tanning chamois leather.

There was also spermaceti, the oil from the head of the animal. This was used initially for making candles — indeed the definition of a 'standard candle' (the first unit of light used in science) was a pound's weight of candles made from spermaceti that burned at a certain rate. Later it was used in the manufacture of polishes, soaps, crayons and pencils, and in various food coatings. Spermaceti has also been used as a wax base for a wide variety of cosmetics from lipstick, rouge and eyeshadow to cold and cleansing creams, shampoos and antiperspirants. But spermaceti has also been used in some cleansing emulsions and preparations for protecting skin that have undoubtedly been of medical value.

A mixture of sperm whale oil and spermaceti was called sperm oil. At first it was used to make candles. More recently it has been converted to produce germicides, detergents and antifoams. Sulphur can be attached to the oil components to make sulphurised sperm oil, as well as sulphated and sulphited oils (sulpho oils). Sulphurised sperm oil is an excellent antiwear additive in lubricants used under extreme pressure and temperature. It has had a high value in wartime. Sulpho oils are used to finish leathers and as lubricants in metal cutting and wiredrawing processes, where they have been invaluable. In recent years substances to replace sperm oil have been introduced with some success. Some industrial firms have tried to avoid sperm oil, but often it is difficult for them to ascertain whether is has been included in a particular product.

Residues left after the extraction of oils and wax are high in protein content and can be turned into nutritious meat stock and soup cubes, which might become valuable stock feeds for animals were it not for the high mercury content. Sperm whale meat is not delicious, and cannot be made so by any cook, but people in some places chew away on sperm whale steaks for lack of anything better. The belly blubber is a delicacy in Iceland,

The Whaling Museum, New Bedford, Mass.

▲ For much of commercial whaling's long history, sperm whale oil was the single most important product. Oil from sperm whales was used for lighting, and in soap and paint manufacture. Sperm whale oil was without peer for candlemaking, the lubrication of high-speed machinery and as a base for cosmetics.

and raw blubber is served in Japan with pungent sauces.

The teeth and the bones were carved and decorated to make snuffboxes, jewel cases, buttons, chessmen, cuff links, brooches and other fancy articles, known as scrimshaw. Tendons were used for stringing tennis racquets and as 'catgut' for surgical purposes. Whalebone continued to be used to stiffen top boots, guardsmen's busbies and fishing rods, and to make brushes of many types. Whale skin was turned into bootlaces, shoe leather, slippers and coverings for cases, radios, bicycle saddles and so on. Skeletal remains were made into fertiliser and the connective tissue was rendered into glue or into gelatine for use in the photographic and food industries. In addition to the use of by-products in food manufacture, vitamins were obtained from whale livers; and hormone preparations made from extracts of the endocrine organs.

Finally, there was one interesting sperm whale product that could be obtained without killing, or even encountering, the animal. Ambergris (grey amber) is a wax-like, flexible substance with an ashy or brown colour, found floating in tropical seas or sometimes washed ashore; it originates in the intestines of sperm whales. Bits of the harder tissues from cuttlefish have been found in ambergris and experts think that it is formed in the intestine by a pathological process involving faeces. It smells of musk; Alexander Pope observed that 'a little whiff of it . . . is very agreeable'. It was used in love-philtres as an aphrodisiac, in cooking and then as a fixative in high-quality perfumes and soaps. It was once worth its weight in gold, but there are now many synthetic substitutes, so it is no longer as valuable or as sought after.

In recent years there has been a great decline in the use of whale products for three reasons — the moratorium on whaling, acceptable substitutes for most whale oil products, and the prohibition of trade in whale products by an increasing number of countries. Yet there are a few countries, determined to take whales for 'research' purposes that will at the same time export the meat and oil products. There have also been clandestine free whalers who have utilised the market. How many are active now or who plan to become active is not known; the future will depend on the success of the International Whaling Commission in obtaining general agreement on what should happen to all whales.

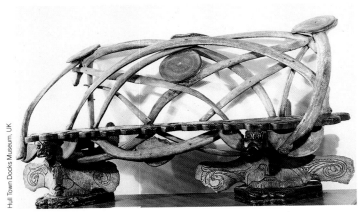

Hull Town Docks Museum, UK

▲ A triumph of ingenuity if not of taste, this nineteenth century love seat is constructed of whale ribs and carved vertebrae. Much 'artistic' use of whale products was of similar questionable quality, though whalemen often produced delicate chessmen or finely etched scrimshaw during their long periods of idleness at sea.

▲ Although it has been criticised by both cetologists and conservationists, the International Whaling Commission was the world's only means of supervising whalers whose declining profits led them to pursue almost any whale of any species in a desperate attempt to cover spiralling costs.

Where was this sanctuary? What could an inspector do in such a huge area of ocean, and without any means of enforcement? It was hoped there would be an overall limit to the total Antarctic catch, and indeed in 1944, because many of the whaling factory ships had been sunk during the war, it was possible to put a realistic ceiling on the total catch. Post-war whaling began in the Antarctic in 1945, initially on a small scale. An effort was made to limit overall catches in terms of 'blue whale units' (1 blue = 2 fin = 2.5 humpbacks = 6 sei, though it was not necessary to take any blue whales at all). Sadly, this scheme indicated the way catches were to go in the future: one stock after another, followed by one species after another, were to be relentlessly exploited.

ironic blow to the efforts of the IWC. In 1946 the average tonnage of factory ships was a little over 13 000; by 1955 the average capacity was some 16 000 tonnes. The number of catchers per factory ship increased from nine to fifteen, and their horsepower by nearly 50 per cent. Although hunting and striking ability had improved with better technology. a limiting factor to increased harvesting (called at one time 'Number of Blue Whale Units per Catcher's Day's Work') was the inability of a factory ship to process more than so many whales during any period of time. Another problem was to get dead whales to the factory ships — while a catcher was acting as buoy-boat, it could not catch another whale, and carcasses had to be processed within 33 hours of death — so there were several practical problems that put a brake on operations. Appalling weather conditions affected more than one season.

After 1945, British participation was reduced and finally ceased in 1965; Norwegian activity has also lessened, but has not ended altogether. It was the Japanese (also with North Pacific activities) and the Russian industries that grew post-World War II, and went on growing into the 1960s. Apart from Antarctic whaling, fair-sized industries were built up in Peru, South Africa, Chile and Australia (much reduced after 1963). Smaller and less regular interests were stationed in Argentina, Brazil, Canada, Denmark, the Faroe Islands, France, Iceland, Newfoundland, New Zealand, Panama, Portugal, Scotland, Spain and the United States.

The total world catch of whalebone whales from 1956 to 1965 amounted to 403 490, and that of sperm whales during the same period to 228 328. Annual catches were greatest for whalebone whales in 1960 and 1961, with more than 40 000 whales each year and more than 29 000 sperm whales were taken in 1964.

Humpback whales had first shown signs of excessive exploitation in 1910, and this species gained some protection in 1946. Blue whales were taken in large numbers from 1925 to 1940, and again in the 1950s, but were protected from 1967. The industry had been affected by a decline in blue whale stocks and turned to fin whales until catches of this species slumped in the 1960s. It was then the turn of sei whale populations to be plundered, until by the early 1970s only the small minke whales were left in any number.

In 1975 the IWC evolved a New Management Policy that divided whales into Protection Stocks, Sustained Management Stocks or Initial Management Stocks. The object was to obtain even greater restriction of quotas, eventually to gain a Maximum Sustainable Yield from any given stock. It was claimed that powerful computers and mathematical models derived from fish population studies gave all the necessary data to ensure successful management. Later, a more severe conservationist attitude was introduced

▲ Despite its lack of enforceable authority over member nations, the IWC (founded in Washington, DC, in November 1946) at least provided a public forum for discussion, international observation of whaling practices, and for attention to the continued 'harvesting' of declining whale stocks.

▶ The rain-washed bones of an antarctic whale, neatly arranged by some forgotten visitor to King George Island, provide an eerie memorial to the thousands of 'units' taken by the Southern Ocean whalers from the late nineteenth century to the early 1960s.

In 1946 there occurred what has been called a creditable act of international statesmanship; the establishment in Washington of the International Whaling Commission (IWC). The IWC was to achieve the maximum sustainable utilisation of whale stocks, and by definition to protect the future of the stocks as a resource. It has met annually since 1949 to assess statistics and to set limits and quotas on catches.

Agreement has been difficult and not always honoured; some countries refused to sign or left the commission later. Most experts feared that even had the IWC quotas been adhered to, there were too many adverse, uncontrollable factors that were to bring about the inevitable. If the IWC is to be accused of doing much too little far too late to prevent the whaling industry destroying whale populations, it must also be asked in its defence what other practical actions were available that would have had the slightest effect. The IWC was given no powers of enforcement whatsoever.

Whaling techniques changed radically from 1950 to 1960, in a series of changes that dealt an

▲ When the International Whaling Commission agreed to demands from scientists and conservationists to restrict the exploitation of cetaceans, small island communities were exempted from the ban because they are dependent on food from the ocean and because their hunting techniques (such as the open-boat whaling practised by sperm-whalers in the central Atlantic Azores) pose no threat to whale populations.

ESTIMATES OF TOTAL POPULATION SIZES

SPECIES	AREA	ORIGINAL[a]	PRESENT
Sperm	Southern Hemisphere	1 250 000	950 000
	Northern Hemisphere	1 150 000	1 000 000
Blue	Southern Hemisphere	220 000	11 000
	Northern Hemisphere	8 000	3 000
Fin	Southern Hemisphere	490 000	100 000
	Northern Hemisphere	58 000	20 000
Sei	Southern Hemisphere	190 000	37 000
	Northern Hemisphere	66 000	17 000
Bryde's	Southern Hemisphere	30 000	30 000
	Northern Hemisphere	60 000	60 000
Minke	Southern Hemisphere	436 000	380 000
	Northern Hemisphere	140 000	125 000
Grey	Southern Hemisphere	—	—
	Northern Hemisphere	20 000 +	18 000
Right	Southern Hemisphere	100 000	3 000
	Northern Hemisphere	—	1 000
Bowhead	Southern Hemisphere	—	—
	Northern Hemisphere	30 000	7 200
Humpback	Southern Hemisphere	100 000	3 000
	Northern Hemisphere	15 000	7 000

(a) 'Original' means the best estimate of the population before intense exploitation began.

Note: Calculation of the numbers of whales around the world have been made by members of the IWC Scientific Committee for many years. Recently, however, doubts have been expressed by some scientists on the precise values and accuracy of these estimates, because of the nature of the data used and their analysis. The following figures are, therefore, given as indications of the orders of magnitude of the stock sizes, based on recent published estimates.

▼ Although some whales that were formerly hunted in great numbers are regaining their population sizes quickly, many others, such as this fin whale being processed at a shore station in Iceland, are still under threat from illegal hunting and ocean pollution.

Rose Bierce, Centre for Environmental Education

with the intention by the IWC that all pelagic whaling should cease, in a kind of moratorium, until it could be shown 'scientifically' that whale stocks had recovered.

A moratorium on factory ship whaling was adopted eventually in 1979. Just how and by whom it would be decided that any stock had recovered — and just who would be allowed to kill the whales in the future — was not made clear. In reality, the concern of the IWC with the regulation of whaling was becoming synonymous with that of conserving all the stocks of whales in the world. An indefinite moratorium on commercial whaling, as advocated by the IWC, came into effect in January 1986. While many countries and their scientific advisers supported a temporary cessation in whaling, some individuals were puzzled about whether the IWC was pursuing a purely conservationist or a more extreme — even emotional — anti-whaling attitude.

In 1987, Norway, Japan, Iceland and South Korea indicated their intention to continue whaling for 'scientific purposes'. This is in fact a loophole in the ban, allowed by the IWC, so that information on reproduction, age distribution and the state of stocks can be obtained. However, the number of fin, sei, and minke whales to be killed by these countries is excessive and unnecessary when other assessment methods of a more observational type are available.

More thought on how to establish the present and future states of the world's stocks of whales is required, and more effective international agreement on what to do about all whales is imperative.

Should commercial whaling begin again, a less cruel way of slaughtering whales must be developed. Technology has done much to remove whales from our oceans, and it is essential that technology should help to end 'the war of the whales' so that whale populations can be sustained to the benefit of both whales and mankind.

▲ At the same time as fuel and labour costs were rising, the value of whale products fell as substitutes were developed. At one time even the bones of whales processed at Port Lockroy, in Antarctica's Graham Land, would have been ground for fertiliser — as whaling's profitability declined, they were left as mute testimony to a dying industry.

WHALES AND DOLPHINS IN CAPTIVITY

VICTOR MANTON

When a child comes up to a window and a dolphin swims down to open its mouth and goggle its eyes at the fascinated child, the reaching out to another species begins.

▼ Early attempts to maintain cetaceans in captivity were hampered by a lack of knowledge of their biology. In the past 20 years, however, we have learned a great deal not only about the healthy maintenance of captive cetaceans, but also about the biology of free-living whales.

Unlike seals and sealions, who haul themselves onto dry land for long periods, whales and dolphins spend all their time in the water, so that few people are able to see them in their natural environment.

For most people it is only possible to encounter these marvellous animals in fairly close and confined conditions. In 1985, one hundred million people visited live marine displays in the USA alone. Audiences of over 1000 at a time watch three orcas (*Orcinus orca*) perform at Sea World, San Diego. It would be impossible for even a tiny fraction of this number of people to go on expeditions to the North Atlantic, for example, to witness the breaching of a humpback whale (*Megaptera novaeangliae*). It is, therefore, important that we maintain captive collections of a representative sample of these superb and uniquely adapted animals.

HISTORY

Records show that, to date, at least 2700 bottlenose dolphins (*Tursiops truncatus*) have been taken into captivity worldwide. Other cetaceans in captivity include 250 pilot whales (genus *Globicephala*), 150 spotted dolphins (genus *Stenella*),120 orcas, (*Orcinus orca*), 100 belukhas (*Delphinapteras leucas*), over 80 harbour porpoises (*Phocoena phocoena*), numerous common dolphins (*Delphinus delphis*), Amazon dolphins (*Inia geoffrensis*), false killer whales (*Pseudorca crassidens*), finless porpoises (*Neophocaena phocoaenoides*) and a few Chinese river dolphins (*Lipotes vexillifer*).

In the 1870s, five belukhas were on display to the public in England, and bottlenose dolphins and harbour porpoises were kept in the Battery Aquarium in New York in 1913. However, the latter were not very popular due to a tendency to exhibit 'overt sexual behaviour' regardless of the age of the audience. In the 1930s, the Aquarium of the Marine Biological Association of the United Kingdom at Plymouth periodically displayed animals rescued from live strandings, but did not

Australian Picture Library/Volvox

◄ Belukhas are hardy animals — the first dolphins on public display were five belukhas shipped to England in the 1870s — and captive belukhas have provided valuable insights into the physiology, behaviour and reproductive biology of a species whose arctic habitat precludes extended field research.

begin to keep animals permanently until about 1962, when two female bottlenose dolphins were obtained.

In 1938, a Hollywood film company, Marine Studios, set up a marine tank in Florida, primarily to shoot underwater footage of dolphins. Finding the dolphins to be a big tourist attraction, a curator

EARLY DEVELOPMENTS IN MARINE MAMMAL FACILITIES

Marineland of Florida

▲ Adolph Frohn, the world's first dolphin trainer, works with Flippy at Marine Studios, Florida in the 1940s.

1938   Marine Studios, St Augustine, Florida, (later called Marineland of Florida) displayed bottlenose dolphins — 27 dolphins were born there between 1939 and 1963.

1954   Marineland, Pallos Verdes, California, opened. Two bottlenose dolphins born at Marine Studios were displayed at the opening.

1955   Miami SeaAquarium displayed bottlenose dolphins.

1956   Fort Worth Zoological Park, Texas, displayed an Amazon dolphin.

1957   Zeedierenpark Harderwijk, The Netherlands, displayed harbour porpoises.

1961   Chicago Zoological Park, Illinois, displayed bottlenose dolphins.

1963   New York Aquarium displayed a belukha.

1965   Zeedierenpark Harderwijk, Barcelona Zoo, Spain, and Duisberg Zoo, West Germany, displayed bottlenose dolphins.

1965   Seattle Aquarium, Washington, displayed an orca called Namu.

1965   Enoshima Aquarium and Marineland, Japan, exhibited bottlenose dolphins and Risso's dolphins (*Grampus griseus*) — both species successfully mating and giving birth to young that survived to adulthood.

1965   Marineland, Pallos Verdes, displayed pilot whales and Pacific white-sided dolphins (*Lagenorhynchus obliquidens*).

1967   Sea World of California, San Diego, displayed Pacific white-sided dolphins and an orca named Shaun (later joined by two more).

1968   Royal Zoological Society of Antwerp, Belgium, displayed bottlenose dolphins and tucuxi (*Sotalia fluviatilis*).

1969   Flamingoland, England, displayed an orca and bottlenose dolphins.

1969   Duisberg Zoo displayed a belukha.

of animals was appointed to train them — an easy task. More importantly, it was the first prolonged observation of dolphins' social life and behaviour. This signalled the beginning of the development of marine mammal facilities all over the world.

A survey in 1976 showed that 365 cetaceans were on display in North America, including 299 bottlenose dolphins, 17 orcas, 10 belukhas, 14 Pacific white-sided dolphins, 12 spotted dolphins, 7 pilot whales, 2 false killer whales and 4 harbour porpoises. This figure had risen to 376 in 1983 and included 304 bottlenose dolphins. By 1984, 1341 marine mammals of 27 species were listed as being exhibited in North America, but this would have included pinnipeds (sealions and seals) as well as cetaceans.

WATER CONTROL

Initially, the techniques of water control, and the feeding and hygiene of cetaceans, owed much to previous experience with seals and sealions, with little appreciation of the differences between the orders. Seals and sealions spend much of their time on land so that accurate minute-by-minute water control is not essential. Moreover, the structure of the skins of these two orders is different. The skin of a cetacean is composed of living nucleated cells, hence long immersion in water of a salinity level less than 1 per cent will cause a patchy necrosis and ulceration. Indeed, after about three weeks of such immersion, 'ballooning' degeneration of epidermal cells would commence. Seals and sealions on the other hand have been kept successfully in fresh water for many years.

A dolphin produces approximately 4 litres of urine and 1.4 kilograms of faeces per day. This equals the load put on an equivalent swimming pool filtration system by up to 70 human swimmers! Excretions by the animal, including skin and food debris, and any foreign objects thrown in by the public or blown in by the wind pollute the water and have to be removed. Since the majority of these objects are organic in origin, under the right temperature conditions, putrefaction will take place and many pathogenic bacteria, fungi and plants will develop.

Oxidation of the potentially noxious substances will convert them to harmless molecules, which may be filtered out. Early filtration systems were designed and installed by swimming pool engineers, who were not accustomed to dealing with the corrosive properties of chlorinated saline solutions nor with the situation where the water was being polluted 24 hours a day. Some of the original marine tanks were unfiltered, requiring the water to be completely replaced every 7–10 days, as is the case with many seal and sealion arrangements. Today, most systems are more adequate and attempts have been made to utilise a chemical biological system that will cope with the

massive load put upon it by cetaceans. Of course, these remarks apply mainly to 'closed systems'. 'Open systems' on the coast or near unlimited supplies of unpolluted water, where the pool water can be refreshed continuously or at least frequently, do not require such costly filtration systems. However, the water must still be monitored constantly.

PUBLIC AWARENESS

Public awareness of any species is a prerequisite for adequate conservation control. In 1954, at the request of the Icelandic government, a group of soldiers armed with rifles and machine guns put to sea and, in one morning, destroyed 100 orcas. Until orcas were kept in captivity where people could learn more about them, they were considered to be undesirable predators and competitors to fishermen. They were shot and maimed indiscriminately. In the early 1960s, the US Federal Department of Fisheries considered mounting machine guns at Seymour Narrows, between Vancouver Island and mainland British Columbia, in order to reduce the numbers of these whales.

However, in 1964–65 the first live orcas were captured and maintained in captivity. This created enormous popular interest and before long, boat trips were taking tourists into the wild to see the orca in its natural habitat. A mood of protection and conservation followed and protective regulations were created in Canada, and in the USA where a Marine Mammal Commission was established. In 1985–86, the number of orcas along the British Columbian coast was apparently stable.

The two live orca exhibits at Sealand in British Columbia and the Aquarium in Vancouver continue to sustain public interest and sympathy for these animals. The successful birth of an orca in Orlando, Florida, suggests that with improved facilities it may be possible to breed these animals, and have a self-sustaining captive population. The maintenance of orcas and for that matter all cetaceans, under optimal captive conditions, is necessary to sustain public awareness of the plight of whales in the wild — an environment where they are continually threatened by some fishermen.

There is also concern over the number of black dolphins (*Cephalorhynchus eutropia*) and Burmeister's porpoises (*Phocoena spinipinnis*) being killed for use as crab bait in Chile. Although this is illegal, between mid-1976 and late 1979, more than 7000 dolphins were caught for this purpose in Chilean waters. In 1980–81, it was estimated that some 204 tonnes of dolphin meat was used for bait. The weight of a dolphin is approximately 40 kilograms, which meant that more than 5000 animals were being killed per year. The official crab bait is mutton, but the cost of obtaining dolphin meat is considerably cheaper.

Marty Synderman

▲ Until 1965, when Namu was introduced to audiences at Seattle Aquarium, orcas were regarded as competitors of commercial fishermen and as unbridled killers of seals and dolphins. Namu's charm and grace soon swayed public opinion in favour of the conservation and further study of this species in its natural habitat.

Randy Wells

▲ All whales have sensitive skins and despite their adaptation to the dangers of marine life, are easily injured. Although captive dolphins rarely suffer wounds as severe as this animal, whose dorsal fin was slashed by a boat's propeller, incompetence or wilfully malicious acts by members of the public can harm or kill captive dolphins.

Ben Cropp

Neither the black dolphin nor the Burmeister's porpoise are common in captivity. By increasing the number in captivity we could increase public awareness, which may eventually put pressure on governments to reduce this unnecessary slaughter.

RESEARCH IN CAPTIVITY

By using cetaceans in captivity, accurate information has been obtained about their breeding behaviour and the reproductive cycle — without which estimates of population dynamics in the wild are very unreliable. Studying whales and dolphins has also made it possible to learn about how their senses work, how they echo-locate, how they dive, and how they integrate with one another.

Critics maintain that normal behaviour cannot be studied in captivity as the animals in the wild are very free-ranging but, in fact, work in the wild appears to indicate that where marked animals have been monitored they often remain within 5 kilometres of the marking site, and, although they can dive to vast depths, they seem to prefer depths of 2–6 metres. Studies made of animals in captivity can produce very detailed data whereas the best information obtainable at sea can only provide

▲ Their playfulness and apparently smiling faces, as well as their willingness to learn new tasks and 'tricks', have made bottlenose dolphins favourites not only with oceanarium audiences but with scientists interested in cetacean biology, behaviour, communication and intelligence.

199

broad outlines of behaviour. It is obviously important for scientific research to have a combination of both. Thus, although erysipelas, for example, has been found to be a disease affecting animals in the wild, it can only be studied and the vaccines developed and monitored successfully in captivity.

As early as 1961, Sealife Park, Oahu, Hawaii, started research into the behaviour of cetaceans, and vocalisation and echolocation are currently being studied at Marineland Africa USA, California. Recent work carried out at the Seven Seas Panorama of Brookfield, Chicago, enabled scientists to identify how dolphins listen to the ultrasonic pulses emitted for echolocation. They found that if the lower jaw of an animal was covered by a soundproof hood, the ability of the animal to distinguish between a ring and a cylinder was no better than that expected by chance. However, if a hood was used that did not cover the lower jaw, the accuracy of responses was in the region of 70 per cent. Although this does not prove that the animal always uses its lower jaw for echolocating, it does show that this animal was able to distinguish between two shapes better with an unobstructed lower jaw.

Most of the work on the echolocation of dolphins has been done in captivity, although recently some comparative work has been done with single animals in the wild. (The experiments in the wild have to be confined to fairly shallow estuaries.) It has been reported that dolphins in captivity become deafened by the sound of their echolocation clicks and a recent comparative study in France has shown that the recording of sound emission from one particular animal in the wild was not as loud as sound emission in captivity. However, in the wild, more efficient use of the band width was made.

The dolphin is rated by many as highly intelligent but it was shown using animals in captivity in Germany, that the Californian sealion was able to select a variety of shapes with 100 per cent accuracy after 60 attempts whereas dolphins only reached 90 per cent accuracy after 120 attempts.

By comparing the behaviour of different mothers with captive-born offspring it is possible to illustrate how individuals vary in their ability to care for their young. The suckling behaviour of newborn animals has also been studied and, with the increasing numbers of young born in captivity, the literature on this subject is now expanding rapidly.

Other interesting experiments carried out with individuals in captivity have been on the differentiation in taste between sour, saline, bitter and sweet substances, and on the sense of smell. Recent research on captive animals has also suggested that dolphins do not dream while asleep — an insight impossible to gain in the wild.

Marineland of Florida

▲ Research experiments on captive dolphins have enabled scientists to solve some of the mysteries of echolocation. Here, hydrophone tape recordings are being made of the sounds — whistles, clicks and jaw clacking — made by 'Dolphin 232'.

► 'Performing' dolphins provide a valuable educational resource, giving thousands of people who would otherwise never see a whale the chance to reach out to another species, to begin to understand the way other animals live and to appreciate the importance of their protection and conservation.

Australian Picture Library

has been observed in the wild. Here an adult tosses a calf into the air by lifting its head suddenly under the calf's body. This could, of course, be a 'punishment' for the calf but illustrates yet another activity regarded by many as only 'captive induced'. Interference with dinghy mooring ropes is a nuisance to those on board but shows the inquisitive nature of these animals, which is often harnessed in captive displays.

PRESENT SITUATION

In 1983, 32 per cent of all captive bottlenose dolphins in the USA were born in captivity compared with only 18 per cent in 1979. This percentage could only be achieved when animals were kept alive to reach their age of sexual maturity. Males become sexually mature at 10–12 years of age and females at 5–12 years of age depending on the origin and upbringing of individuals. From captive work, population dynamics in the wild can be extrapolated. Studies on the rings of dentine laid down in the teeth have shown the maximum recorded age of male bottlenose dolphins to be 25 years, and of females to be 30 years. Details published in 1985 reveal the presence, in captivity, of a 30-year old bottlenose dolphin who was captive born and is now a grandmother.

Some of the original work on releasing animals in the wild has met with problems. There are reports from the USA and from the United Kingdom of animals either soon after release into the wild (or still in captivity) being offered live fish, which they refuse to eat, returning the bait to their trainers in exchange for pieces of dead fish to which they have become accustomed. Also, if the animal encounters a strange school of animals in the area of release immediately outside the captive pen, it will probably return very quickly to captivity. Some individuals may suffer aggressive attacks if they try to join a 'strange school' to which they are not related. A number of individuals in the wild have been monitored and photographed with the teeth marks fresh on their skins. An American survey in 1985 showed that most carcasses washed ashore on the coast of the USA had injuries on them that may or may not have been related to the cause of death, and there are certainly a very high rate of still births and neonatal deaths in the wild. Indeed, it may be that the average mortality rate for cetaceans in the wild, without the pressures of whaling, may exceed 15 per cent.

In addition to the natural hazards facing cetaceans in the wild, humans have unfortunately decided that the oceans, which cover so much of our planet, are ideal dumping grounds for pollutants, and this, of course, can have disastrous effects on marine life. Using heavy metals, such as mercury, as an indicator of this pollution, it was shown in 1970 that cetaceans that had been in

▼▶ Critics of the captivity and public display of dolphins often point to the 'degrading' or 'offensive' nature of the performances they give. However, recent research has shown that many aspects of behaviour once thought restricted to captive animals, for example, 'jumping for joy', or ball tossing, are also common in free-living animals.

Hugh Edwards

Hugh Edwards

CAPTIVE DISPLAYS

Concern has been expressed about the indignity that dolphins allegedly suffer giving 'performances' for the public. Fortunately, these are generally extroverted animals that respond to applause or public enthusiasm. Displays in captivity often simulate displays in the wild, for example, dolphins leaping out of the water or 'spy hopping' with their bodies in a vertical position and their heads above the water. They will 'Medusa toss' — kicking jellyfish out of the water with their tails — much as they would in captivity with a ball. On several occasions 'calf throwing'

Pat Morris/Ardea London Ltd

captivity for a number of years after arriving from the wild with elevated levels of mercury in the blood, showed a decrease in these levels the longer they stayed in captivity, and that this drop in mercury levels has continued up until the present day. It is, therefore, interesting to postulate that if pollution continues, it may be necessary for some of these species to be kept and bred in captivity to provide a nucleus of unpolluted stock for release into fresh water at a much later date.

Marine zoological parks are and can continue to be a bridge between humans and nature. In my opinion we should concentrate on improving this bridge rather than plotting to burn it.

▲ The exigencies of life in captivity inspire some odd friendships among captive cetaceans. An orca and a Pacific white-sided dolphin would be predator and prey in the wild, but in captivity they have become inseparable companions.

HUMAN CONTACT

ROBERT MORRIS

Mankind's preoccupation with cetaceans goes back many thousands of years. Cetaceans have featured in folklore, myths and legends since the earliest period of recorded history. Many of the larger whales live predominantly in the offshore regions of the oceans, and our ancestors had only infrequent contact with them. Some species of dolphins, however, live almost entirely in coastal waters and it is these animals that humans were first able to observe closely.

Since first contact with dolphins, humans have held them in high esteem and there have been many accounts of intimate relationships between humans and these creatures of the sea.

One account of this is given in a letter from Pliny the Younger written around 109 AD. It concerns the friendship between a local peasant boy and a dolphin called Simo. The boy lived in the small town of Hippo on the North African coast of Tunisia and had befriended the dolphin after it had saved him from drowning. The two would regularly play together in the bay, the dolphin often giving the boy rides on its back. The local townsfolk got to hear of the dolphin and would gather to watch them at their games. Gradually the fame of the dolphin spread until people from miles around started coming to see the dolphin. The town became very crowded and many of the local tradespeople realised that they could make a lot of money from the new visitors. As the numbers of visitors grew, the facilities of the town could no longer cope with the crowds and there were serious shortages of accommodation, toilets, water and food. Many arguments broke out among the locals, causing unpleasant divisions in the community. Eventually the town elders realised that something had to be done in order to save the stability of their community: they killed the dolphin.

▲ With the help of more sophisticated diving equipment, today's skindiver can observe more easily the world of the dolphin.

► Although orcas have on rare occasions attacked and damaged sailing boats, their reputation as a 'killer whale' comes not from attacking or killing humans but other cetaceans.

This tale may sound fanciful, but it is more than plausible; there have been many other accounts during the intervening centuries of similar friendships. The sad tale of Simo graphically illustrates the dangers faced by dolphins when they entrust their friendship to us.

Dolphins are found either living with others of their kind in social groups or as solitary individuals having only occasional contact with their own species. The term 'sociable' implies friendliness and is used to describe those dolphins who actively seek to make contact with humans.

The type of contact can range from animals following in the wake of vessels or riding their bow wave, to an individual animal spending long periods in the water with swimmers and allowing direct touching. In the latter case, the dolphin may restrict intimate contact to certain selected people apparently being able to quickly recognise familiar persons. It is likely that a person's voice, appearance or mannerisms could be used as signals by the dolphin but, in addition, the possession of a sophisticated sonar system enables the animal to obtain a detailed, three-dimensional anatomical picture of a swimmer for identification purposes.

Although contact between humans and dolphins might appear commonplace to any of

us who have visited dolphinaria, it must be remembered that captive dolphins have a limited choice and their 'sociability' is continually being encouraged by careful attention, and regular training and feeding. In the wild, dolphins have the freedom of being able to swim away from anyone with whom they do not wish to make contact. The intimate relationships that have occurred between humans and sociable dolphins in the wild are, therefore, of the dolphin's own choosing and as such are remarkable.

PERCY

Percy was a very large, fully mature male bottlenose dolphin (*Tursiops truncatus*) first seen off the north coast of Cornwall in January 1981. For four years he occupied one small coastal area that included about 25 kilometres of coast.

Initially Percy was quite aloof. He showed a clear interest in diving activities and often followed local boats, but close contact with people was not made until 1983. During that year he built up a close relationship with a local diver and spent long periods in his company, allowing a good deal of close contact. But in September 1983 he became extremely wary of any close encounter and it was seen that he had a large fish hook embedded in his

Horace E. Dobbs

▲ Percy, an adult male bottlenose dolphin, provided cetologists with a rare opportunity to establish contact with a dolphin on the animal's own terms, when he frequented the inshore waters off Cornwall between 1981 and 1984, making contact with swimmers and divers.

▼ It soon became apparent that Percy demanded control of his relationships with humans: he would accept food or stroking only from his favourites. Unwelcome attention was rebuffed with sharp butting or with light warning bites.

head near his right eye. There were fears that he might have been blinded in this eye and during the winter nobody managed to get close to him. By the following spring, however, the hook had disappeared, with apparently no harm done, and he renewed contact.

Percy had one major fishing site in his territory — a narrow channel between Godrevy Point and Godrevy Island where the tidal currents were fierce. He would occupy this site at mid-tide for periods of an hour or more. He had little competition from people or other animals here but on one occasion a local fisherman rigged a gill net across the channel. The fisherman had possibly heard that the dolphin regularly fished this channel and concluded that what was good for the dolphin was also good for him. Deprived of his favourite fishing site, Percy began biting and tearing the net until he had managed to separate one of the mooring buoys from it.

The local fishing boats were regularly accompanied by Percy as keep-pots were tended and lobster pots rebaited. Percy was apparently able to associate particular fishing buoys with particular boats and we sometimes observed him moving from one buoy to another ahead of the fishing boat concerned. When he was alone he would frequently play with the moored keep-pots on the sea floor, entangling their lines. We would often see him doing this during our observations from nearby cliffs. On one occasion he had managed to get a set of pots into such a mess that the fisherman was unable to raise or disentangle the lines. The fisherman called upon a local diver for help. The diver happened to be Percy's special 'friend', and while he was struggling to sort the

lines out Percy appeared to indicate individual lines with his jaws, apparently in the reverse order in which he had initially tangled them up. The diver was then able to disentangle the lines without having to sever any.

On another occasion the same diver was in the water with Percy when the dolphin suddenly started to push him back to his moored boat. When he attempted to resist, the dolphin grasped his hand roughly in his jaws, drawing blood, and forcibly propelled him to the boat where he waited until the diver climbed out of the water. The diver was shaken because Percy had never behaved like this in the several years of their acquaintance, but after 20 minutes he re-entered the water. Percy immediately made contact but this time his mood was extremely gentle and friendly. We assumed that for some reason the dolphin had not wanted his 'friend' in the water earlier. We can only speculate why, but sharks had been seen in the area shortly before.

Percy spent many hours in the water with us or alongside our boat and always tried to get involved in any tasks we were carrying out. He particularly liked watching the anchor being paid out or raised. Being a very powerful animal Percy soon learnt how to dive down, pick up the anchor and bring it back to us at the surface. With the anchor retrieved, we were then often treated to a free ride as he towed our large heavy inflatable around at speed.

During the spring and early summer of 1984 Percy was generally placid and friendly. He would allow his body to be touched and stroked and would regularly give individuals rides while they hung onto his dorsal fin. Now that we could inspect his body marks and scars closely, we were able to see that he had had recent, regular contact with other bottlenose dolphins, other whales and possibly even otters — he was not a truly solitary animal.

As the summer passed more and more people came to the coast of Cornwall to see Percy. Local and national newspapers published articles on his activities and television film crews appeared. On one occasion his photograph was published in a daily national paper apparently drinking a cup of tea with some of his admirers. Percy had become a celebrity and during the day he was surrounded by large numbers of people.

During this period his mood changed dramatically. What can only be described as aggressive or 'warning-off' behaviour was commonplace, often involving a firm butt with the snout in the chest or on the arm. The cause of this behaviour could have been either overexcitement or, with so many people in the water around him, fear, leading to attempts to exercise dominance. He became very possessive of certain individuals in the water and on occasions other people seemed to be regarded as intruders who

Horace E. Dobbs

Robert Morris

threatened to disrupt his play or even to remove his 'playmate'. Biting became quite a frequent occurrence and sometimes Percy would attempt to stop his 'favourites' from leaving the water by pushing them out to sea. Luckily his chosen companions were strong swimmers and those on the receiving end of his displeasure suffered at worst some bruises. It could, however, have been more serious.

Percy also started to exhibit quite indiscriminate sexual behaviour. For example, in one incident witnessed by the entire crew of a fishing vessel, Percy was reported to have attempted to insert his erect penis into a hosepipe 5 centimetres in diameter hanging over the side of the vessel. At least five separate approaches were made. Another curious incident was reported by four members of another fishing boat. Percy was swimming with the boat when he suddenly veered away, swam some 12 metres, turned and rushed at the boat. As he closed with the boat he rolled onto his back and from his extended penis directed a stream of urine into the stern of the boat and onto the rather startled helmsman.

Other aspects of his behaviour became

violent. One incident involved a windsurfer on holiday in the area who had not heard of the dolphin. Percy often chased windsurfers and on this occasion the windsurfer was in full sail, well out to sea, when Percy arrived and attempted to jump over the sailboard. Either by accident or design, he landed right across the front of the board. Not surprisingly, with Percy weighing approximately 400 kilograms, the fibreglass hull broke up and the terrified surfer was thrown into the sea. The surfer, obviously in panic, released an emergency flare and the local lifeboat was called out to rescue him. The story received national coverage on radio and television and further increased Percy's fame.

At this stage conflicts started to erupt between groups of locals as to how the dolphin should be treated. Percy was the cause of a number of acrimonious encounters that took place at sea and to most it was a relief when that particular summer came to an end.

As the the summer ended and the number of tourists declined, Percy gradually reverted to his gentle, placid and friendly nature. He disappeared from the area later that winter.

▲ Scientists attempt to distance themselves from emotional identification with their subjects, but some admit to being seduced by their charm, good humour and curiosity, as well as by the deep level of trust they appear to place in their human 'friends'.

Claire Leimbach

THE MONKEY MIA DOLPHINS

HUGH EDWARDS

On a hot summer's night in 1964, Ninny Watts was on a boat anchored off the jetty at Monkey Mia, Shark Bay, Western Australia. 'It was a hot, still night, and a full moon,' she recalls. 'I couldn't sleep, and this porpoise (as fishermen call dolphins) was splashing and blowing around the boat. I took a fish out of the ice-box and threw it to him.'

Soon the dolphin was taking fish right out of Ninny's hand. She called him Charlie and he became an identity and a favourite at the jetty. Charlie bought other dolphins in to the bay and a bond with the locals was established. In the 1970s, after Charlie had died his friends continued to visit the locals, so forming the nucleus of the group who are found at Monkey Mia today.

Every year fascinated tourists flock to Monkey Mia to see these wild bottlenose dolphins (*Tursiops truncatus*) in their natural environment. The dolphins are free to come and go as they please — there are no established incentives or constraints. They do not jump through hoops or perform tricks to amuse human audiences. Visitors are able to pet and handle the dolphins.

From quiet beginnings, Monkey Mia (which consists of a caravan park and fishing jetty on the east side of the remote and arid Denham Peninsula) now has more than 40 000 visitors a year — some coming from as far away as Europe, Japan and North America. In 1986, because of increasing crowd pressure, rangers were stationed at Monkey Mia to ensure the safety and welfare of the dolphins. An information centre, part of a half-million dollar program to provide tourist facilities, was completed by the Western Australian Government in conjunction with the Shark Bay Shire in 1986. When the then Western Australian Premier Brian Burke opened the centre, he described the dolphins' unusual choice of human friends as a miracle'.

Scientists, more cautious in their terminology, concede that it is indeed a phenomenon, for the Monkey Mia dolphins are the only herd of wild dolphins in the world to have befriended people.

In the past, individual dolphins have usually had a special affinity for one human friend, just as today captive dolphins relate to their trainers. Most recorded dolphin-human relationships have been brief and all too often they have ended sadly; for example, the tragic case in New Zealand of the dolphin 'Opo', who attracted world news headlines during her single summer with people in 1956.

There is certainly no doubt that dolphins *do* like people. They cheerfully come up alongside boats, often accompany fishermen, and seem to like jumping and showing-off when

Claire Leimbach

Claire Leimbach

Claire Leimbach

◄▲ An obvious rapport exists between the cetacean and the human visitors to Monkey Mia, on the shores of Shark Bay in Western Australia.

▶ The bottlenose dolphins at Monkey Mia 'strand' themselves willingly, vocalising and accepting pieces of fish from tourists before using their flukes to propel themselves backward into deeper water.

Jean-Paul Ferrero/Auscape International

people are around. At times, dolphins even seem to strand themselves, lying half-in, half-out of the water, for a closer touch with people. The Monkey Mia dolphins have evolved their own technique of dealing with stranding by developing a 'reverse gear'. Arching their tails they pull backwards to help themselves back into the water.

The bottlenose dolphin abounds in Australian seas, from the kelp water fringes of Victoria and South Australia to the warm coffee-coloured tidal reaches of the Gulf of Carpentaria. The herd at Monkey Mia, however, are the only dolphins who have established regular contact with humans. About twenty dolphins have come in to the bay and up to the jetty at various times, with eight to ten who come in close to the beach most days. Some dolphins have been born during visits to the bay and one calf is third generation.

From the 1970s to when rangers were introduced, the dolphins' unofficial guardians were Wilf and Hazel Mason, who ran the caravan park. Hazel named most of the dolphins and her initial favourite was 'Speckeldy Betty', a very tame old female dolphin who was almost toothless. 'She was so tame,' Hazel

recalls, 'that once when she got a fishhook in her mouth she came in to the beach for Wilf to get it out. It was deeply embedded and must have really hurt when he got it out with a pair of pliers. But she just lay there trusting him with her mouth open until he got it free.'

Some caravan park proprietors, with an apparent dolphin bonanza in their front yard, would have sought to exploit the situation by turning it into a dolphin show with hoops and balls and, inevitably, captive dolphins. But Wilf and Hazel Mason discouraged tourists' attempts to teach the dolphins games. They instituted a number of regulations, requesting visitors not to sit children on the dolphins' back, because dolphins' ribs are delicate and can break easily; not to pull dolphins' fins; not to allow dogs into the water, since they may nip or bite the dolphins.

Visitors are also told that dolphins like to be stroked on the side or on the belly. I have photographed dolphins at length underwater and have observed that they do not seem to like rapid or staccato movement. They are also particularly averse to being patted on the 'melon' on their forehead, which shields their sensitive echolocation centre.

The most important requests, however, are connected with food. Dolphins have a small gullet, and swallow their fish head-first. The wrong kind of food could kill them. They should be fed small fish, especially bony herring, which they love. People have, however, offered them chicken bones, even T-bones from steaks off the barbeque! Other objects, including bottle tops, have also been thrown to them. So far the dolphins have resisted taking them but every zoo director has stories of favourite creatures being killed by swallowing foreign objects.

Since Charlie's first contact with Ninny Watts, fish has always been a link between the dolphins and humans at Monkey Mia. If you go down to the water's edge, with the right kind of fish, a dolphin will swirl up, cock a bright eye at you and take it from your fingers. Woe betide the joker who teases and pulls a fish away at the last moment, or is only pretending that he has a fish for the dolphin. The dolphins can lose patience and nip the hand.

The tourist supplement of fish is appreciated but not

DOLPHINS ARE VERY INTELLIGENT MAMMALS
IF YOU WISH TO COMMUNICATE WITH THEM
IT IS IMPORTANT TO REMEMBER THESE GUIDELINES

Do be kind to the dolphins DO NOT harm them
There is no reason to be afraid of them
Let the dolphins approach you, stroke their sides
DO NOT PAT DOLPHINS ON THEIR HEADS
DO NOT feed them anything other than fresh fish

PLEASE DO NOT try to catch them, ride on them or hold on to a fin
ENJOY YOUR EXPERIENCE IN MEETING THESE
WONDERFUL CREATURES

WORMALD A COMPANY WHO SPECIALISE IN SAVIING LIVES

Huan Edwards

▲ Until rangers were stationed at Monkey Mia, caravan park proprietors Wilf and Hazel Mason took responsibility for harmonious and safe contact between people and the 'resident' bottlenose dolphins.

Benn Cropp Productions/Auscape International

▲ Diver Lyn Cropp proffers fresh fish to a bottlenose dolphin at Monkey Mia.
Although dolphins appear to enjoy being stroked on the flanks, they dislike being patted
on the forehead, perhaps because it interferes with their echolocation ability.

essential. Often the dolphins cruise among the people when they are not hungry, and take the fish simply to flick playfully in the air. 'It is more like a courtesy, a lot of the time,' says Wilf. 'You've made the effort to bring a fish. They make an effort to be sociable in return. Like humans shaking hands it's an introduction.'

Sometimes the dolphins reciprocate by bringing fish in for the tourists. On several occasions they have herded in snapper — a fish dolphins never eat but tourists value — to the shallows. They shepherd them like marine sheepdogs to the feet of the visitors.

The Monkey Mia dolphins fascinate the crowds that line the water's edge to see them, and television cameras and crews often come to film this phenomenon. As Soichiro Tabizaki, director of a Japanese documentary for an audience of 20 million explained: 'The Japanese people have never seen the expression in a wild dolphin's eye. It is quite wonderful . . .'

What will the future hold for the Monkey Mia dolphins? There are obvious concerns that crowd pressure or irresponsible behaviour could destroy the current harmony that exists between humans and dolphins at Monkey Mia. The crowds are increasing, but the public education program carried out by the rangers appears to be working well, and the dolphins remain unconcerned by the increasing pressures. We can only watch and wonder, and hope that this remarkable contact between humans and dolphins remains unspoiled.

Don Croll

▲ 'Whale watching' has become a successful tourist industry in areas where grey whales breed.
Obviously used to the sound of outboard engines, the whales do not appear to be disturbed by such contact.

EYEBALL TO EYEBALL WITH A 40 TONNE WHALE

MARTY SNYDERMAN

I am not sure that anyone fully understands the affinity humans feel for whales. Perhaps we feel some sense of kinship with creatures that, like ourselves, are mammals, or maybe we feel some sense of guilt for the cruelties we have imposed on so many whale species. There are other reasons, too, that help explain the intense interest: the fascinating natural history of whales, their sheer size, and our admiration of their ability to survive in the harsh conditions imposed by life in the sea. For divers and professional underwater film makers like myself, this intense interest is dramatically increased.

I have had a lifelong dream of swimming with a whale, not just catching a fleeting glimpse, but spending some time with the animal. I have always wanted to know what it would be like to look directly into the eye of a whale, and I have fantasised about capturing the moment on film. To me, swimming with a whale would be the ultimate diving experience.

In my dreams, I swim next to the whale in the clear, calm waters of some tropical paradise; I can swim as fast as it can, hold my breath as long, and dive as deep. In my dreams the whale is as curious about me as I am about it, so I am able to swim eyeball to eyeball with my photographic subject for hours on end.

But my first extended encounter in the water with a real whale differed considerably from my dreams. The water was cold and rough, the wind was howling, the current was ripping and visibility was less than 3 metres — common conditions in Magdalena Bay where I was attempting to film a grey whale (*Eschrichtius robustus*). Magdalena Bay, a remote but well-known breeding and calving ground for grey whales, is located approximately halfway down the Pacific side of Mexico's Baja peninsula. Howard Hall and I were not on assignment, but in Magdalena Bay specifically to chase our dreams and swim with a whale.

On any winter day, a visitor to Magdalena Bay is likely to see dozens of grey whales, but getting close to one underwater is difficult. Conditions are extremely demanding. Other film teams had spent a season in the series of Pacific lagoons used by grey whales and all they had to show for their efforts were a few barely useable sequences of film.

Spotting the whales was easy, but chasing them in the water would be impossible. Howard and I realised that we must either find a whale 'resting' at the surface or wait for an unusually curious whale to approach us. One afternoon I spotted a lone grey whale that appeared to be frolicking at the surface rolling over and over.

We had been taking it in turn to film the whale while free-diving, or snorkelling. It was my turn to try to swim with the whale and, as I entered the water, I remember seeing the animal roll over on the surface, and although it appeared to change direction I could not be sure. Howard pointed towards the whale, and I thought how ridiculous it was that he should have to point out a 15-metre-long whale that was less than 14 metres from the boat. I could not see over the waves and underwater I was hampered by the limited visibility.

I swam, head down, in the direction Howard pointed and suddenly found myself staring at a wall of whale, round and mottled grey. The whale was enormous. I had no idea where I was along its body since every part I glimpsed at looked the same.

When fully grown, grey whales attain a length of almost 15 metres, and at that length they weigh approximately 40–50 tonnes. This whale was obviously an adult. I had anticipated some problems in filming a whale, but had never considered the possibility that I would not recognise where I was in relation to the whale's body. To understand what I was looking at, I had to try to create the whale in my mind's eye to orientate myself. I did the best I could, made a decision and swam down the body looking for that large eye and massive head. The whale disappeared and then, just as suddenly, reappeared in the cloudy water as the 4-metre-wide tail stopped right in front of my face mask; I had travelled in the wrong direction.

The whale moved as though it was aware of my presence, repeatedly bringing its powerful flukes within centimetres of me, but never making contact. I, on the other hand, could not resist the urge to reach out and touch the animal's rubbery skin. After a few moments, I swam back up the body towards the head. The great creature rolled as I reached its pectoral flippers and I suddenly realised what the dimensions 15 metres long and 40 tonnes meant. The pectoral flipper, like the tail, was only a body part but it was larger than I. Yet it was not the whale's size that impressed me so much as its body control and grace. There was now no question in my mind that the whale was aware of me. The flippers, too, came within a few centimetres of my body but did not touch me.

I moved along the whale's body and finally found myself at the surface of the sea looking into a tennis-ball-sized eye. I did not feel any sense of impending danger, instead I felt an incredible sense of elation. Upon reflection, I find it strange that I was eyeball to eyeball with a creature that weighed almost 500

◄▲ The awesome dimensions of a grey whale at close range are enough to confuse a diver who is no more than an eighth the whale's length and less than 4 per cent of its weight — although whales are careful not to injure fellow swimmers with their fins or flukes.

times as much as I did, and yet I was afraid I was going to frighten it. I did not want the moment to end too soon. I remember trying to look for any clue — a facial expression, a movement — that would give me some idea about what the whale was thinking, but I did not perceive anything I could understand. I decided that as long as the whale saw me, which it obviously did, and did not swim away, it was not disturbed by my presence. This gave me a sense of relief, for I often fear that those of us who profess to love and respect wildlife, create situations that annoy the very creatures we so admire when we attempt to film them. Perhaps, in this case, the great creature was as curious about me as I was about it.

The whale suddenly rose above the surface of the water and, as I looked up, I realised that the horizon was changing shape. We were so close to each other that the whale blocked a portion of the sky from my view. Then it dropped down below the surface and I quickly followed. We were only 2 metres deep when the whale rolled over and eyed me for the final time. After a few seconds it descended and disappeared into the murky waters.

I do not know how long I had been able to swim with the whale but I estimated it to be around three minutes. Although I had always dreamed of filming a whale at close range I had taken only a few pictures. I had tried to enjoy the moment and not allow my camera to rob me of that pleasure.

◄ To swim with a whale is to realise a dream held by many, yet as underwater cameraman Marty Snyderman discovered, the experience is one of elation and wonder: fear is banished in the face of the whale's gentle and expressionless curiosity, and the sheer majesty of its nearness.

STRANDINGS — FACT AND FICTION

MARGARET KLINOWSKA

There is no mystery about the vast majority of whale, dolphin and porpoise strandings — they are simply the bodies of dead animals washed ashore by tides and currents. The animals have died through all the hazards of life in the wild (which may include entanglement in fishing nets as well as disease, old age and other more 'natural' causes). It is important to note that only a proportion of the animals that die will be washed ashore, and that only a proportion of those washed ashore are likely to be recorded. Therefore, it is not possible to relate changes in the numbers of dead animals reported on beaches to changes in the population alive at sea.

British Museum (Natural History)

▲ Live strandings are rare but dramatic events that have always attracted public interest, as shown by this group in Cornwall, United Kingdom. Many theories have been advanced to explain why whales strand, but it is only recently that the suggestion of cetacean direction-finding mechanisms has provided some testable pointers to reasons why strandings occur.

▶ Offshore toothed whales strand in large numbers more often than inshore species, and their highly social nature may encourage 'rescue' or support behaviour that only exacerbates the problem, leading more group members on to the shore.

LIVE STRANDINGS

The cause of live strandings, where individuals or groups of animals seem to swim ashore deliberately, has been the subject of much speculation over the years. Live strandings are very rare: for example, in the 70 years of the United Kingdom's strandings recording system only 137 events (out of a total of almost 3000 records, not all of which refer to animals found on beaches) could be identified as live strandings. These included 28 group strandings (with 3 or more animals involved) 96 single and pair strandings, and 13 group near-strandings. The latter are cases with all the preliminary features of a live group stranding, but ending in the escape of all or most animals. Such events begin to resemble 'sightings' rather than classic 'strandings' and illustrate the fact that not all groups of cetaceans that appear to be about to strand do so; nor is it necessarily true that if one animal is beached the rest of the group will follow. Further, in about half the cases where attempts were made to rescue single stranded animals, the

results seem to have been successful (in that no animal of that description was reported as having been stranded, alive or dead, within the following weeks).

The low proportion of live stranding events is not unique to the United Kingdom, similar proportions of live stranding events are observed elsewhere in the world, wherever suitable systematic records are kept. All species (except, perhaps, for some river dolphins) live strand, but proportionally offshore species do so more frequently than inshore species. The number of animals involved depends on the social habits of the species — those that live in groups tend to live strand in groups. This explains why baleen whales, with small social groups, do not live strand in large groups (often called 'mass strandings'), although individuals and small groups do live strand.

LIVE STRANDING THEORIES

So why do these animals, which normally spend all their lives in water, come ashore? Aristotle, who was probably one of the first to record this aspect of cetacean behaviour, simply said that he did not know the answer. Others, however, have put forward a variety of explanations including suicide, entering shallow water to rest or rub the skin, reversion to a primitive instinct to seek safety on land, confusion of sonar echoes by shallow water, inner ear parasites preventing proper reception of sonar echoes, brain infections leading to disorientation, attempts to use ancient migration paths now closed by geological changes, population pressure, noise from modern shipping and other activities, pollution, radar, television and radio transmissions, earthquakes, storms phases of the moon.

The recent increase in interest in these events may give the impression that live strandings, especially live group strandings, have increased, but records over the last few hundred years do not bear this out. Modern human activities, therefore, have not affected the live stranding rate, ruling out

some of the postulated causes. Some of the other possible causes can also be eliminated. Only about two thirds of live strandings in the United Kingdom are on the sloping sandy shores thought to confuse sonar echoes; the remaining third are on exactly the steep shores that ought to give good echoes. Furthermore, baleen whales do live strand, but they do not have sonar like some toothed whales. Some live stranded animals do have parasites or brain lesions but others seem to be perfectly healthy. Some live strandings occur at places that were never seaways at any relevant point in geological time, so it seems unlikely that an ancient memory of previous routes is to blame.

The theory that population pressure results in live strandings is based on the observation that group strandings of long-finned pilot whales (*Globicephala melaena*) in Canada increased after catching ceased. From records of sightings, live strandings and catches of long-finned pilot whales

▲ It has been proposed that sloping sandy coastlines confuse sonar echoes and lead to strandings. This explanation does not account for mass strandings on, for example, the rocky coast of Tasmania, especially by long-finned pilot whales.

Dave Watts/Australasian Nature Transparencies

in the United Kingdom and Ireland, going back to 1602, reports of group strandings and sightings do indeed appear to increase as catching ceased around 1900. However, this is not surprising as in former times schools near the coast were pursued, thus providing a 'catch' record. When catching ceased, observations were then noted as 'sightings' or 'strandings'. There is, in fact, some decline in the number of reports of long-finned pilot whale schools in the United Kingdom after catching ceased, because there was no longer any financial reward involved, and few people were interested in recording their observations. Population pressure, then, is not a plausible cause for live strandings.

The ideas of suicide or reversion to a primitive behaviour are not testable, but seem unlikely. Resting in shallow water is not normal cetacean

behaviour and, although some groups of orcas (*Orcinus orca*) do use 'rubbing areas', this has never been observed to result in live strandings; other cetaceans do not use rubbing areas. In fact, as scientists in the USSR have recently shown, cetaceans have evolved a very interesting way of sleeping in the water without any danger of drowning. The animals only sleep with one side of the brain at a time — the other side is awake, and controls movement and respiration.

Craig Matkin/Earthviews

If earthquakes were the cause, we would expect more live strandings in areas particularly prone to earthquakes, but this is not the case. Weather patterns around the time of live strandings do not seem to show any common factor, either.

One might argue that all that this demonstrates is that no single explanation is enough to account for the variety of live stranding events we see among cetaceans. However, there is an explanation that does seem to account for all live strandings. This explanation emerged from investigations of another long-standing mystery — how cetaceans find their way about.

HOW CETACEANS FIND THEIR WAY ABOUT
Whales use the total geomagnetic field (flux density) of the earth to supply them with both a simple map, and a timer that allows them to monitor their position and progress on the map.

▲ The rarity of baleen whale strandings can be explained in part by the infrequency with which even healthy baleen whales are seen close to shore.

They are not using the directional information of the earth's field, as we do with our magnetic compasses, but small relative differences in total local field. This explanation was obtained from a detailed analysis of the original United Kingdom strandings records, which are kept by the British Museum (Natural History), but so far it has been confirmed by at least two groups in the United States (using their stranding records). Similar work is in progress in other parts of the world.

The total magnetic field of the earth is not uniform. It is locally distorted by the magnetic characteristics of the underlying geology, forming a topography that may be thought of as 'hills and valleys'. The cetaceans appear to move parallel to the contours, keeping higher field to the left and lower field to the right, or vice versa (rather like walking across the slope of a hill, with one foot up the slope and one foot down). In the oceans, the movements of the continents have produced series of almost parallel magnetic hills and valleys, which could be used as 'motorways'.

Unfortunately, problems may arise near shore because the magnetic formations do not end at the beach, but continue on to the land — and sometimes so do the whales. All the live strandings in the United Kingdom occur at places where the magnetic contours are perpendicular to the coast. Dead bodies, on the other hand, wash up with equal frequency in places with parallel and perpendicular geomagnetic contours.

Live strandings, then, seem to be the

DETAILS OF ONE UK LIVE STRANDING SITE

This area illustrates most of the detailed features of stranding sites. It is all 'classical' live stranding coast, with gently sloping beaches, yet the live strandings are grouped, not scattered. There are very few dead strandings within the Wash, as would be expected from the general set of local currents. The three live strandings toward the top of the map are at a site where there is also a major deposition of dead strandings, and there is an adjacent Coastguard establishment. The site, however, has geomagnetic contours perpendicular to the coast, and illustrates the fact that live strandings, dead strandings and recorders (Coastguards) can sometimes be found together. The dead stranding sites to the east are in areas with contours both parallel and perpendicular to the coast. The density of dead strandings here is typical for southern United Kingdom areas, and many sites are associated with Coastguard establishments.

Analysis of stranding records for the whole United Kingdom coastline from the Wash to the Solway Firth has shown a very clear pattern. The coast was divided into 5-kilometre grid squares, and each of the 600 squares independently scored as to whether the geomagnetic contours were in general perpendicular or parallel to the coast (from the sea). The records of dead strandings were found in both perpendicular and parallel squares, in about the expected proportions, and they were also strongly related to recorder distribution, as represented by the Coastguard establishments. Live strandings, on the other hand, were *only* recorded in perpendicular squares, and their positions had no relationship to the distribution of Coastguard establishments. This very strong relationship between live (but not dead) strandings and geomagnetic contours perpendicular to the coast can be explained only if the animals are moving parallel to the geomagnetic contours.

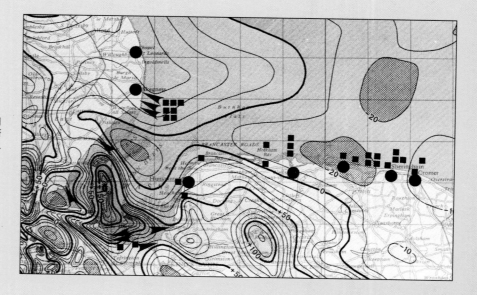

► The Wash area of the British Geological Survey geomagnetic topography map. The live stranding positions are shown by arrows, the dead strandings by squares and the position of the Coastguard establishments by circles. The Coastguard are the most important reporters of strandings in the United Kingdom. Geomagnetic contours are at 10 nanoTesla intervals and grid squares at 10 kilometre intervals.

Jiri Lochman/Auscape International

◄ Disorientation, exhaustion, panic, shock and, possibly, an instinctive urge to respond to distress calls possibly combine to cause 're-stranding' behaviour, where animals already pushed back to sea return to the shore and to other members of the group still trapped. Patience and careful supervision are needed to reduce the incidence of repeated strandings.

equivalent of road accidents, due to mistakes in map-reading. This explains why offshore species, which would not be familiar with the problems of using their system close to shore, live strand more frequently than inshore species, which would be familiar with the problems. The young, the old, the sick, the healthy, singles or groups may be involved — accidents can happen to anybody. If they are accidents, this would explain why live stranded animals appear to be shocked and may require assistance to leave the beach. An accident in their map-reading would explain why they sometimes try to return to the same beach, or strand again at the next 'magnetic trap' along the coast; they are travelling in what seems to them to be an appropriate direction and the fact that there is another beach in the way comes as another nasty surprise.

HOW MISTAKES ARE MADE

But where and why do the animals make the mistake, or take the wrong turn, that leads them into unfamiliar waters?

The total geomagnetic field fluctuates in a fairly regular manner each day, providing a time cue each morning and evening, rather like dawn and dusk. There are also irregular fluctuations, caused by solar activity; these tend to occur more often at night than during the day. Irregular night-time fluctuations usually obscure the regular evening cue, but the morning signal is normally available and the cetaceans use it to reset a

biological travel 'clock'. This 'clock' seems to be used to tell them how long they have been travelling; if they have some idea of how fast they have been moving, they can then work out where they are.

The fluctuations do not affect the basic shape of the geomagnetic topography, rather they are a local distortion of the total field through the magnetic characteristics of the local geology. The situation is rather like that of a boat in tidal waters — the depth of water under the keel varies regularly with the tide, and the wave height will change irregularly with the weather, but the boat still floats at the surface.

The fluctuations in the geomagnetic field do reflect lunar, seasonal and sunspot cycles. Live strandings should thus be related to these events, but unfortunately the United Kingdom data set is too small to demonstrate such long-term changes. Records from elsewhere are also insufficient, being too short, not sufficiently detailed or not systematically collected. However, with more worldwide interest in recording these events, this problem should be overcome in future.

This picture of the cetacean travel strategy emerged from a series of calculations based on the behaviour of the geomagnetic field around the dates of United Kingdom live strandings, using the dates of dead strandings as a control. Days when the morning travel cue is obscured by the irregular fluctuations are associated with live strandings. However, it is only on the Irish and North Sea

▶ No matter how great the rescuers' commitment may be, it is rarely possible to return every whale to the sea. Length of time out of the water, stress, overheating and lack of assistance may contribute to the deaths of many animals.

Steven French

coasts that the strandings tend to occur on the day the cue was lost: in the south the strandings happen about two days later, while in the north they happen about a day and a half later. Inspecting geomagnetic topography maps revealed that there are two major 'crossroads' in the system — one about two days' steady swimming time from the south coast and another about a day and a half's swimming time from the Scottish coast. The North and Irish Seas are too narrow for animals to be more than about a day's travel from the coast.

This suggests that the primary mistake may be made some distance from land. The animals simply continue the wrong way until they encounter the shore. Of course we do not know how many times such mistakes are made, or how many are corrected before any problems arise. (The near-strandings may represent 'last moment' error corrections.) We do know that uncorrected mistakes resulting in live strandings are very rare — of all the hundreds of thousands of cetaceans in the seas, very few indeed end up alive on the shore. This shows that the animals are usually very good at finding their way about. Their simple travel system, involving only a map and a timer, with information supplied by a single

▶ Live strandings appear to be the marine equivalent of road accidents — potentially fatal incidents that stem from navigational errors, sometimes having their genesis one or two days before the actual stranding takes place.

source, is applicable to journeys of any length anywhere on the earth at any time. No compass is involved, so no compensation is needed for magnetic pole wanderings or even for reversals of the entire geomagnetic field. The animals do need to be familiar with the geomagnetic area they use, but this learning could begin while the young whale accompanies its mother during lactation. Later this familiar area can be extended, through individual exploration or travel with more experienced animals.

CAN WE PREVENT LIVE STRANDINGS?
Unfortunately, the explanation does not provide any hope of preventing live strandings. However, loss of individuals or groups in this way is not a threat to the survival of any species, except perhaps the rare and endangered Chinese river dolphin (*Lipotes vexillifer*). The rescue of live stranded cetaceans is, therefore, not a species conservation issue, but a question of the welfare of the individual animals concerned. It may be possible to refloat smaller species without risk of injury either to the cetaceans or to their human helpers. Sometimes animals can be removed for rehabilitation at suitable premises. However, in

cases where the animals are very large, ill, injured or in places where there is no possibility of rescue, humane destruction by an expert is the only solution to prevent further suffering.

THE MAGNETIC SENSE

Almost nothing is known about how cetaceans 'read' geomagnetic information, but they must have a very sensitive receptor system to be able to detect these tiny changes in the local geomagnetic field. They are picking up changes of 1 nanoTesla or so, for comparison (the total geomagnetic field is about 50 000 nanoTesla). So far, the only geomagnetic receptor system that has been fully documented is that used by some bacteria and algae. They contain small magnetic iron-oxide (magnetite) crystals, which serve as passive devices to direct the organisms down into their muddy habitat. The organism provides the swimming power, but the magnetite crystals act like a small magnet, directing the movement along the force lines of the geomagnetic field. Magnetite has been reported in a variety of organisms, including cetaceans, although it appears that early investigations often suffered from contamination and inappropriate methodology (which identified iron in general, not magnetite in particular).

However, although the small magnetite crystals are, in theory, capable of detecting these tiny fields, it is not clear that such a system would be sufficient to sustain the features we see in the cetacean travel strategy. Here, a total field detector is needed, but the magnetite system has so far only been shown to be able to pick up the directional information — magnetite can work like a compass, but can it 'read' the map? Also, loss of geomagnetic time information on one day is enough to upset the travel 'clock'. This means that cetaceans must be able to store the time information for twenty-four hours, but then need an external cue to reset the system. We do not yet know whether a magnetite-based system would be capable of this. Larger magnetite crystals could do such a job, but the animals would need to encounter huge electromagnetic forces (for example, being struck by lightning) to reset these large crystals. It might even be that magnetite is not the answer where higher animals are concerned.

Evidence is accumulating from research in West Germany that the retina, which contains no magnetite, is sensitive to these small magnetic fields. Cetaceans, unfortunately, are extremely inconvenient animals for this kind of detailed anatomical and physiological research, so we may have to wait for information from other species before we can fully understand the mechanism of the magnetic sense of cetaceans. Analysis of live stranding patterns also has its limitations, and we now need to look at the living animals at sea for confirmation of the behaviour indicated by the strandings.

► It is virtually impossible to refloat very large stranded cetaceans — the necessary equipment is rarely available, topography usually prevents its use, and damage from overheating and pressure on the lungs is almost inevitable. Painless destruction by someone with an expert knowledge of cetacean anatomy is the most that can be done to relieve an animal's distress in such cases.

Jonathan Player/Ardea London Ltd

WHAT TO DO IF YOU FIND A STRANDED CETACEAN

1. **Do not panic.**
2. **Find out whether the animal is alive or dead.** In most cases this is obvious — the animal is either moving about or already decaying. However, if the animal is not moving but seems in good condition, it should be approached cautiously from the front — keep away from the tail at this stage, as it may move suddenly and hit you. Listen for any respiration; this may take ten minutes or more with some species. In the meantime, look at the eyes (without touching them). If they are open, and the animal is alive, they may follow a finger moved gently across the line of sight. However, take care that the animal cannot roll on to you or be washed on to you by waves.
3. If you are sure the animal is dead, **take a careful note of the position and report it as soon as possible** to the local recording scheme, which will deal with it. If in doubt about where to report, try local police, coastguards, lifeguards, school teachers, museum staff or even the tourist information office. In many areas it is forbidden by law to damage any stranded animals, or to remove them or any parts, without permission. Souvenirs of the occasion should, therefore, be confined to photographs or drawings.

   However, if there is no prospect of contacting a recorder, if the tide is about to wash the body away, or there are other circumstances that clearly mean that nobody else will be able to arrive in time to make observations, you should do your best to make a record of the animal. Photographs are ideal — as they provide enough information to identify the animal and the site. Photographs should not be 'artistic' but carefully planned shots with some kind of scale included (a person, an object or even a shoe of known size). One photograph must be at right angles to the body, showing the full length (one of each side is better), then photograph the head, the dorsal fin (if there is one), the tail and the flippers. Close-ups of any marks, scars or parasites can also be useful. Do not forget a frame or two including some local landmarks so that the place can be identified. If there is no camera, record the same things using a notebook and some means of measurement (your pace, a piece of string). Sketch the parts and add measure as best you can.

   If possible, bury the body (or at least the head) well above the high tide line, marking the place (bearings on landmarks are best for this; other people tend to move or take away things like sticks and piles of stones) so that it can be found again. If this is not practical, the whole head is the most useful part to remove for identification by an expert, but the lower jaw (or half the jaw), a tooth or a plate of baleen is almost as good. If you can see the belly, try to find out the sex of the animal — in males the urogenital slit is some distance from the anal opening, in females it appears to be continuous with the anal opening (if in doubt take a photograph or make a drawing).

   Report your find promptly to the appropriate people, giving your name and address in case they need to contact you for more information.
4. If the animal is alive, or you are not quite sure whether it is dead, **get help** quickly — after taking a careful note of the rough size and shape of the animal, and of the place. The

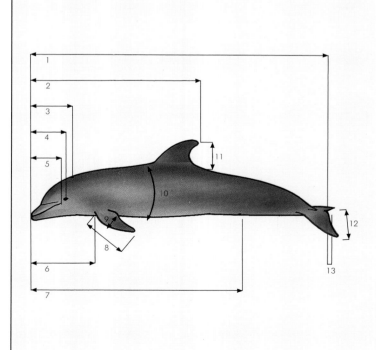

Small cetaceans can be especialy difficult to identify, and good quality photographs can be very helpful. If possible, photograph the entire animal from the side and take close-ups of the head (from the side, from the front and from above), the dorsal fin, flukes, flippers and the genital region.

Basic measurements also help to identify the species. All measurements, except the girth (10), should be taken in straight lines — do not follow body curves.

1. Total length from tip of upper jaw to deepest point of notch between flukes;
2. Tip of upper jaw to tip of dorsal fin (if present);
3. Tip of upper jaw to blowhole;
4. Tip of upper jaw to centre of eye;
5. Tip of upper jaw to corner of mouth;
6. Tip of upper jaw to front of flipper (where it joins body);
7. Tip of upper jaw to anus, measured along belly or side;
8. Length of flipper from tip to body, measured along leading edge;
9. Maximum width of flipper;
10. Maximum girth (give distance from tip of upper jaw to point where girth measurement taken);
11. Height of dorsal fin from tip to base;
12. Width of flukes;
13. Depth of notch between flukes, from deepest point to main curve of trailing edge.

Many of these measurements will be difficult or impossible to take in large whales, because they are too heavy to move. For identification purposes the most useful measurements of large whales are 1, 4, 6, 8 and 12. The distance between the genital slit and the anus is valuable in determining the sex of the animal.

◄ A stranded whale will overheat quickly and can suffer cracked skin if not kept moist and cool. Protect the animal if possible, using hessian or beach towels (take care not to cover the blowhole) and moisten regularly with seawater.

more time the animal has to spend on the beach, the more difficult it will be to help it. If you have to leave the animal alone while you get help, do what you can to make it comfortable before you leave. For example, prop it up so that the blowhole is in no danger of filling with water; remove any objects such as stones, which may damage the skin; try to find something cool and wet with which to cover it for the time being (a wet sheet, seaweed). **Be careful** not to get anything into the blowhole (usually on top of the head) — water in here can drown the animal, while sand will damage the lungs. Also, do not let anything get in the eyes.

While waiting for help to arrive, **keep the animal cool, calm and comfortable.** Cetaceans are built for life in water and quickly begin to overheat on land, even if the weather is cool. They use a heat exchange system in their flippers, fin and tail for cooling, so these parts are the most important to keep cool. It is a good idea to keep the flippers as free as possible, for example, by scooping out the sand beneath them and letting them hang in a hole filled with water — this helps with cooling, too. Also, their delicate skin soon begins to dry out in the air, so all parts need to be kept damp. An animal that is upset and rolling about is likely to damage both itself and any people in the way. Everyone trying to help should, therefore, keep calm and behave quietly, soothing the animal as best they can. It is a good idea to organise helpers into teams, with one person acting as 'beachmaster'. For example, one team fetches water for cooling the animal, another team deals with bystanders to keep them out of the way, others soothe the animal or take records. Teams should be changed around, so that nobody gets too tired and everyone who wishes gets a chance to help. The beachmaster hands over to the experts when they arrive. If experienced help is on the way, resist the temptation to try to get the animal back to the water — you may accidentally harm it.

If it is quite clear that you are on your own without expert help, you will need to **make careful assessment of the situation.**

(a) If you are completely alone, with no prospect of getting any help and the animal is too large for you to lift easily, there is nothing you can do except make the animal as comfortable as possible (see above), record as much information about it as you can and report it promptly, so that at least the record is not lost.

(b) If the animal is so large that there is no prospect of moving it with the help available, again there is nothing more to be done than to keep it comfortable, record details and report promptly.

(c) If it looks as if there is enough help available to lift the animal, and the sea condition is such that people would be able to support the animal in the water without undue risk to themselves, start planning the move, in particular working out who is to do what. You will also need to think about whether the tide will be able to help and whether there is enough daylight left to complete the job. In cool conditions, an overnight wait may be possible and preferable.

(d) Before returning any animal to the sea, take photographs and records in the same way as for dead strandings. In particular, note any marks that could identify it again at sea or on shore.

▲ Attendants at a stranding may be able to get help from a nearby farm or town — a tractor or front-end loader can increase the speed and efficiency of moving numbers of stranded animals, especially when there is a risk they may strand themselves again if other group members are still in difficulty.

▲ Wherever possible, stranded animals should be moved using improvised stretchers or slings. Never lift a whale by its fins or flukes, these are heavy animals and must be lifted with care.

▲ Whales that have been stranded for some time will probably be disorientated and confused, and must be supported until they have regained their balance and can swim freely by themselves.

(e) **The greatest care is needed when returning an animal to the water.** The flippers must never be pushed or pulled — they are easily injured or dislocated. The skin is also easily damaged, so some kind of sling is needed that will support the bulk of the body without cutting it. The animal is lifted on to the sling, or the sling is worked carefully under the body. Then the animal is carried into water deep enough to support its own weight. The sling is released once it is clear that the animal can keep itself upright and swim. Take great care that it does not fall on its side and that water does not enter the blowhole. The animal may be stiff after lying on the beach and need support for a while in the water. Sometimes gentle rocking helps overcome this stiffness. Never grab at the flippers or tail but push on the sides or at the base of the dorsal fin.

(f) If the animal insists on returning to the beach and seems unable to swim properly even after your best efforts, it is not worth continuing to try to push it out to sea. Just make it as comfortable as possible on the shore.

(g) **Never make any attempt to kill a cetacean humanely,** even if it is in great distress. Only an expert can do this because cetacean anatomy and physiology are very different from those of land mammals and you are most likely only to cause further suffering through not finding a vital part quickly. In particular, resist any temptation to try to shoot the animal — the bullet is very likely to be deflected by the shape of the skull and emerge to damage onlookers.

However, do try to accept the situation if an expert decides that humane destruction is the best option for the animal. It is simply not possible to save every animal and in this case the suffering should not be prolonged.

5. While single live animals are very often too ill to swim, it is likely that the vast majority of the members of a group stranding will be in good health and can be successfully returned to the water (if they are not too large to handle). One difficulty, however, is that the group social bonds are very strong and it can be very difficult to get one or two

animals to swim away while the rest are alive ashore. The other major difficulty is that there are simply a lot of animals to deal with. This is a situation where, if anything useful is to be done, many well-organised helpers are needed, as well as the guidance (even by telephone) of experts familiar with the social structure of the species. Lifting equipment, and people experienced in its safe use, can be invaluable if you can make your slings strong enough to take the strain and rigid enough not to squash the animals during transport.

The most successful strategy for dealing with group strandings seems to be:

(a) Assess the resources in terms of helpers and equipment available. Deploy equipment and organise helpers into teams, with well-defined tasks and good leaders. Arrange for communications between each team and the beachmaster, for relief teams and for the deployment of new helpers and equipment.

(b) Try to prevent any animals still in the water from getting on to the beach — not by dashing about and shouting, but by using boats and/or people to keep this group quietly bunched together in sheltered, shallow water.

(c) Get the beached animals back into the water with the others.

(d) Guide the entire group back to sea together.

(e) This is all obviously easier said than done! However, large groups very often contain smaller subgroups, with strong social bonds. If these can be identified, each subgroup can be treated in turn, starting with the group containing the least damaged and easiest to handle animals. If the group leader can be identified (in case of doubt try the largest animals) and moved a little way out, the others sometimes follow. It may be necessary to secure these 'leaders' carefully to a boat to prevent them returning to shore, taking care that their blowholes are above water at all times. **Never** tow an animal behind a boat by the tail — the blowhole will be forced underwater and the animal will drown. Many of the sounds that cetaceans make are highly directional, so in order for the animals near shore to hear the leaders, the leaders need to be held with their heads toward the shore.

(f) Animals that are awaiting refloating and any that clearly cannot be refloated need care too, with priority given to those that can be rescued. It is often said that humane killing of beached animals, which cannot be rescued, facilitates the return of the rest to the water. However, unless there is an expert present this is not an option, for the reasons given above.

(g) Even with all the difficulties in helping a group of stranded animals, recording should not be forgotten. If possible record all the details as for any other stranding, but at least try to get a note of the numbers and of the position of each animal. Also try to get as clear an account as possible of the sequence of events leading to the stranding, and, in particular, of the order in which the animals arrived on the beach. This information can help to identify subgroups and group leaders, as well as providing a valuable record of the event. (Very few good accounts of group strandings are available, probably because everyone is too busy trying to help the animals. However, if we knew more about how strandings begin we could probably get some valuable clues about how to reverse the situation.) Press and media people are often most helpful here, if you explain the kind of information required. This is also a good job for bystanders who are unable to help with the heavy work.

6. In trying to help the animals, do not forget the people. They are going to be tired, cold and hungry — there may even be injuries. Appoint someone to organise this aspect as soon as you can; everyone will appreciate it. This is particularly important if you are returning to a stranding alone after calling for help — arrange for someone to visit you every few hours, to carry messages and food, and to check there have been no accidents.

Simon Cowling/Horizon

▲ The ideal refloating situation is one where attendants outnumber stranded whales — but co-ordination and definition of tasks by a 'beachmaster' are essential if rescue efforts are not to be wasted. The safety and care of rescue personnel should be regarded as being more important than the welfare of stranded animals.

British Musem (Natural History)

CHECKLIST OF LIVING CETACEANS ORDER CETACEA

Attempts to classify Cetacea are difficult because, for the most part, they are poorly known. Some live almost entirely on the high seas, or in remote or inaccessible parts of the ocean. Whale carcasses are difficult and expensive to collect, and to preserve for investigation by biologists, trained in the classification of living things.

For these reasons, any classification and list of names of Cetacea can be regarded only as provisional. The classification and the scientific names used here follow those agreed, for the most part, among marine mammalogists at present. Some remain controversial and future studies will, almost certainly, lead to changes.

SUBORDER MYSTICETI — BALEEN WHALES

FAMILY BALAENIDAE — RIGHT WHALES

Balaena mysticetus . . . . bowhead (Greenland right whale)
Eubalaena glacialis . . . . northern right whale
(black right whale, Biscayan right whale, North Atlantic right whale)
Eubalaena australis . . . . . . southern right whale (black right whale)

FAMILY NEOBALAENIDAE — PYGMY RIGHT WHALE

Caperea marginata . . . . pygmy right whale

FAMILY ESCHRICHTIIDAE — GREY WHALE

Eschrichtius robustus . . . . grey whale
(Pacific grey whale, California grey whale)

FAMILY BALAENOPTERIDAE — RORQUALS

Balaenoptera musculus . . . . blue whale (sulphur bottom)
Balaenoptera physalus . . . . fin whale (finback, finner)
Balaenoptera borealis . . . . sei whale
Balaenoptera edeni . . . . Bryde's whale
Balaenoptera acutorostrata . . . . . minke whale (little piked whale)
Megaptera novaeangliae . . . . humpback

SUBORDER ODONTOCETI — TOOTHED WHALES

FAMILY PHYSETERIDAE — SPERM WHALES

Physeter catodon . . . . sperm whale (cachalot)
Kogia breviceps . . . . pygmy sperm whale
Kogia simus . . . . dwarf sperm whale

FAMILY MONODONTIDAE — WHITE WHALES

Monodon monoceros . . . . narwhal (unicorn whale)
Delphinapterus leucas . . . . belukha (beluga, white whale, sea canary)
Orcaella brevirostris . . . . Irrawaddy dolphin
(pesut, Irrawaddy River dolphin)

FAMILY ZIPHIIDAE — BEAKED WHALES

Tasmacetus shepherdi . . . . Shepherd's beaked whale
(Tasman beaked whale)
Berardius arnuxii . . . . Arnoux's beaked whale
(southern giant bottlenose whale)
Berardius bairdii . . . . Baird's beaked whale
(North Pacific giant bottlenose whale)
Indopacetus pacificus . . . . Longman's beaked whale
(Pacific beaked whale)

Mesoplodon bidens	Sowerby's beaked whale (North Sea beaked whale)
Mesoplodon densirostris	Blainville's beaked whale (dense-beaked whale)
Mesoplodon europaeus	Gervais' beaked whale (Antillean beaked whale)
Mesoplodon layardii	strap-toothed whale
Mesoplodon hectori	Hector's beaked whale
Mesoplodon grayi	Gray's beaked whale (scamperdown whale)
Mesoplodon stejnegeri	Stejneger's beaked whale
Mesoplodon bowdoini	Andrews' beaked whale
Mesoplodon mirus	True's beaked whale
Mesoplodon ginkgodens	ginkgo-toothed beaked whale
Mesoplodon carlhubbsi	Hubbs' beaked whale
Ziphius cavirostris	Cuvier's beaked whale (goose-beaked whale)
Hyperoodon ampullatus	northern bottlenose whale
Hyperoodon planifrons	southern bottlenose whale

FAMILY DELPHINIDAE — DOLPHINS AND OTHER SMALL, TOOTHED WHALES

Peponocephala electra	melon-headed whale (electra)
Feresa attenuata	pygmy killer whale
Pseudorca crassidens	false killer whale
Orcinus orca	orca (killer whale)
Globicephala melaena	long-finned pilot whale (pothead, pilot whale, common blackfish)
Globicephala macrorhynchus	short-finned pilot whale
Steno bredanensis	rough-toothed dolphin
Sotalia fluviatilis	tucuxi (river dolphin)
Sousa chinensis	Indo-Pacific humpback dolphin (Indo-Pacific sousa)
Sousa teuszii	Atlantic humpback dolphin (West African sousa)
Lagenorhynchus albirostris	white-beaked dolphin
Lagenorhynchus acutus	Atlantic white-sided dolphin
Lagenorhynchus obscurus	dusky dolphin
Lagenorhynchus obliquidens	Pacific white-sided dolphin
Lagenorhynchus cruciger	hourglass dolphin
Lagenorhynchus australis	Peale's dolphin
Lagenodelphis hosei	Fraser's dolphin (shortsnouted whitebelly)
Delphinus delphis	common dolphin
Tursiops truncatus	bottlenose dolphin

Grampus griseus	Risso's dolphin (grey grampus)
Stenella attenuata	pantropical spotted dolphin (bridled dolphin)
Stenella clymene	clymene dolphin (Atlantic spinner dolphin)
Stenella frontalis	Atlantic spotted dolphin
Stenella longirostris	spinner dolphin
Stenella coeruleoalba	striped dolphin (streaker, blue-white dolphin)
Lissodelphis peronii	southern right whale dolphin
Lissodelphis borealis	northern right whale dolphin
Cephalorhynchus heavisidii	Heaviside's dolphin
Cephalorhynchus eutropia	black dolphin (Chilean dolphin)
Cephalorhynchus hectori	Hector's dolphin (whitefront dolphin)
Cephalorhynchus commersonii	Commerson's dolphin (piebald dolphin, le jacobite)

FAMILY PHOCOENIDAE — PORPOISES

Phocoena phocoena	harbour porpoise (common porpoise)
Phocoena spinipinnis	Burmeister's porpoise
Phocoena sinus	vaquita (cochito)
Australophocoena dioptrica	spectacled porpoise
Phocoenoides dalli	Dall's porpoise (whiteflank porpoise)
Neophocaena phocaenoides	finless porpoise (black finless porpoise, South-East Asia porpoise, river pig)

FAMILY PLATANISTIDAE — RIVER DOLPHINS

Platanista gangetica	Ganges River dolphin (Ganges susu, gangetic dolphin, blind dolphin)
Platanista minor	Indus River dolphin (Indus susu)

FAMILY INIIDAE — AMAZON RIVER DOLPHIN

Inia geoffrensis	Amazon River dolphin (bouto)

FAMILY LIPOTIDAE — CHINESE RIVER DOLPHIN

Lipotes vexillifer	Chinese river dolphin (baiji, Yangtze River dolphin, white dolphin, Chinese lake dolphin)

FAMILY PONTOPORIIDAE — FRANCISCANA

Pontoporia blainvillei	franciscana (La Plata River dolphin)

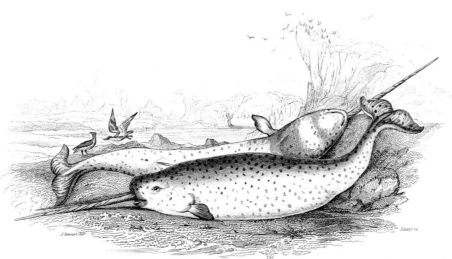

THE NARWHAL OR SEA UNICORN
F. Cuvier

British Musem (Natural History)

BIBLIOGRAPHY

Much of the information in this book derives from original research undertaken by the contributors. However, the following publications may be of value to those readers who would like to explore more fully the fascinating world of whales, dolphins and porpoises.

Baker, A.N. 1983. *Whales and Dolphins of New Zealand and Australia: An Identification Guide.* Victorian University Press, New Zealand.

Baker, M.L. 1987. *Whales, Dolphins and Porpoises of the World.* Doubleday, New York.

Bryden, M.M. and Harrison, R.J. (eds). 1986. *Research on Dolphins.* Clarendon Press, Oxford.

Bullen, F. 1898. *The Cruise of the Cachelot.* Smith, Elder, London.

Burnham, Burnham 'Dolphin's role in Aboriginal Life'. *Australian Geographic* vol 7, July–Sept, 1987.

Cottrell, L. 1984. *Bull of Minos: Discoveries of Schliemann and Evans.* Bell and Hyman, London.

Ellis, R. 1980. *The Book of Whales.* Alfred A. Knopf Inc, New York.

Evans, P.G.H. 1987. *The Natural History of Whales and Dolphins.* Christopher Helms Ltd, Kent.

Ferguson, G. 1972. *Signs and Symbols in Christian Art.* Oxford University Press, Oxford.

Forster, E.M. 1927 *Aspects of the Novel.* Edward Arnold, London.

Gatenby, Greg. *Whales A Celebration.* Hutchinson, New York, nd

Graves, R. 1955 and 1984. *The Greek Myths.* (2 Vols), Penguin, Harmondsworth, U.K.

Graves, R. 1981. *The Greek Myths* (illustrated and condensed) Cassell, London.

Graves, R. 1982. *The Greek Myths* (illustrated), Doubleday, New York.

Hoyt, E. 1984. *The Whale Watcher's Handbook.* Penguin Books, Canada.

Kaufman, G.D. and Forester, P.H. 1986. *Hawaii's Humpback Whales: A Complete Whalewatchers Guide.* Pacific Whale Foundation Press, Hawaii.

Kelly, J., Mercer, S. and Wolf, S. 1981. *The Great Whale Book.* Center for Environmental Education, Washington D.C.

Klinowska, M. 1985. *Interpretation of the U.K. cetacean stranding records.* Rep. International Whaling Commission. 35:459–67.

Lawrence, D.H. 1964. *The complete poems by D.H. Lawrence.* Heinemann, London.

Lawrence, D.H. 1924. *Studies in classic American literature.* Martin Secker, London.

Lockley, M. 1979. *Whales, dolphins and porpoises.* David and Charles, Newton Abbot, Devon.

Lowell, R. 1973. *The dolphin.* Farrar Straus and Giroux, New York.

Maret, G., Boccara, N. and Kiepenheuer, J. (eds). 1986. *Biophysical effects of steady magnetic fields.* Springer-Verlag.

McIntyre, J. 1974. *Mind in the Waters.* Charles Scribner's Sons, NY.

McNally, R. 1981. *So Remorseless a Havoc.* Little, Brown & Co, Boston, Mass.

Melville, H. 1961. *Moby Dick or The White Whale.* The New American Library edn, New York.

Minasian, S.M., Balcomb, K.C. and Foster, L. 1984. *The World's Whales: The Complete Illustrated Guide.* Smithsonian Books, Washington D.C.

Piggott, J. 1969. *Japanese Mythology.* Hamlyn, London and NY.

Roberts, A. and Mountford, C. 1969. *The Dawn of Time.* Rigby, Adelaide.

Seki, K. (ed). 1963. *Folktales of Japan* (translated by Robert Adams). University of Chicago Press.

Slijper, E.J. 1979. *Whales.* Hutchinson and Co Ltd, London.

Sweeney, J. 1972. *A Pictorial History of Sea Monsters.* Crown Pub. Inc., NY.

Watson, L. 1981. *Sea Guide to Whales of the World.* Hutchinson and Co Ltd, London.

ACKNOWLEDGMENTS

The publishers would like to thank the following people for their assistance in the preparation of this book:
Dr Tim Flannery and Linda Gibson, Australian Museum, for advice on contributors and current research; Dr David Gaskin, Dr Charles Potter, Dr Louis Hermann and Dr William Perrin for assistance with photographs and information; David Phillips for information on the anti-whaling movement. Special thanks to Stanley Minasian who provided valuable help in locating authors, illustrations and photographs. Jennie Phillips, Tracey Peakman, Penny Pilmer and Kate Rogers for administrative assistance; Jane Fraser for initial picture research and continued support and encouragement. Rosemary Wilkinson and Jane Lewis for picture research in London, in particular the British Museum (Natural History).

EVOLUTION
Photographs by D.V. Weston courtesy of the Department of Geology, University of Otago.
Page 14 **Mesonyx**
Savage, R.G. & Long, M.R. 1986. *Mammal Evolution: An Illustrated Guide.* British Museum (Natural History), London.
Page 16 **Protocetus**
Ibid.
Page 18 **Dorudontine**
Kellog, A.R. 1936. *A Review of the Archaeceti.* Carnegie Institute of Washington: publication no 482.
Evolutionary tree
From sketch by R. Ewan Fordyce, based on published literature, including Barnes, L.G., Domning, D.P., Ray, C.E. 1985. 'Status of Studies on Fossil Marine Mammals'. *Marine Mammal Science.* Vol 1 (1). Pages 15–53.
Page 19 **Mammalodon**
Based on an adaptation by Peter Schouten's reconstruction from a sketch by R. Ewan Fordyce, which appears in *Antipodean Ark.* 1988. Angus & Robertson, Sydney.
Gondwana
Adapted from Kennett, J.P. 1980. *Palaeogeography, plaeoclimatology, palaeoceology.* Vol 31. Pages 123–152.
Page 21 **Skull views**
Minasian, *et. al.* 1984. *The World's Whales: The Complete Illustrated Guide.* Smithsonian Books, Washington D.C.
Romer, — 1966. *Vertebrate Paleontology.* University of Chicago Press.

KINDS OF WHALES
Illustrations adapted from Baker, M.L. 1987. *Whales, Dolphins and Porpoises of the World.* Doubleday, New York; Minasian, *et. al.* 1984. *The World's Whales: The Complete Illustrated Guide.* Smithsonian Books, Washington D.C. and Hoyt, E. 1984. *The Whale Watcher's Handbook.* Penguin Books, Canada.

BALEEN WHALES
Page 46 **Difference between baleen and toothed whales**
Adapted from Watson, L. 1981. *Sea Guide to Whales of the World.* Hutchinson and Co Ltd, London. Page 33.

DISTRIBUTION AND ECOLOGY
Photographs by Paul Ensor, supplied by Hedgehog House, New Zealand.
Page 84 **Isothermal ocean regions**
Adapted from Watson, L. 1981. *Sea Guide to Whales of the World.* Hutchinson and Co Ltd, London. Page 50.
Page 88 **Distribution of mesoplodon**
Adapted from Evans, P.G.H. 1987. *The Natural History of Whales and Dolphins.* Christopher Helms Ltd, Kent. Page 88.
Distribution of lagenorhynchus
Ibid. Page 81.
Page 90 **Distribution of cephalorhynchus**
Ibid. Page 82.
Distribution of porpoises
Ibid. Page 87.
Page 98 **Migration of humpbacks**
Ibid. Page 213.
Migration of grey whale
Ibid. Page 215.

ANATOMY
Page 102 **Parts of a whale**
Adapted from Minasian, *et. al.* 1984. *The World's Whales: The Complete Illustrated Guide.* Smithsonian Books, Washington D.C. Page 33.
Page 103 **Comparative Sizes**
Adapted from Kaufman, G.D. and Forester, P.H. 1986. *Hawaii's Humpback Whales: A Complete Whalewatchers Guide.* Pacific Whale Foundation Press, Hawaii. Pages 10–11.
Page 105 **Dorsal fins**
Ibid. Page 33.
Fluke profiles
Ibid. Page 32.
Page 106 **Whale teeth**
Ibid. Page 24.
Page 107 **Telescoping**
Adapted from Slijper, E.J. 1979. *Whales.* Hutchinson and Co Ltd, London. Page 73.
Page 108 **Internal Anatomy**
Adapted from *Australian Geographic.* No 7. July/Sept 1987. Page 59, from an illustration by Peter Schouten.

ADAPTATION
Page 110 **Convergent evolution**
Adapted from Howell, A.B. 1970. *Aquatic Mammals.* Dover Publications, England.
Pages 112–113 **How a dolphin swims**
Based on the work of Peter Purves. 1963. Adapted from a model in British Museum (Natural History).
Page 113 **Blubber**
Based on an illustration in Kelly, *et. al.* 1981. *The Great Whale Book.* Center for Environmental Education, Washington D.C. Page 7.
Page 117 **Diving**
Based on an illustration in Slijper, E.J. 1979. *Whales.* Hutchinson and Co Ltd, London. Page 126.
Page 120 **Retia Mirabilia**
Ibid. Page 161.

THE WORLD OF THE SENSES
Page 122 **Eye**
Adapted from Slijper, E.J. 1979. *Whales.* Hutchinson and Co Ltd, London. Page 230. Originally based on Putter, 1902.
Pages 130–131 **Echolocation**
Based on an illustration by Peter Schouten in *Australian Geographic.* No 7. July/Sept. 1987. Page 56.

REPRODUCTION AND DEVELOPMENT
Page 136 **Male reproductive organs**
Based on an illustration in Slijper, E.J. 1979. Whales. Hutchinson and Co Ltd, London.
Page 137 **Female reproductive organs**
Ibid.

WHALES IN ART AND LITERATURE
Page 169 *Aelian: The Dolphin of Iassos.* Reproduced from McNally, R. 1981. So Remorseless a Havoc. Little Brown & Co., Boston, Mass. Chapter 6.

STRANDINGS
Thanks are due to the H.M. Coastguard and the Receivers of the Wreck for their invaluable assistance in the reporting of strandings: the British Museum (Natural History) for access to unpublished records: and the British Geological Survey for help in locating data. The director of the British Geological Survey kindly gave permission for the use of the geomagnetic map, copyright of which is reserved to the Natural Environment Research Council.
Page 226 **Dolphin measurements**
Adapted from Baker, A.N. 1983. *Whales and Dolphins of New Zealand and Australia: An Identification Guide.* Victorian University Press, New Zealand. Page 47.

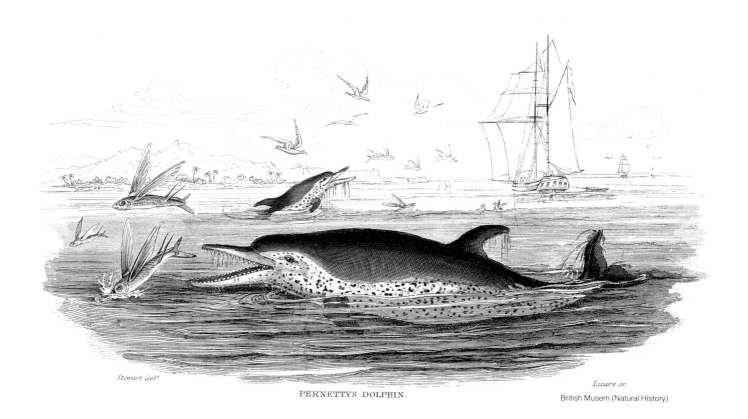

Stewart del^t

PERNETTYS DOLPHIN.

Lizars sc.

British Musem (Natural History)

NOTES ON CONTRIBUTORS

LAWRENCE BARNES

Lawrence Barnes was born in Portsmouth, Virginia, USA, and has had a long interest in the study of whales, dolphins and porpoises and the evolution systems and distribution of fossils and modern marine mammals. In 1972 he completed his Phd in vertebrate paleontology and he has been Curator and Section Head of The Vertebrate Paleontology Section, Natural History Museum of Los Angeles, Los Angeles, California, since 1983. As well as being interested in the study of Cetacea and publishing several articles on the subject, he is also interested in entomology.

M. M. BRYDEN

Professor Michael Bryden was born in Australia and has spent the past twenty years dedicated to the study of whales and dolphins. In 1963–64 he worked as a veterinarian in Tasmania, then spent 16 months as a biologist with the Australian National Antarctic Research Expedition to Macquarie Island, studying growth and development of the southern elephant seal.

Professor Bryden has held academic posts at Cornell University, USA, the University of Sydney and the University of Queensland. He has studied the growth and adaptation of Antarctic seals on four summer research trips to Antarctica, and conducted research on the reproductive biology of cetaceans at the University of Cambridge in 1978 and 1981. In 1988 he took up the Chair of Veterinary Anatomy at the University of Sydney.

Since the mid-1970s Professor Bryden has conducted surveys of bottlenose dolphins and humpback whales as consultant to the Australian National Parks and Wildlife Service. He has been joint editor of two books and author of more than 70 research papers and several government reports.

PETER CORKERON

Peter Corkeron is a Tutorial Fellow in the Department of Zoology at the University of Queensland, Australia, where he obtained his BSc and MSc. He is currently completing his doctorate on the ecology of inshore dolphins in

Moreton Bay, southeast Queensland. He is greatly involved in the study of whales, dolphins and porpoises and has also assisted in research on humpbacks and dugongs.

CARSON CREAGH

Carson Creagh was born in Sydney in 1951 and has been involved with natural history since childhood. His interest in marine biology (especially the anatomy, behaviour and taxonomy of sharks and cetaceans) led to studies at Macquarie University, where he obtained a BSc in 1974 with majors in zoology and geography. For the past six years he has worked as a magazine journalist and production editor, and has written three books on natural history subjects for schools: *The Ones That Got Away* and *Animal Tracks,* which won the Whitley awards in 1987. He is a founder member of Trees On Farms, a Sydney-based volunteer organisation devoted to assisting landholders with tree regeneration, and works as a consultant on a number of large-scale environmental management projects. His wife Joanne is a childbirth educator and they have four children.

WILLIAM H. DAWBIN

William Dawbin, DSc, started his studies of whales in 1948 in Cook Strait, New Zealand, while he was a lecturer in Zoology at Victoria University, Wellington. Biological examination of whale catches at the Perano station led on to the tagging of humpbacks in many locations in the South Pacific, which continued after his move to Sydney University as Senior Lecturer (later Reader) in 1956. Extended periods were spent in whale research at the National Institute of Oceanography, United Kingdom, the British Museum (Natural History) and as Visiting Professor at the Ocean Research Institute, University of Tokyo. He conducted field studies at the Auckland Islands (New Zealand subantarctic) and aboard RSS *Discovery II* in antarctic waters, and made visits to examine whale catches in Norway, Iceland, Canada, South Africa, Japan and Australia. He has published a series of scientific papers on humpbacks, right whales and dolphins and, with others, papers on reptiles (mainly *Sphenodon*), holothurians and plankton. He has also published a number of encyclopedic articles including some for Encyclopaedia Britannica. He was the first President of the Antarctic Society of Australia and served on the Scientific Committee of the International Whaling Commission. Since retiring, he has carried on his whale studies as Honorary Research Associate, Australian Museum.

HUGH EDWARDS

Hugh Edwards is a West Australian diver and marine photographer and the author of nineteen books, mostly about the sea. He began diving with an ex-army gasmask as a boy of twelve after World War II and had his first scuba gear in 1952. In 1958 he was a member of a Cambridge University expedition diving on Greek wrecks off Sicily and exploring the sunken Graeco-Roman city of Apollonia off North Africa. In 1963 he was involved in the discovery of the Dutch treasure ship *Batavia* wrecked in 1629, and was leader of the first expedition to explore the wreck. His book *Islands of Angry Ghosts* won the Sir Thomas White Memorial Prize for the best book by an Australian in 1966. In 1968 he discovered the wreck of the 1727 Dutch ship *Zeewyk* in the Abrolhos Islands and wrote *Wreck on the Half Moon Reef.* But perhaps his most exciting diving period came between 1976 and 1978, filming *The Great White Shark* alongside dead whales off the now-defunct Albany Whaling Station.

R. EWAN FORDYCE

Ewan Fordyce has had a long interest in natural history, especially vertebrates. He attended the University of Canterbury where he completed his doctorate on New Zealand fossil cetacea and then proceeded to carry out research on the Oligocene predecessors of odontocetes and mysticetes at the Smithsonian Institution and at Monash University in Melbourne. More recently, he has become involved in the study of fossil cetacea from New Zealand, Antarctica and Australia and the recovery of scientific material from strandings. Ewan is also keenly interested in the taxonomy, anatomy and evolution of fossil and living cetacea and is also currently working on fossil penguins, fossil seals and fossil marine reptiles. Since 1982 he has been Senior Lecturer, Department of Geology at the University of Otago. In his little spare time he likes to work in his garden and walk in the backcountry.

SIR RICHARD HARRISON

Sir Richard Harrison, MD, DSc, FRS has been Professor of Anatomy in the University of Cambridge and a Fellow of Downing College since 1968. From 1954 he was Professor of Anatomy at The London Hospital Medical College and also Professor of Physiology at the Royal Institution from 1961 to 1966. He has also been Visiting Professor to Universities in Australia, Africa and the United States and has done research at oceanaria in several countries. He is a Trustee of the British Museum (Natural History), is involved in animal welfare and the protection of endangered species especially cetaceans. He has been President of the European Association for Aquatic Mammals and of the Anatomical Society of Great Britain. He is the author of numerous papers on anatomy and reproduction in marine mammals and has written many books, including *Marine Mammals* (1965), *Functional Anatomy of Marine Mammals* (1972), *Handbook of Marine Mammals* (1981) and *Research on Dolphins* (1986).

MARGARET KLINOWSKA

Dr Margaret Klinowska, has specialised in the study of cetaceans for the past ten years. She has produced reports for the Nature Conservancy Council and for the Commission of the European Communities on the status of cetaceans, for the Department of the Environment on the keeping of cetaceans in captivity, and is currently working on the IUCN Cetacean Red Data Book. Her research interests are in the relationships between animals and their environment, particularly where this relates to biological time-keeping. Her current projects include an investigation of the use of the earth's magnetic field as a map and position finding aid and the behaviour of wild and captive dolphins. Dr Klinowska is a member of the Society for Marine Mammalogy, European Association for Aquatic Mammals, British Society for Chronobiology, IUCN Species Survival Commission — Cetacean Specialist Group, Scientific Committee of the International Whaling Commission (UK delegation), European Pineal Study Group, Cambridge Philosophical Society, Groupe d'Etude des Rythms Biologiques, International Society for Biometeorology and of the Shropshire Trust for Nature Conservation. She

currently belongs to the Research Group in Mammalian Ecology and Reproduction at the Physiological Laboratory, University of Cambridge and also acts as a private scientific consultant.

VICTOR MANTON

Victor Manton has been involved in the study of cetaceans in captivity since he qualified as a veterinary surgeon from the Royal Veterinary College, London, in 1953. He has had more than fifty scientific papers published and contributed to chapters in two books, *Research in Dolphins* and *Pere David's Deer — The Biology of an Extinct Species*. He was appointed Deputy Director and Veterinary Officer of Whipsnade Park in 1963 and Curator, Whipsnade Park, in 1968. He is also editor of the journal *Aquatic Mammals*.

ROBERT MORRIS

Robert Morris conceived his love of marine life during his childhood holidays at Dorset, in England, where he now lives between field trips with his Australian wife and their two children. In 1967 he joined the Institute of Oceanographic Sciences in Surrey as a young marine organic chemist, and since then has spent two years in Whitehall as a scientific advisor on environmental matters. He is an Honorary Research Fellow at several universities in the United Kingdom and Australia. He was awarded a D.Sc. in Oceanography at Southampton University in 1981. An inveterate traveller, he has taken part in research cruises to every ocean of the world, working in and establishing links with universities and marine laboratories in Russia, Finland, America, France and Australia. In recent years, his work with whales and dolphins has become his major personal interest.

MARTY SNYDERMAN

Marty Snyderman is a photographer, cinematographer and author specialising in the marine environment who lives in San Diego, California. His photographs have been used by many publications and institutions with interest in marine life, including *National Geographic, Oceans Magazine, Ocean Realm, Skin Diver,* the National Wildlife Federation, Oceanus and Weldon International. Marty's cinematography has been used by the National Geographic Society, Nova, the British Broadcasting Corporation, Mutual of Omaha's Wild Kingdom, and many other organisations that create films about marine life.

Marty is the author of a book entitled *California Marine Life* published by Marcor in Port Hueneme, California.

RUTH THOMPSON

Ruth Thompson grew up in England and came to Sydney in 1973 on a working holiday. She taught for several years while studying part-time at Macquarie University, where she completed her PhD. In 1982 she began recording interviews for the Australia 1938 Oral History Project, a collection of 500 interviews with Australians who had lived through the 1930s. Since 1985 she has worked as a freelance writer and historian for a number of private and government bodies including the Sydney Opera House, the NSW Department of Public Works, the NSW Department of Environment and Planning and the Power House Museum. She is on the editorial committee of the Oral History Association of Australia's *Journal* and is co-author of *Oral History. A Handbook.* Dr Thompson has contributed to the *Australian Dictionary of Biography* and to *Australians: A Historical Library.*

KAIYA ZHOU

Professor Kaiya Zhou is Dean of the Department of Biology at Nanjing Normal University, Nanjing, People's Republic of China. After graduating in 1953 with a BSc in biology, he taught for two years at Jiangsu Normal College in Suzhou. He accepted a position at Nanjing Normal University in 1955 and has been there ever since. His research on vertebrate biology has included each class of vertebrates and he has authored or co-authored 43 scientific papers and co-authored two books on zoology. He rediscovered the baiji or Chinese river dolphin in the lower reaches of the Yangtze River in 1957, which led to his continuing interest in biology of dolphins and porpoises. Since then he has carried out research on the morphology, taxonomy, distribution and ecology of dolphins and porpoises in Chinese waters. Much of his recent work has involved the conservation of the baiji. He is a member of Cetacean Specialist Group of IUCN Species Survival commission, a council member of the Society for Conservation Biology, Mammalogical Society of China, China Wildlife Conservation Association and China Zoological Society. He is also President of the Jiangsu Zoological Society.

METRIC CONVERSION TABLE

QUANTITY	METRIC UNIT	IMPERIAL UNIT	Conversion Factors (Approximate)	
			METRIC TO IMPERIAL UNITS	IMPERIAL METRIC UNITS
LENGTH	millimetre (mm) or centimetre (cm)	inch (in)	1 cm = 0.394 in	1 in = 25.4 mm
	centimetre (cm) or metre (m)	foot (ft)	1 m = 3.28 ft	1 ft = 30.5 cm
	metre (m)	yard (yd)	1 m = 1.09 yd	1 yd = 0.914 m
	kilometre (km)	mile	1 km = 0.621 mile	1 mile = 1.61 km
MASS	gram (g)	ounce (oz)	1 g = 0.0353 oz	1 oz = 28.3 g
	gram (g) or kilogram (kg)	pound (lb)	1 kg = 2.20 lb	1 lb = 454 g
	tonne (t)	ton	1 tonne = 0.984 ton	1 ton = 1.02 tonne
AREA	square centimetre (cm²)	square inch (in²)	1 cm² = 0.155 in²	1 in² = 6.45 cm²
	square centimetre (cm²) or square metre (m²)	square foot (ft²)	1 m² = 10.8 ft²	1 ft² = 929 cm²
	square metre (m²)	square yd (yd²)	1 m² = 1.20 yd²	1 yd² = 0.836 m²
	hectare (ha)	acre (ac)	1 ha = 2.47 ac	1 ac = 0.405 ha
	square kilometre (km²)	square mile (sq. mile)	1 km² = 0.386 sq. mile	1 sq. mile = 2.59 km²
VOLUME	cubic centimetre (cm³)	cubic inch (in³)	1 cm³ = 0.0610 in³	1 in³ = 16.4 cm³
	cubic decimetre (dm³) or cubic metre (m³)	cubic foot (ft³)	1 m³ = 35.3 ft³	1 ft³ = 28.3 dm³
	cubic metre (m³)	cubic yard (yd³)	1 m³ = 1.31 yd³	1 yd³ = 0.765 m³
	cubic metre (m³)	bushel (bus)	1 m³ = 27.5 bus	1 bus = 0.0364 m³
PRESSURE	kilopascal (kPa)	pound per square inch (psi)	1 kPa = 0.145 psi	1 psi = 6.89 kPa
VELOCITY	kilometre per hour (km/h)	mile per hour (mph)	1 km/h = 0.621 mph	1 mph = 1.61 km/h
TEMPERATURE	Celsius temp (°C)	Fahrenheit temp (°F)	$°F = \frac{9}{5} \times (°C + 32)$	$°C = \frac{5}{9} \times (°F - 32)$
ENERGY	kilojoule (kJ)	British thermal unit (Btu)	1 kJ = 0.948 Btu	1 Btu = 1.06 kJ
	megajoule (MJ)	therm	1 MJ = 9.48 x 10⁻³ therm	1 therm = 106 MJ

THE SPERMACETI WHALE
Beale

INDEX